Scarlet Traces

VOLUME ONE

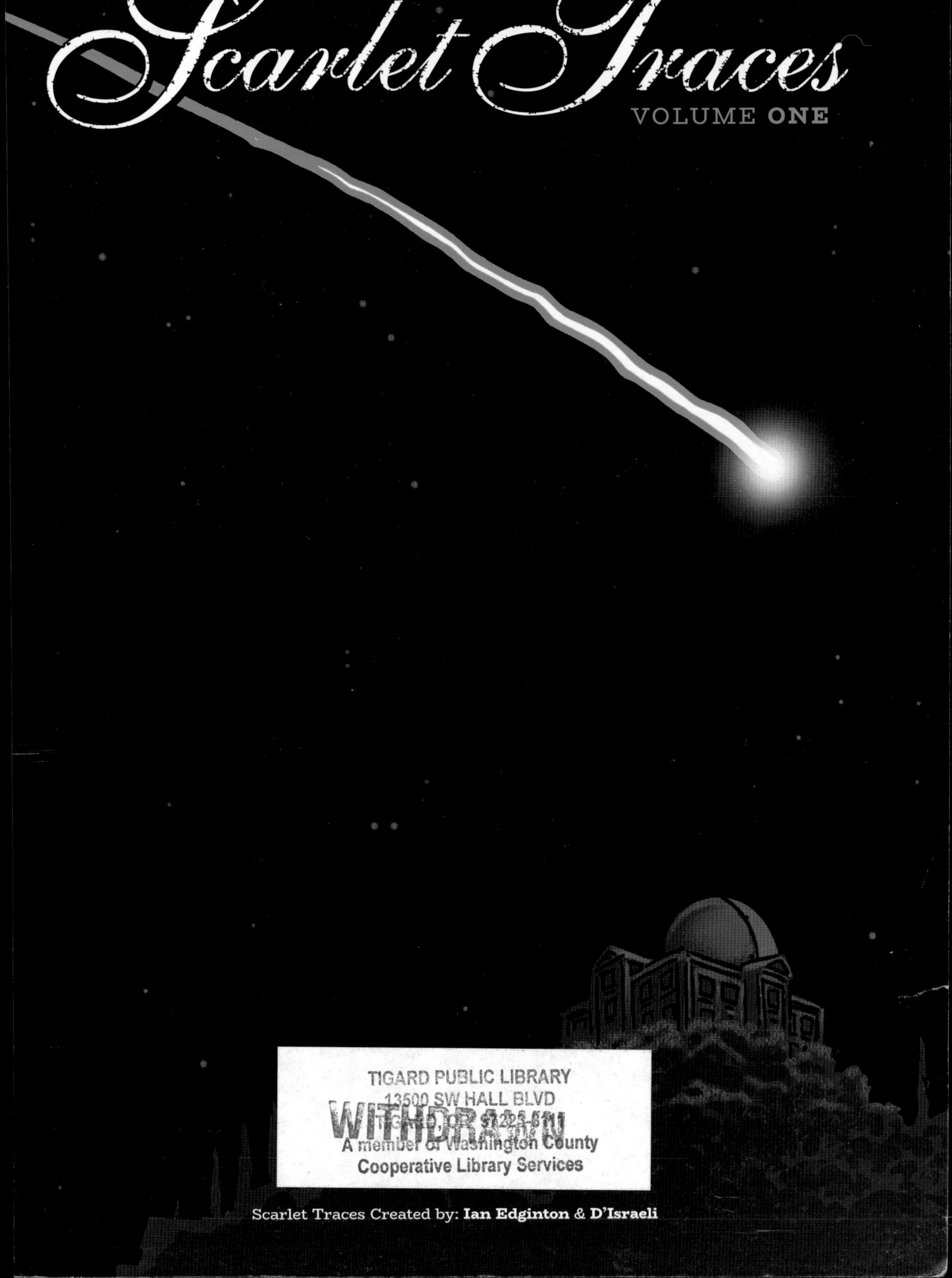

Scarlet Traces Created by: **Ian Edginton & D'Israeli**

I N T R O D

'Funk and Precautions'

Ideas are never forgotten, especially if you're a writer. They're squirreled away, like acorns to be dug up in times of need. I have dozens of notebooks into which I've jotted interesting names, overheard snippets of conversations (writers are aural pickpockets, don't trust them!) intriguing 'What Ifs?' and other assorted gubbins. There's one idea that I never wrote down though, I never really needed to as it loitered around my subconscious for years waiting for its number to be called:

'What happened to all the Martian technology after the end of the War of the Worlds?'

It seemed liked an obvious question but as far as I could tell no one had asked it. In my teens I'd been laid low with glandular fever and to pass the time I read voraciously including a whole swathe of H.G. Wells which was the seed bed for that and many other ideas to come.

Forty years on, that stray thought has had more mileage than I ever could have imagined. Furnished and burnished by the singular visuals of Matt Brooker, aka D'Israeli, *Scarlet Traces* has transitioned through a number of publishers, spawned a sequel and a prequel before settling in here, at Rebellion.

Scarlet Traces was never just about Martian machinery, it's also an observation on Empire and colonialism, on what it means to be a hero, on doing the right thing for the wrong reasons and vice versa. It's the high concept that draws people in but it's the details and subtleties that holds them. Of all the books that Matt and I have worked on, *Scarlet Traces* is the one that people keep asking us for more and now, I'm happy to say, we can oblige them.

I must mention in dispatches the sterling stewardship of Dave Eliot and Steve White of Tundra UK, the late Gary Reed of Caliber Comics, the noble folk at Cool Beans, Randy Stradley at Dark Horse and the redoubtable Alan Barnes who all saw merit in the story and carried it forwards.

By the way, the line 'funk and precautions' isn't a George Clinton track but spoken by the shell-shocked Artilleryman in Wells novel:

'No proud dreams and no proud lusts; and a man who hasn't one or the other… what is he but funk and precautions.'

Ian Edginton
Birmingham, October 2016

U   C   T   I   O   N

'It All Comes Back to Scarlet Traces'

Scarlet Traces? Let me tell you what it means to me.

For nearly a decade it was nothing more than Ian Edginton's inspired ideas and my photocopied scribbles making the rounds of submissions editors. But when it finally took off, it changed my life.

I'd been his middling, sorta-doing-okay artist for years - in the 80's and 90's I did few high profile things (such as colouring on *Miracleman* and inking on *Sandman*) but I'd still never managed to pay the bills regularly. I even worked for 2000 AD as a colourist, but I never quite managed to work my way up to Art Droid, despite doing a couple of Future Shocks.

The *Scarlet Traces* came along. At first for ahead-of-its-time online comics publisher Coolbeans, who folded halfway through the project, then by 2000 AD's sister publication, The Judge Dredd Megazine, who published *Scarlet Traces* in their reprint slot. The reprint fee was just enough for us to live on while we finished the book, and meanwhile, 2000 AD editor Matt Smith saw some of the pages and commissioned *Leviathan* from us. And that was the real start of my 2000 AD Art Droid career.

Scarlet Traces went on to Dark Horse where they commissioned a sequel, *The Great Game*, and acquired rights to do the source novel, War of the Worlds, which also appears in this volume.

But it's *Scarlet Traces* that changed my life; my first long-form project working digitally, the one where I finally worked out who I was as an artist and really showed what I could do.

Now *Scarlet Traces* has come back to 2000 AD, and Ian and I and producing new chapters for the first time in a decade. I am where I hoped I would be, back in those days of inspired ideas and photocopied scribbles.

THE WAR OF THE WORLDS

Script: **Ian Edginton** Art: **D'Israeli** Letters: **D'Israeli**

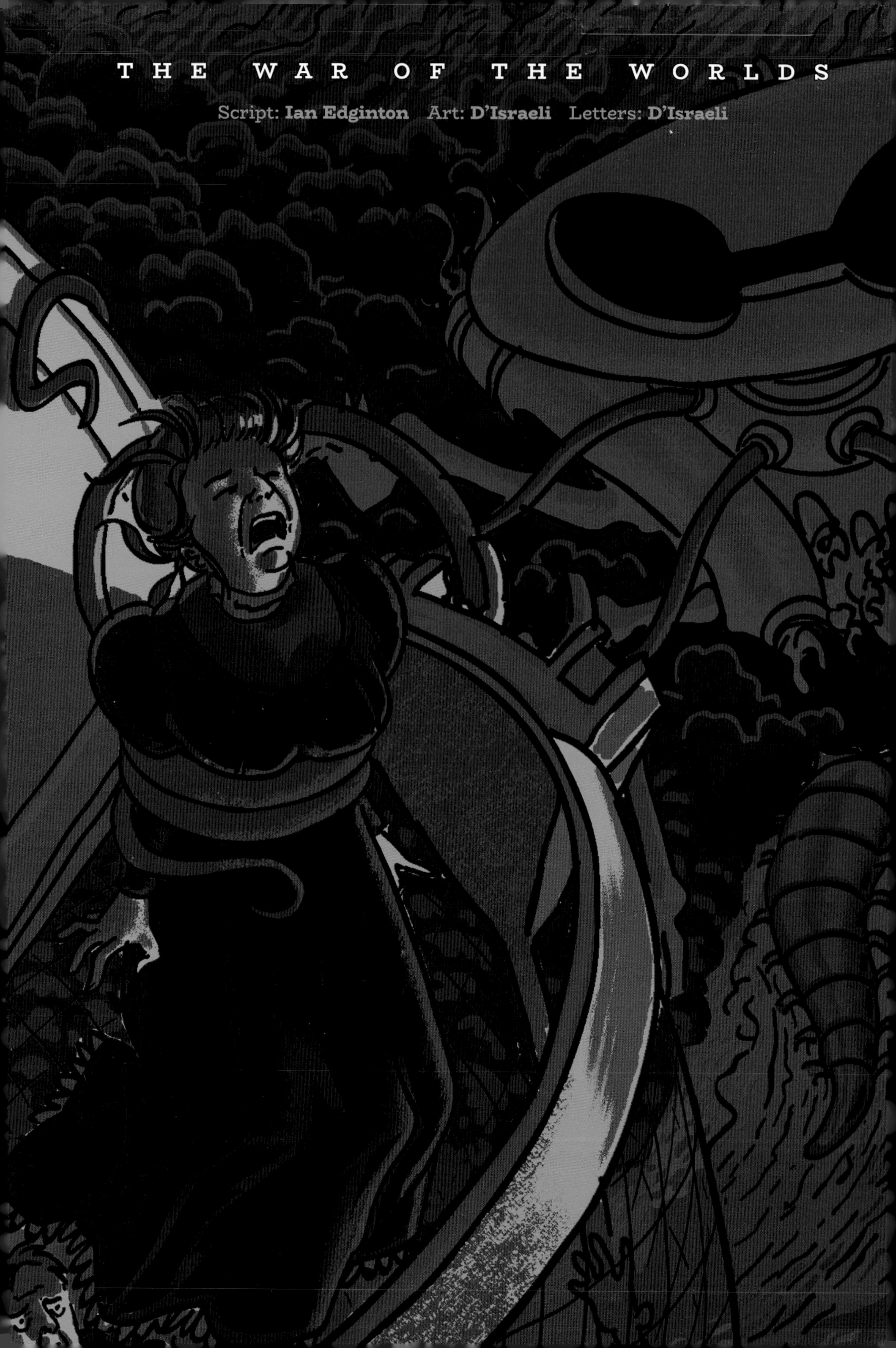

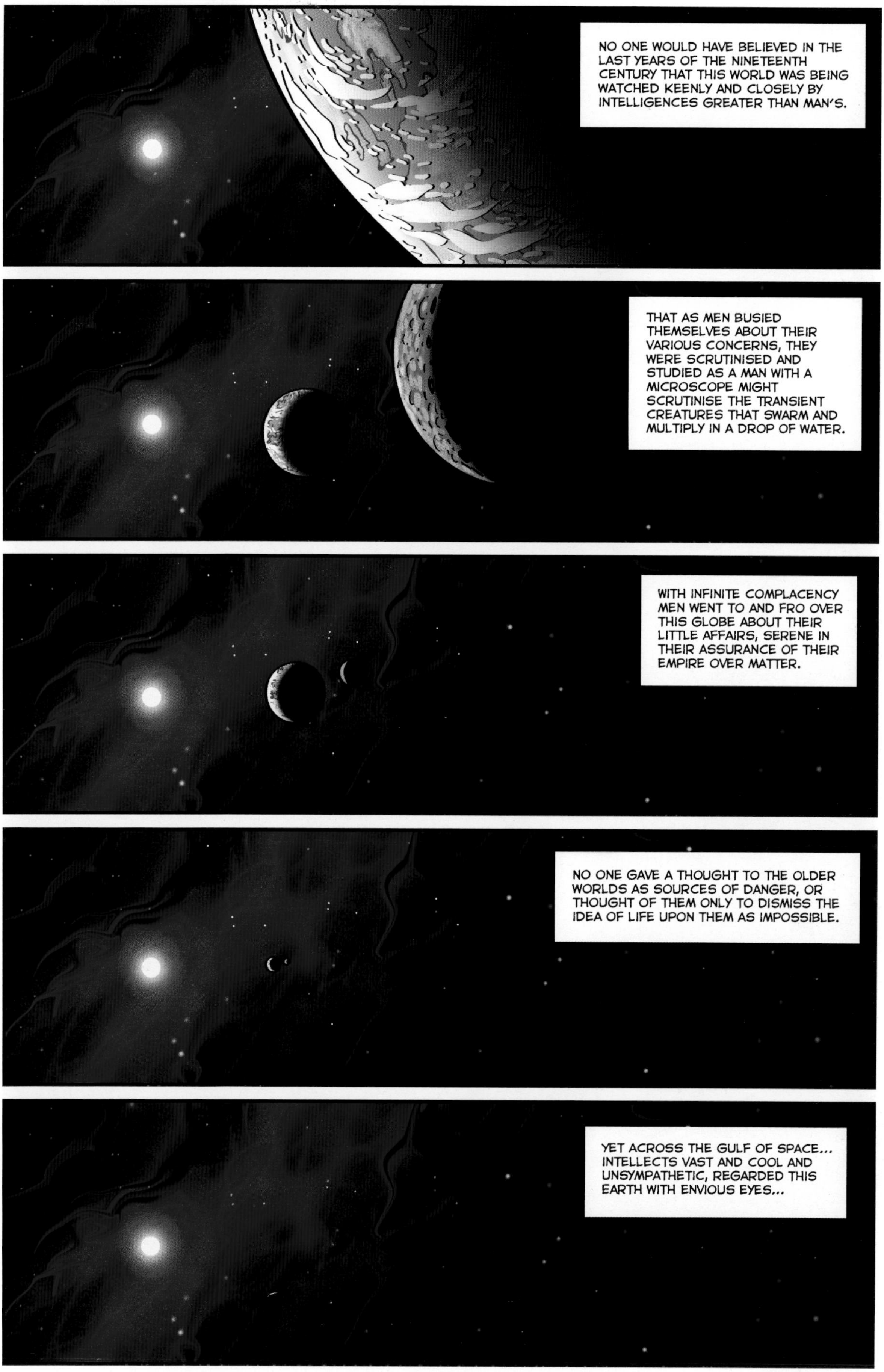
NO ONE WOULD HAVE BELIEVED IN THE LAST YEARS OF THE NINETEENTH CENTURY THAT THIS WORLD WAS BEING WATCHED KEENLY AND CLOSELY BY INTELLIGENCES GREATER THAN MAN'S.
THAT AS MEN BUSIED THEMSELVES ABOUT THEIR VARIOUS CONCERNS, THEY WERE SCRUTINISED AND STUDIED AS A MAN WITH A MICROSCOPE MIGHT SCRUTINISE THE TRANSIENT CREATURES THAT SWARM AND MULTIPLY IN A DROP OF WATER.
WITH INFINITE COMPLACENCY MEN WENT TO AND FRO OVER THIS GLOBE ABOUT THEIR LITTLE AFFAIRS, SERENE IN THEIR ASSURANCE OF THEIR EMPIRE OVER MATTER.
NO ONE GAVE A THOUGHT TO THE OLDER WORLDS AS SOURCES OF DANGER, OR THOUGHT OF THEM ONLY TO DISMISS THE IDEA OF LIFE UPON THEM AS IMPOSSIBLE.
YET ACROSS THE GULF OF SPACE... INTELLECTS VAST AND COOL AND UNSYMPATHETIC, REGARDED THIS EARTH WITH ENVIOUS EYES...

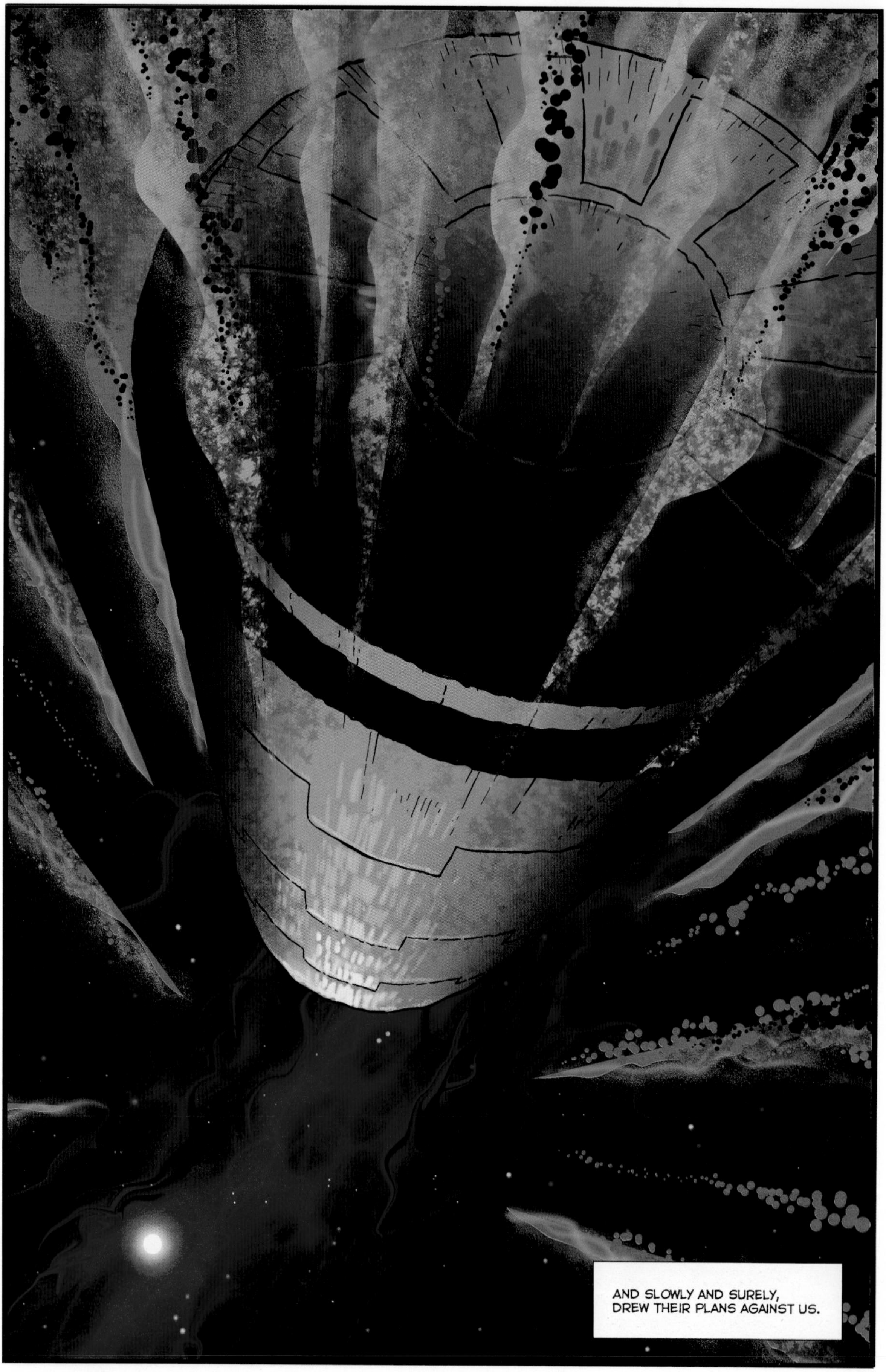
AND SLOWLY AND SURELY,
DREW THEIR PLANS AGAINST US.

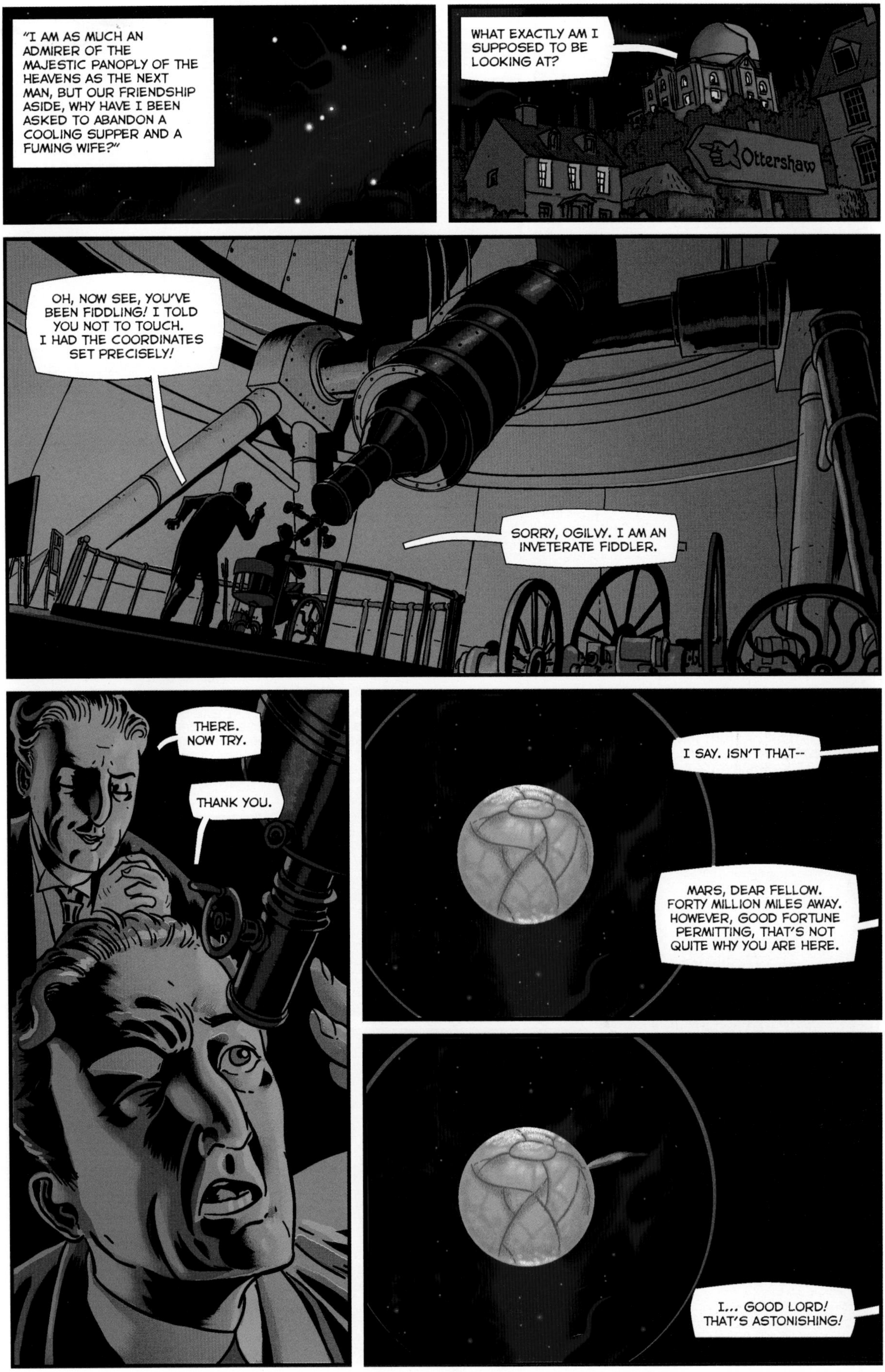
"I AM AS MUCH AN ADMIRER OF THE MAJESTIC PANOPLY OF THE HEAVENS AS THE NEXT MAN, BUT OUR FRIENDSHIP ASIDE, WHY HAVE I BEEN ASKED TO ABANDON A COOLING SUPPER AND A FUMING WIFE?"
WHAT EXACTLY AM I SUPPOSED TO BE LOOKING AT?
Ottershaw
OH, NOW SEE, YOU'VE BEEN FIDDLING! I TOLD YOU NOT TO TOUCH. I HAD THE COORDINATES SET PRECISELY!
SORRY, OGILVY. I AM AN INVETERATE FIDDLER.
THERE. NOW TRY.
THANK YOU.
I SAY. ISN'T THAT--
MARS, DEAR FELLOW. FORTY MILLION MILES AWAY. HOWEVER, GOOD FORTUNE PERMITTING, THAT'S NOT QUITE WHY YOU ARE HERE.
I... GOOD LORD! THAT'S ASTONISHING!

WHAT?! WHAT?! LET ME SEE!

CAPITAL! MOST CAPITAL! IMPECCABLE TIMING, GEORGE. IMPECCABLE!

IS THAT WHAT YOU WANTED ME TO SEE?

IT'S WHAT I'D HOPED, YES. I NEEDED A WITNESS, SOMEONE I TRUSTED, TO OBSERVE THE PHENOMENON.

I'M FLATTERED... BUT WHAT IS IT?

FOR A TIME NOW, WHEN MARS WAS IN OPPOSITION TO THE EARTH, BURSTS AND BLISTERS OF LIGHT HAVE BEEN OBSERVED ON ITS SURFACE. FIRST BY THE LICK OBSERVATORY, THEN BY PERROTIN OF NICE --

-- HOWEVER, IT WAS LAVELLE OF JAVA WHO SET THE WIRES OF THE ASTRONOMICAL EXCHANGE PALPITATING!

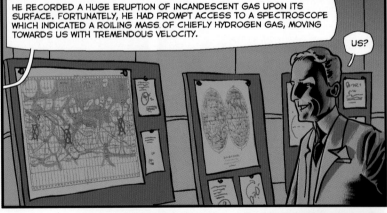

HE RECORDED A HUGE ERUPTION OF INCANDESCENT GAS UPON ITS SURFACE. FORTUNATELY, HE HAD PROMPT ACCESS TO A SPECTROSCOPE WHICH INDICATED A ROILING MASS OF CHIEFLY HYDROGEN GAS, MOVING TOWARDS US WITH TREMENDOUS VELOCITY.

US?

THE EARTH, DEAR FELLOW, DO KEEP UP.

HE LIKENED IT TO THE FLAMING GASES THAT RUSH OUT OF A FIRED GUN. EVEN SO, THERE WAS NO WORD OF IT IN THE PRESS -- BAR A SMALL SIDEBAR IN THE DAILY TELEGRAPH!

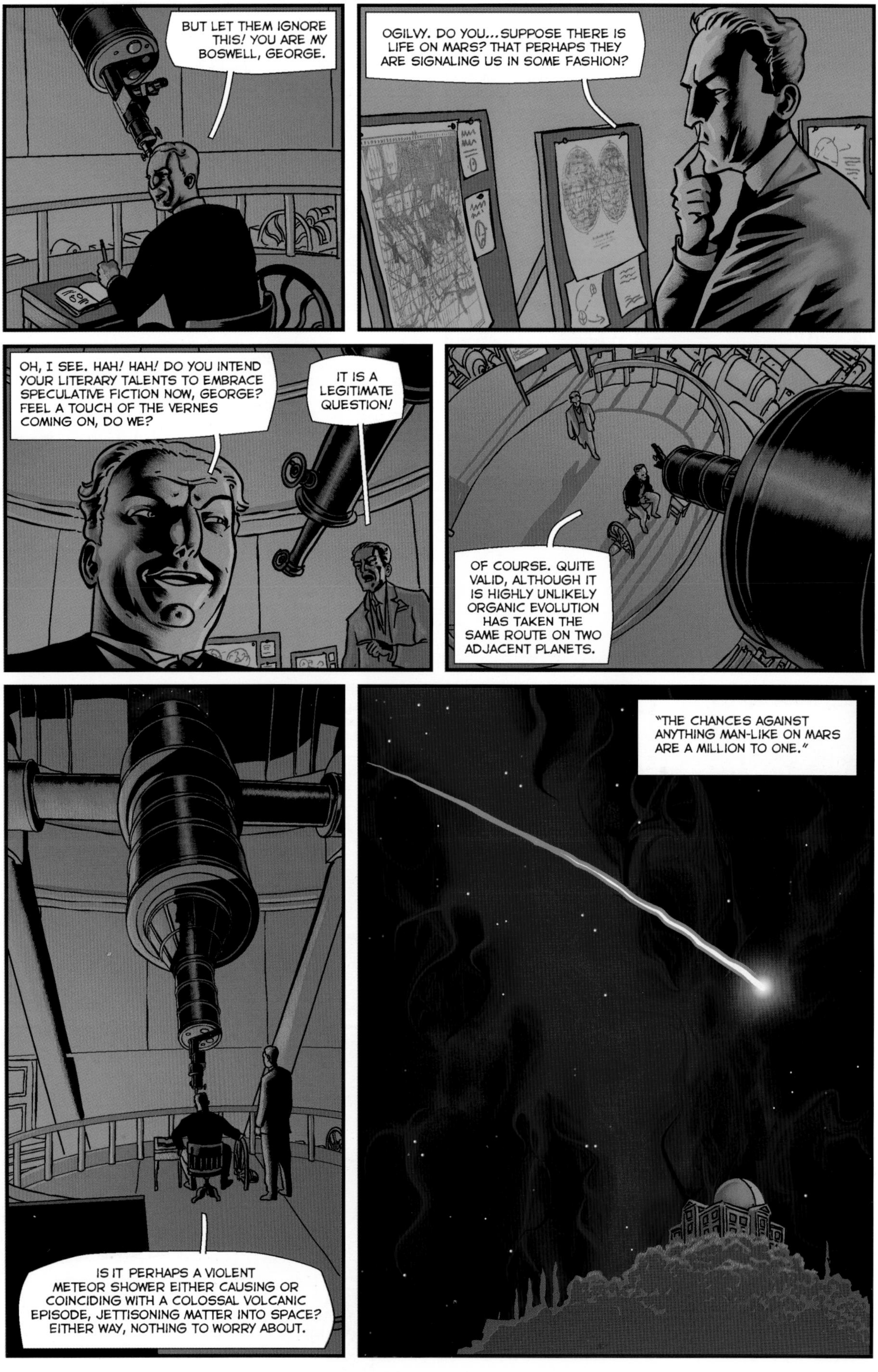
BUT LET THEM IGNORE THIS! YOU ARE MY BOSWELL, GEORGE.
OGILVY. DO YOU...SUPPOSE THERE IS LIFE ON MARS? THAT PERHAPS THEY ARE SIGNALING US IN SOME FASHION?
OH, I SEE. HAH! HAH! DO YOU INTEND YOUR LITERARY TALENTS TO EMBRACE SPECULATIVE FICTION NOW, GEORGE? FEEL A TOUCH OF THE VERNES COMING ON, DO WE?
IT IS A LEGITIMATE QUESTION!
OF COURSE. QUITE VALID, ALTHOUGH IT IS HIGHLY UNLIKELY ORGANIC EVOLUTION HAS TAKEN THE SAME ROUTE ON TWO ADJACENT PLANETS.
IS IT PERHAPS A VIOLENT METEOR SHOWER EITHER CAUSING OR COINCIDING WITH A COLOSSAL VOLCANIC EPISODE, JETTISONING MATTER INTO SPACE? EITHER WAY, NOTHING TO WORRY ABOUT.
"THE CHANCES AGAINST ANYTHING MAN-LIKE ON MARS ARE A MILLION TO ONE."

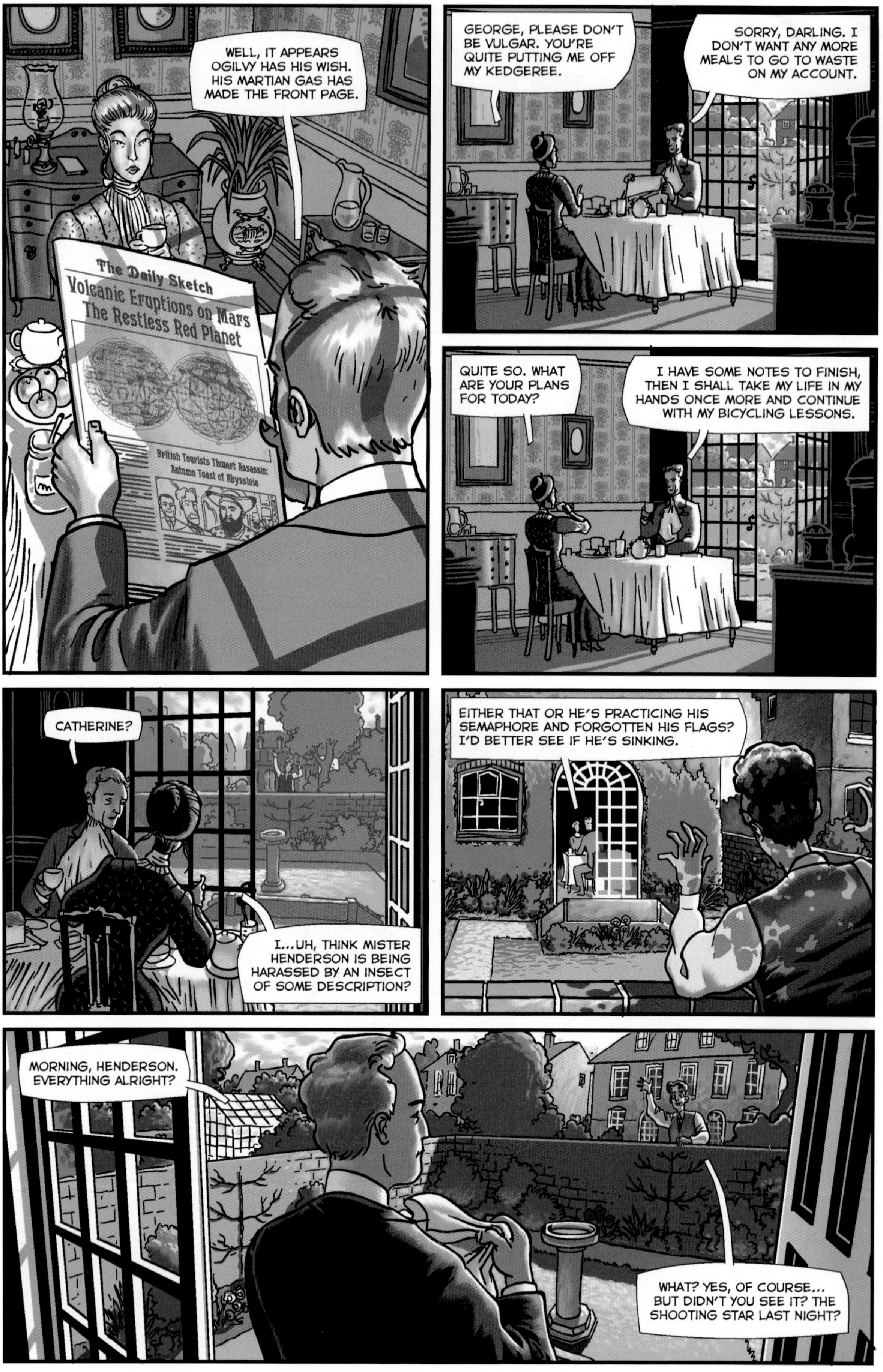
WELL, IT APPEARS OGILVY HAS HIS WISH. HIS MARTIAN GAS HAS MADE THE FRONT PAGE.
The Daily Sketch
Volcanic Eruptions on Mars
The Restless Red Planet
British Tourists Thwart Assassin: Autumn Toast of Abyssinia
GEORGE, PLEASE DON'T BE VULGAR. YOU'RE QUITE PUTTING ME OFF MY KEDGEREE.
SORRY, DARLING. I DON'T WANT ANY MORE MEALS TO GO TO WASTE ON MY ACCOUNT.
QUITE SO. WHAT ARE YOUR PLANS FOR TODAY?
I HAVE SOME NOTES TO FINISH, THEN I SHALL TAKE MY LIFE IN MY HANDS ONCE MORE AND CONTINUE WITH MY BICYCLING LESSONS.
CATHERINE?
I...UH, THINK MISTER HENDERSON IS BEING HARASSED BY AN INSECT OF SOME DESCRIPTION?
EITHER THAT OR HE'S PRACTICING HIS SEMAPHORE AND FORGOTTEN HIS FLAGS? I'D BETTER SEE IF HE'S SINKING.
MORNING, HENDERSON. EVERYTHING ALRIGHT?
WHAT? YES, OF COURSE... BUT DIDN'T YOU SEE IT? THE SHOOTING STAR LAST NIGHT?

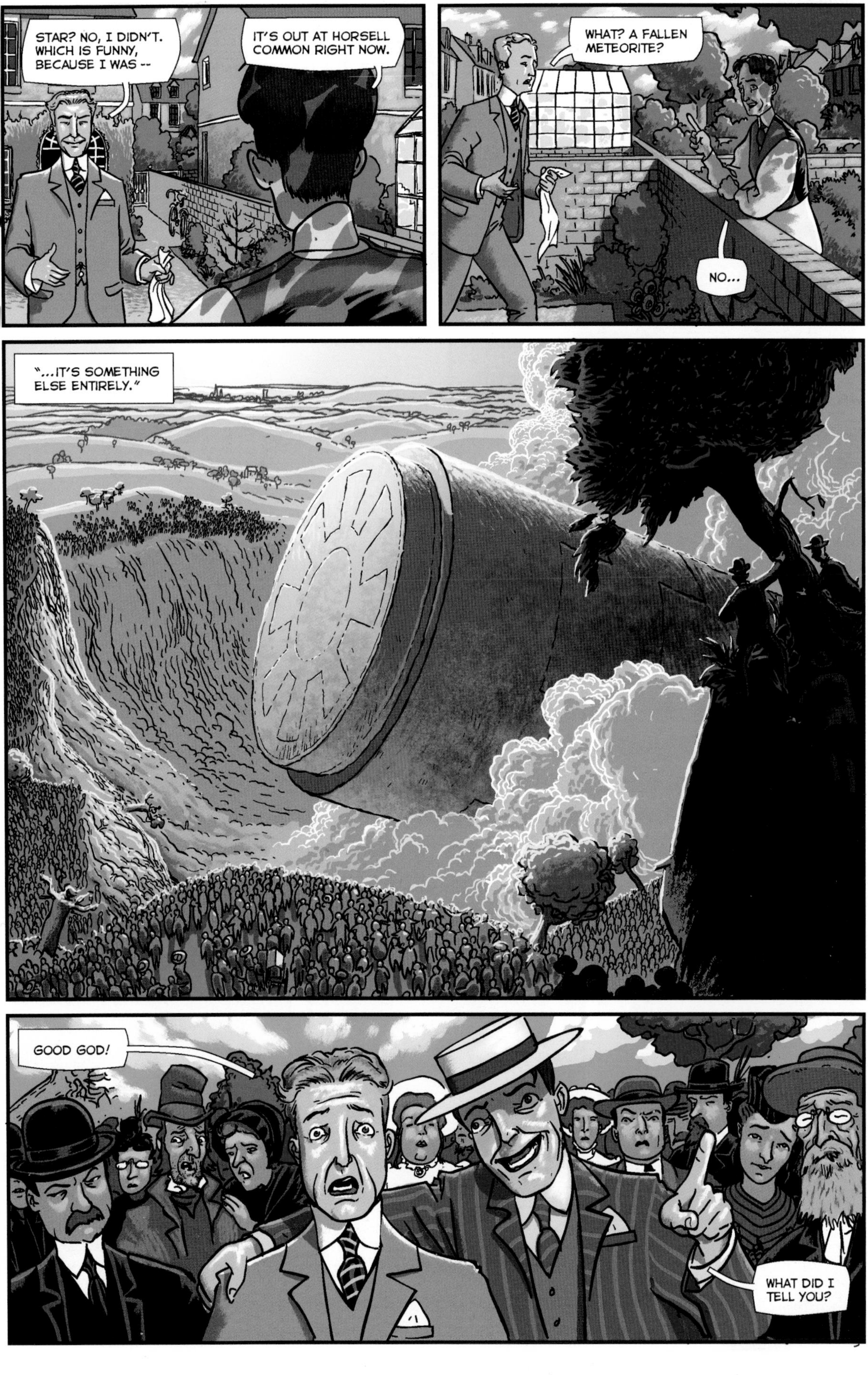
STAR? NO, I DIDN'T. WHICH IS FUNNY, BECAUSE I WAS --
IT'S OUT AT HORSELL COMMON RIGHT NOW.
WHAT? A FALLEN METEORITE?
NO...
"...IT'S SOMETHING ELSE ENTIRELY."
GOOD GOD!
WHAT DID I TELL YOU?

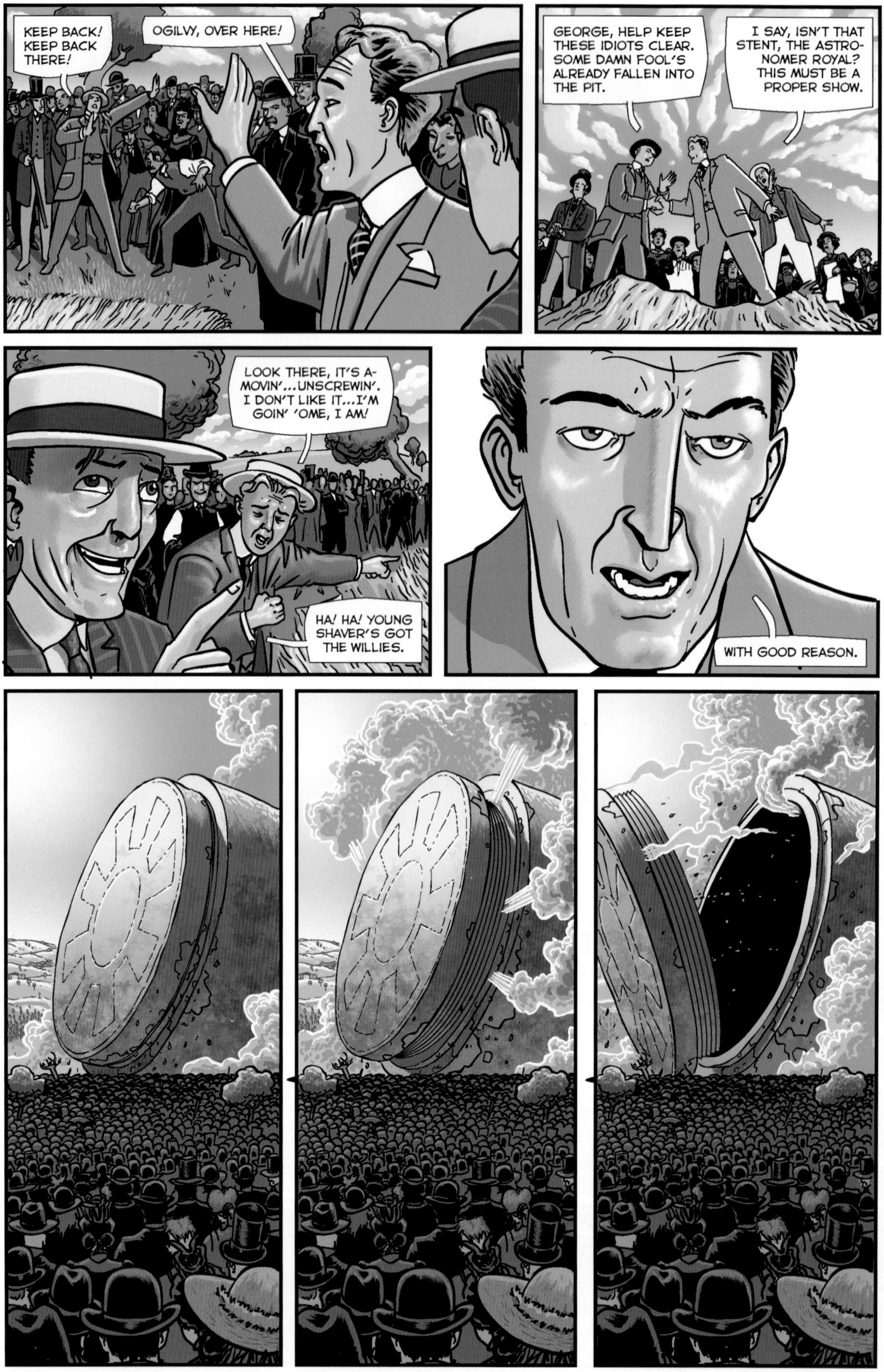
KEEP BACK! KEEP BACK THERE!
OGILVY, OVER HERE!
GEORGE, HELP KEEP THESE IDIOTS CLEAR. SOME DAMN FOOL'S ALREADY FALLEN INTO THE PIT.
I SAY, ISN'T THAT STENT, THE ASTRONOMER ROYAL? THIS MUST BE A PROPER SHOW.
LOOK THERE, IT'S A-MOVIN'...UNSCREWIN'. I DON'T LIKE IT...I'M GOIN' 'OME, I AM!
HA! HA! YOUNG SHAVER'S GOT THE WILLIES.
WITH GOOD REASON.

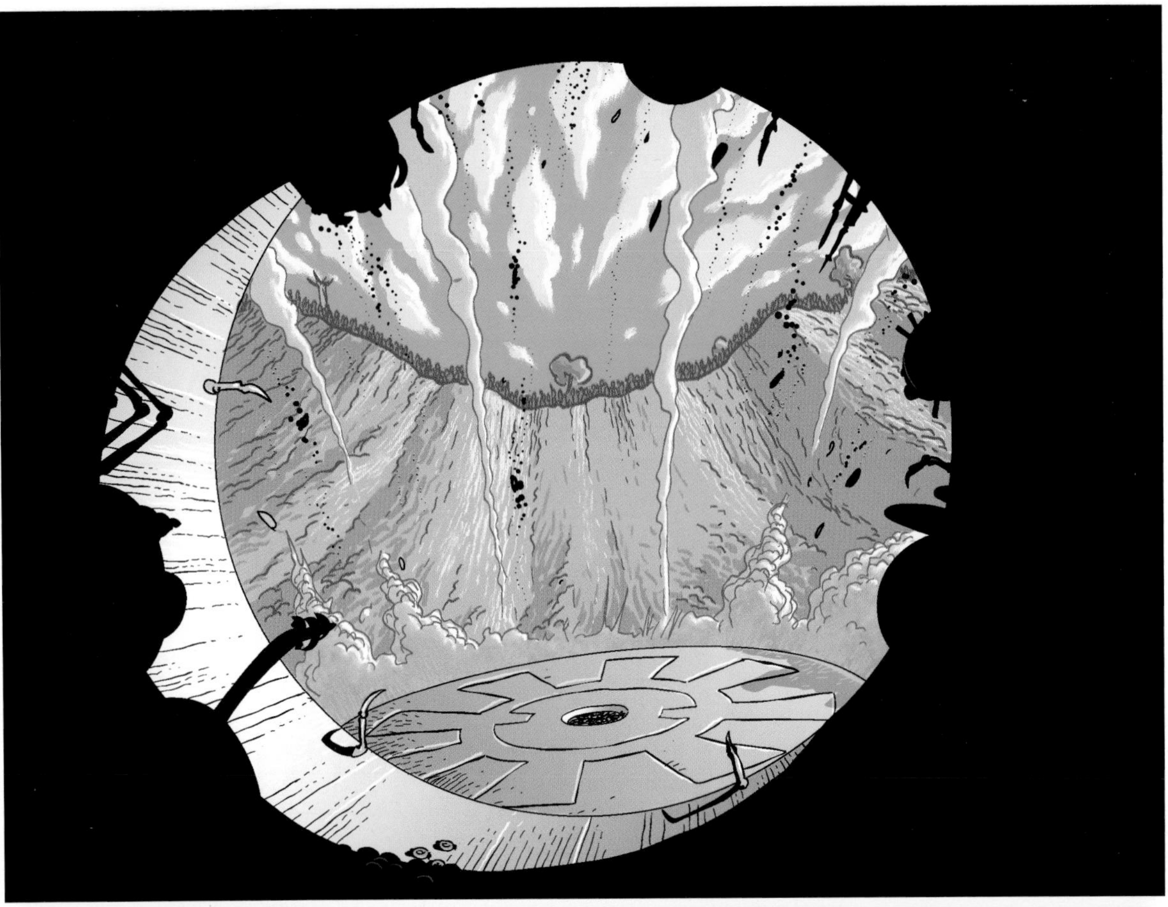

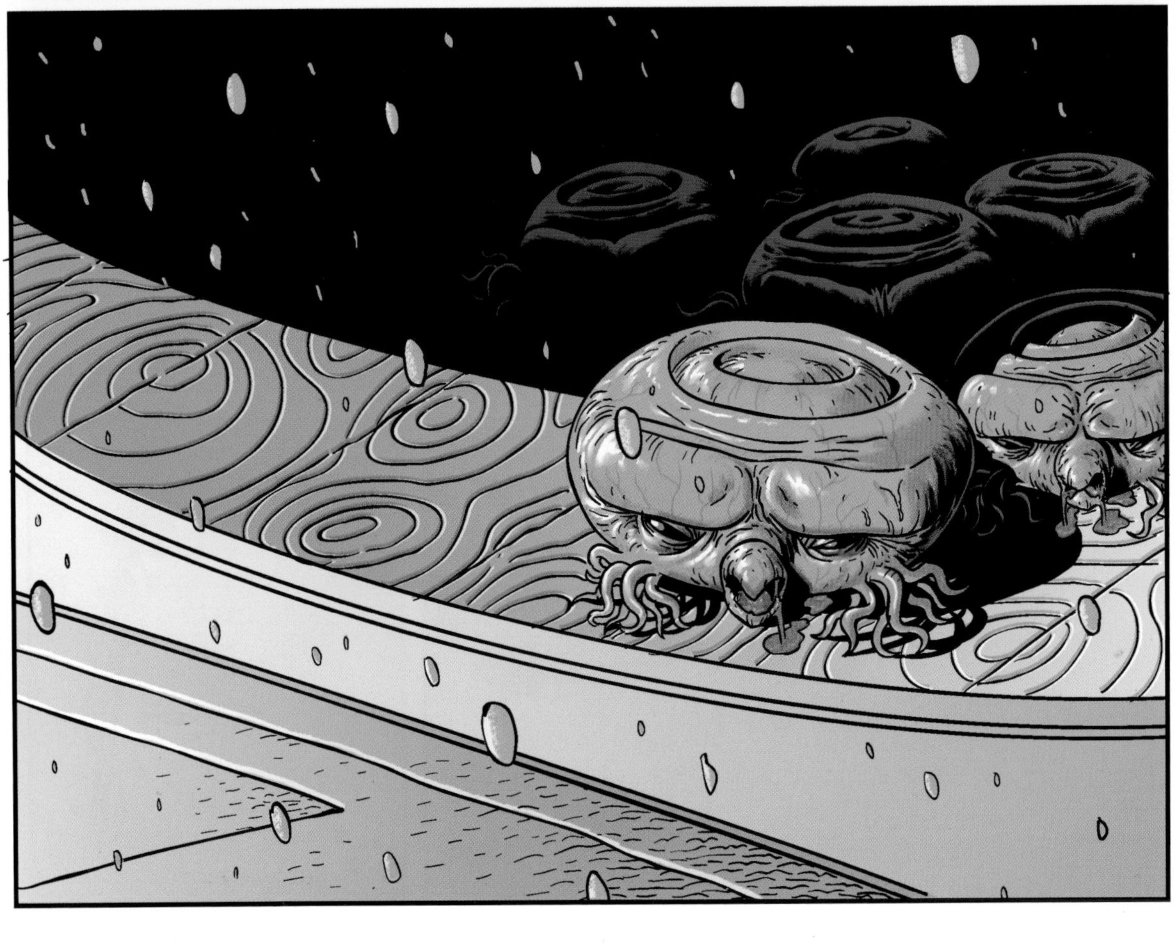

WHAT BRUTES. WHAT UGLY BRUTES!
YET TO HAVE JOURNEYED THIS FAR, THEY ARE CLEARLY OF NO SMALL INTELLECT.
WE MUST ATTEMPT TO COMMUNICATE. ASSURE THEM WE MEAN NO HARM.
QUITE RIGHT.
AREN'T YOU COMING, GEORGE? IT'S THE STORY OF THE CENTURY!
NO...NO, I'LL STAY HERE, IF IT'S ALL THE SAME.
SUIT YOURSELF.
IT'S ENORMOUS!
UH, HELLO IN THERE? WE COME IN PEACE.

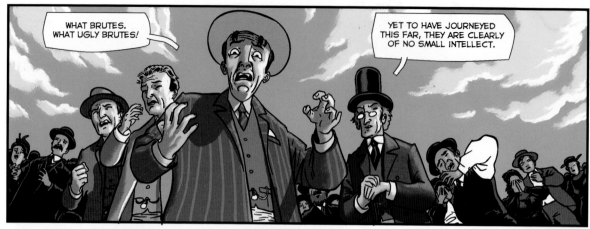

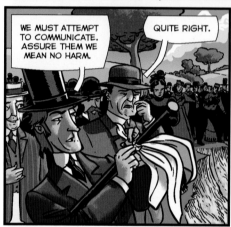

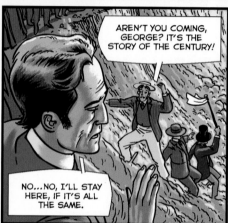

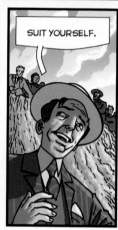

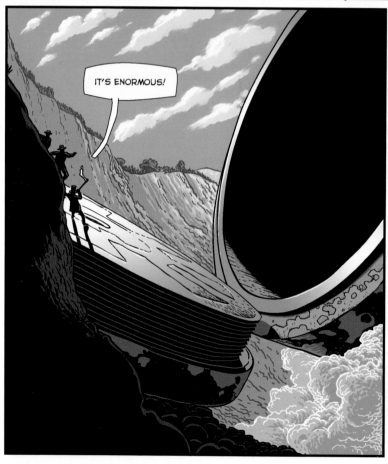

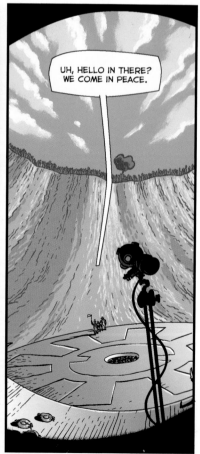

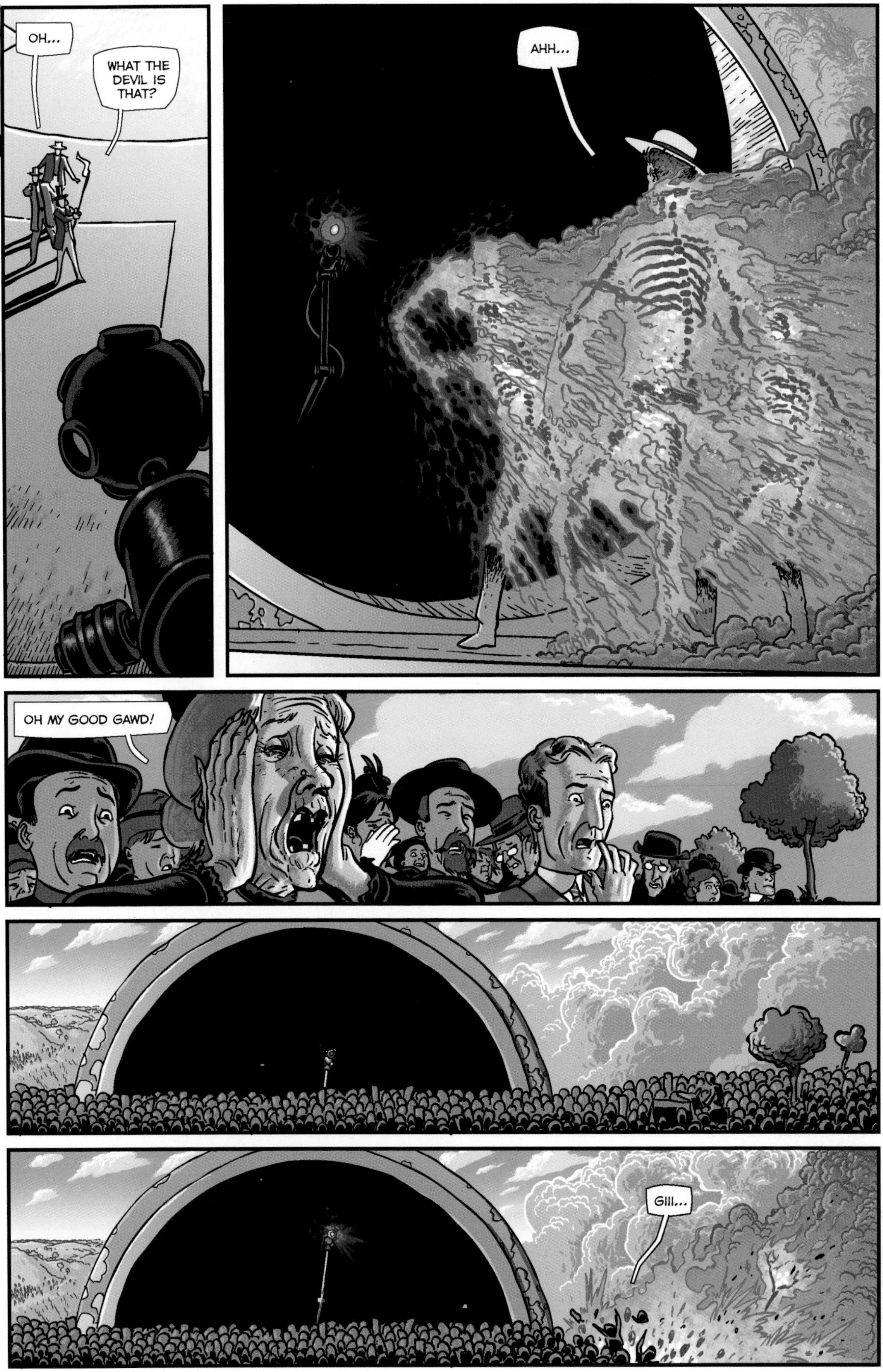
OH...
WHAT THE DEVIL IS THAT?
AHH...
OH MY GOOD GAWD!
GIII...

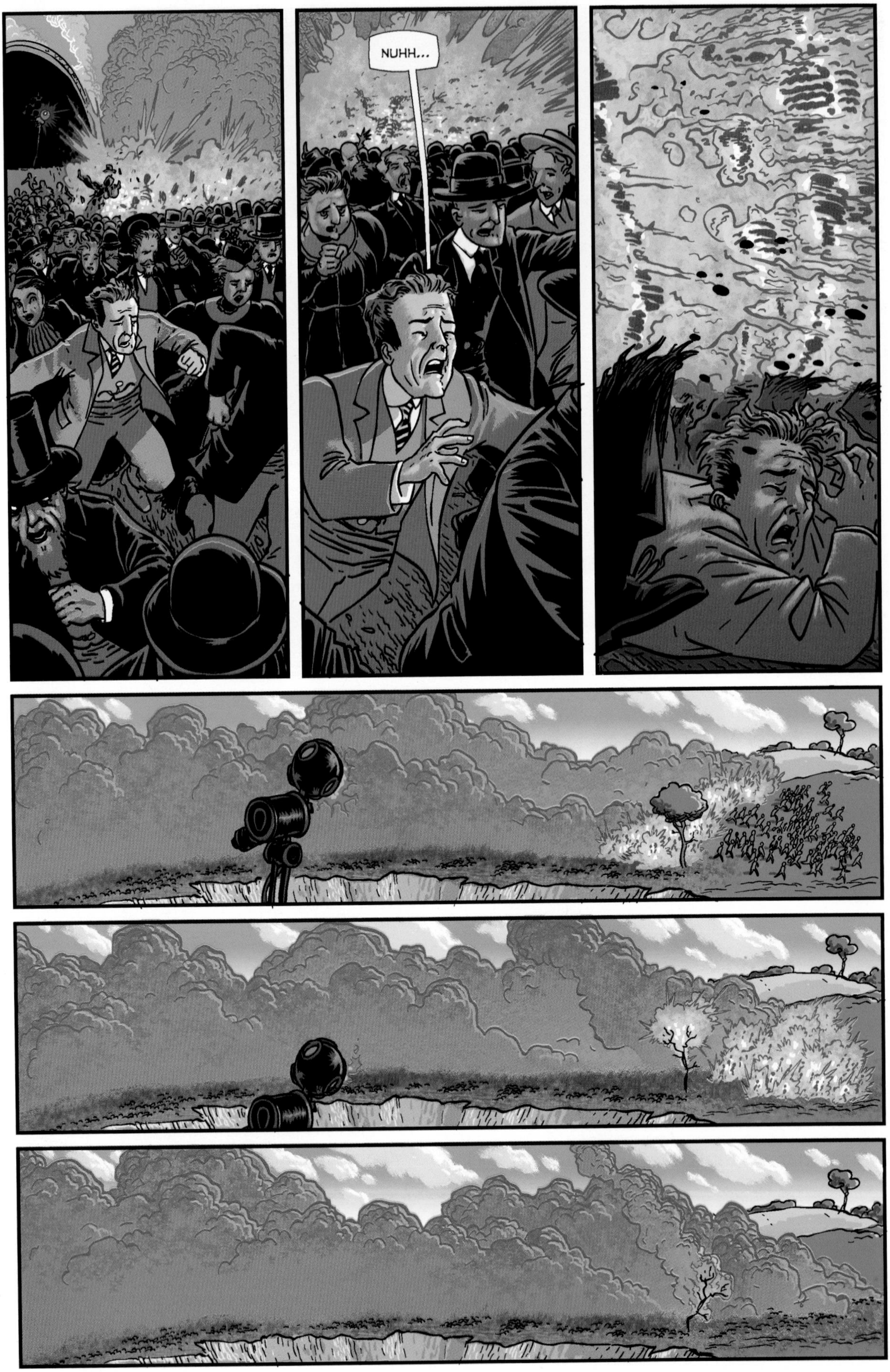
NUHH...

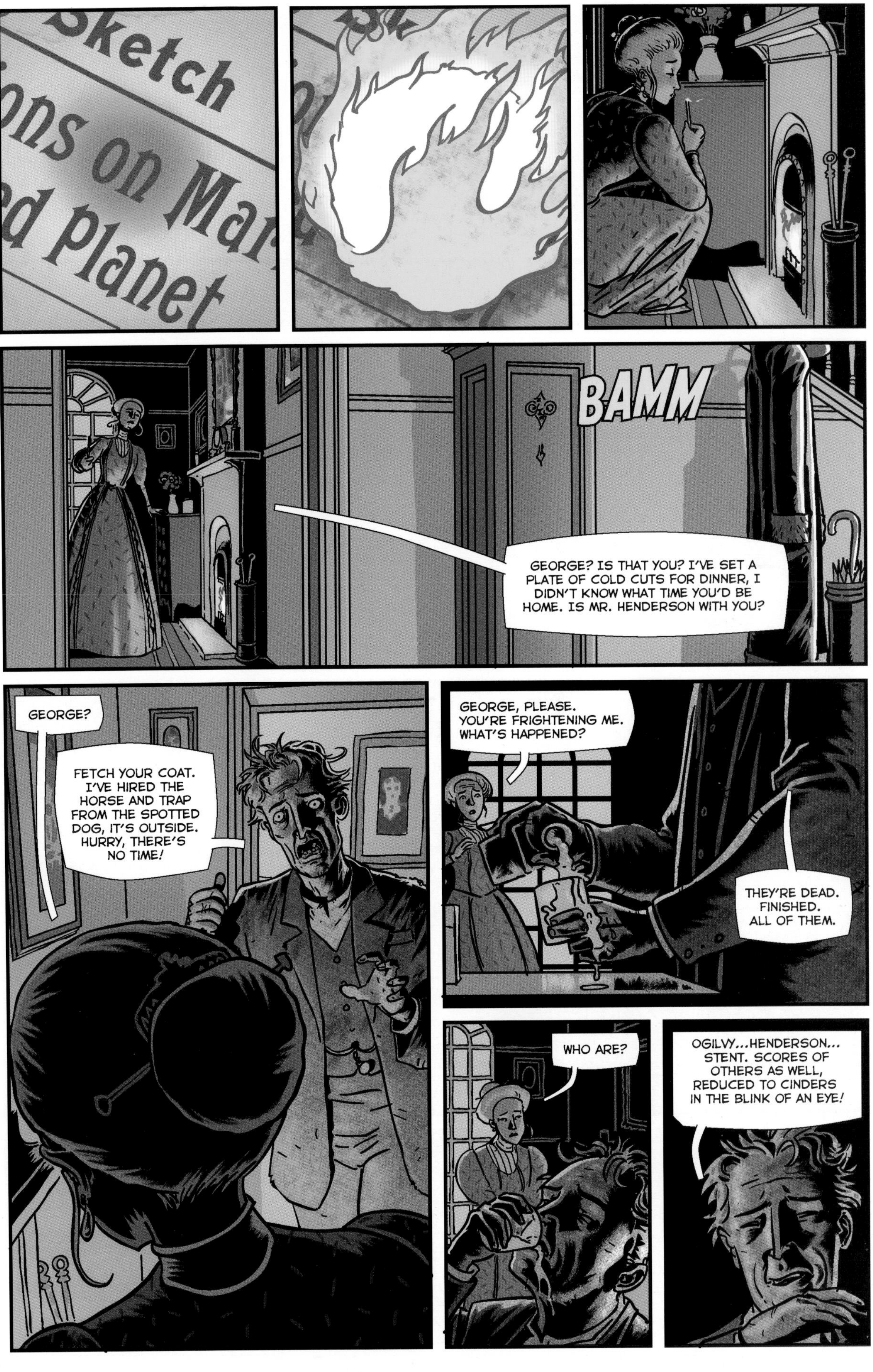
Sketch
ons on Mar
ed Planet
BAMM
GEORGE? IS THAT YOU? I'VE SET A PLATE OF COLD CUTS FOR DINNER, I DIDN'T KNOW WHAT TIME YOU'D BE HOME. IS MR. HENDERSON WITH YOU?
GEORGE?
FETCH YOUR COAT. I'VE HIRED THE HORSE AND TRAP FROM THE SPOTTED DOG, IT'S OUTSIDE. HURRY, THERE'S NO TIME!
GEORGE, PLEASE. YOU'RE FRIGHTENING ME. WHAT'S HAPPENED?
THEY'RE DEAD. FINISHED. ALL OF THEM.
WHO ARE?
OGILVY...HENDERSON... STENT. SCORES OF OTHERS AS WELL, REDUCED TO CINDERS IN THE BLINK OF AN EYE!

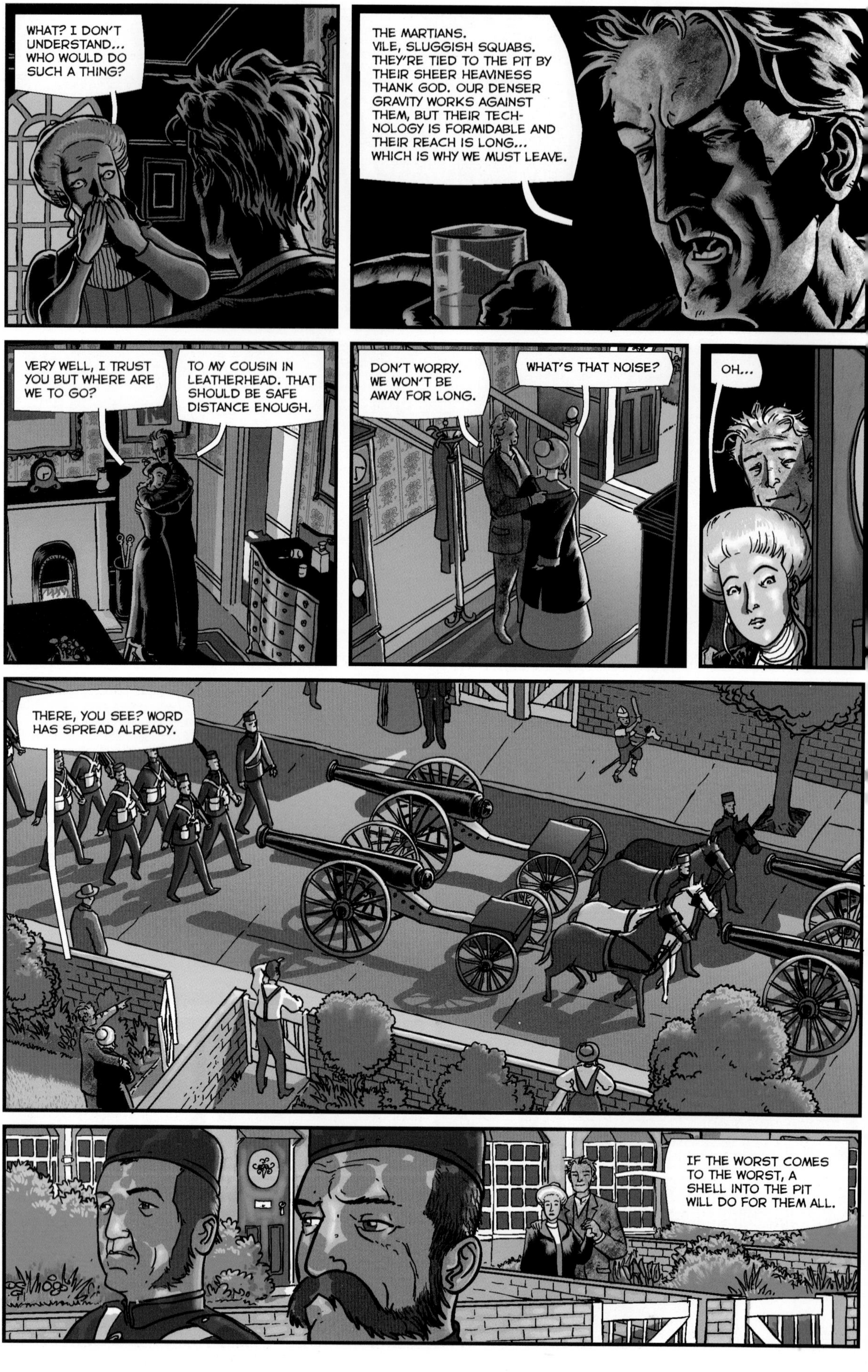
WHAT? I DON'T UNDERSTAND... WHO WOULD DO SUCH A THING?
THE MARTIANS. VILE, SLUGGISH SQUABS. THEY'RE TIED TO THE PIT BY THEIR SHEER HEAVINESS THANK GOD. OUR DENSER GRAVITY WORKS AGAINST THEM, BUT THEIR TECH-NOLOGY IS FORMIDABLE AND THEIR REACH IS LONG... WHICH IS WHY WE MUST LEAVE.
VERY WELL, I TRUST YOU BUT WHERE ARE WE TO GO?
TO MY COUSIN IN LEATHERHEAD. THAT SHOULD BE SAFE DISTANCE ENOUGH.
DON'T WORRY. WE WON'T BE AWAY FOR LONG.
WHAT'S THAT NOISE?
OH...
THERE, YOU SEE? WORD HAS SPREAD ALREADY.
IF THE WORST COMES TO THE WORST, A SHELL INTO THE PIT WILL DO FOR THEM ALL.

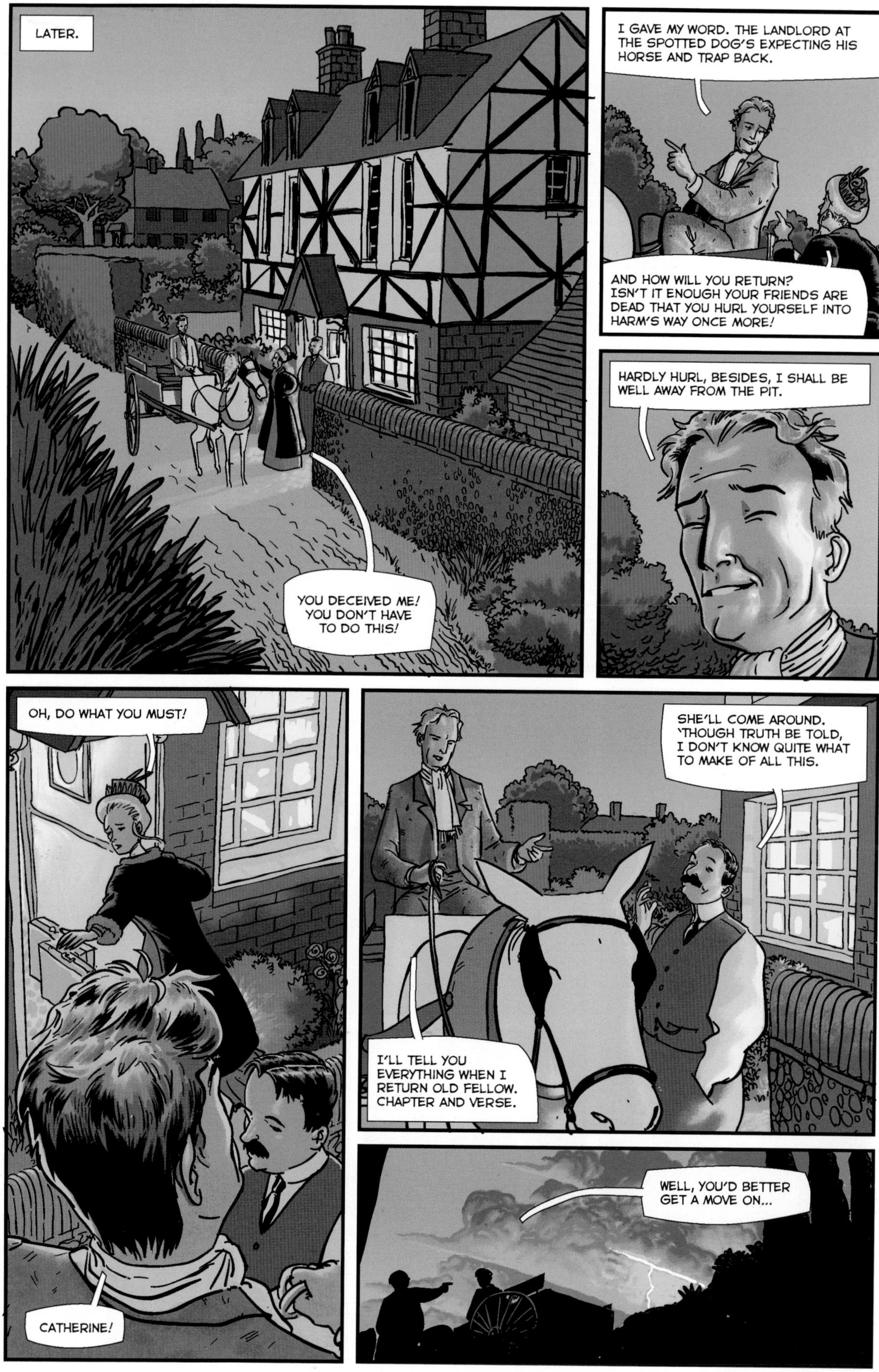
LATER.
YOU DECEIVED ME! YOU DON'T HAVE TO DO THIS!
I GAVE MY WORD. THE LANDLORD AT THE SPOTTED DOG'S EXPECTING HIS HORSE AND TRAP BACK.
AND HOW WILL YOU RETURN? ISN'T IT ENOUGH YOUR FRIENDS ARE DEAD THAT YOU HURL YOURSELF INTO HARM'S WAY ONCE MORE!
HARDLY HURL, BESIDES, I SHALL BE WELL AWAY FROM THE PIT.
OH, DO WHAT YOU MUST!
CATHERINE!
SHE'LL COME AROUND. 'THOUGH TRUTH BE TOLD, I DON'T KNOW QUITE WHAT TO MAKE OF ALL THIS.
I'LL TELL YOU EVERYTHING WHEN I RETURN OLD FELLOW. CHAPTER AND VERSE.
WELL, YOU'D BETTER GET A MOVE ON...

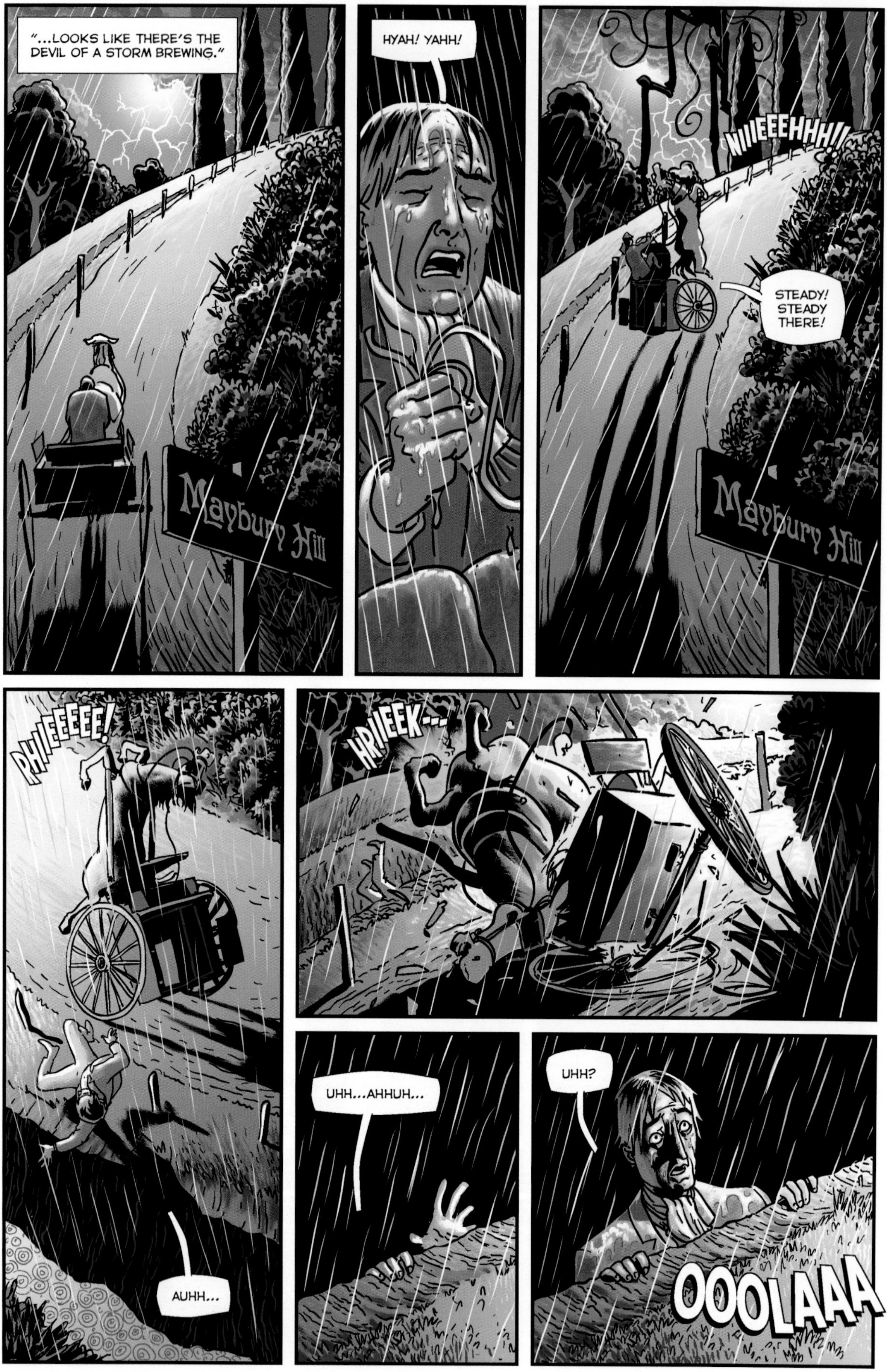
"...LOOKS LIKE THERE'S THE DEVIL OF A STORM BREWING."
Maybury Hill
HYAH! YAHH!
WIIIEEEHHH!!
STEADY! STEADY THERE!
Maybury Hill
RHIEEEEEE!
AUHH...
HRIIEEK...
UHH...AHHUH...
UHH?
OOOLAAA

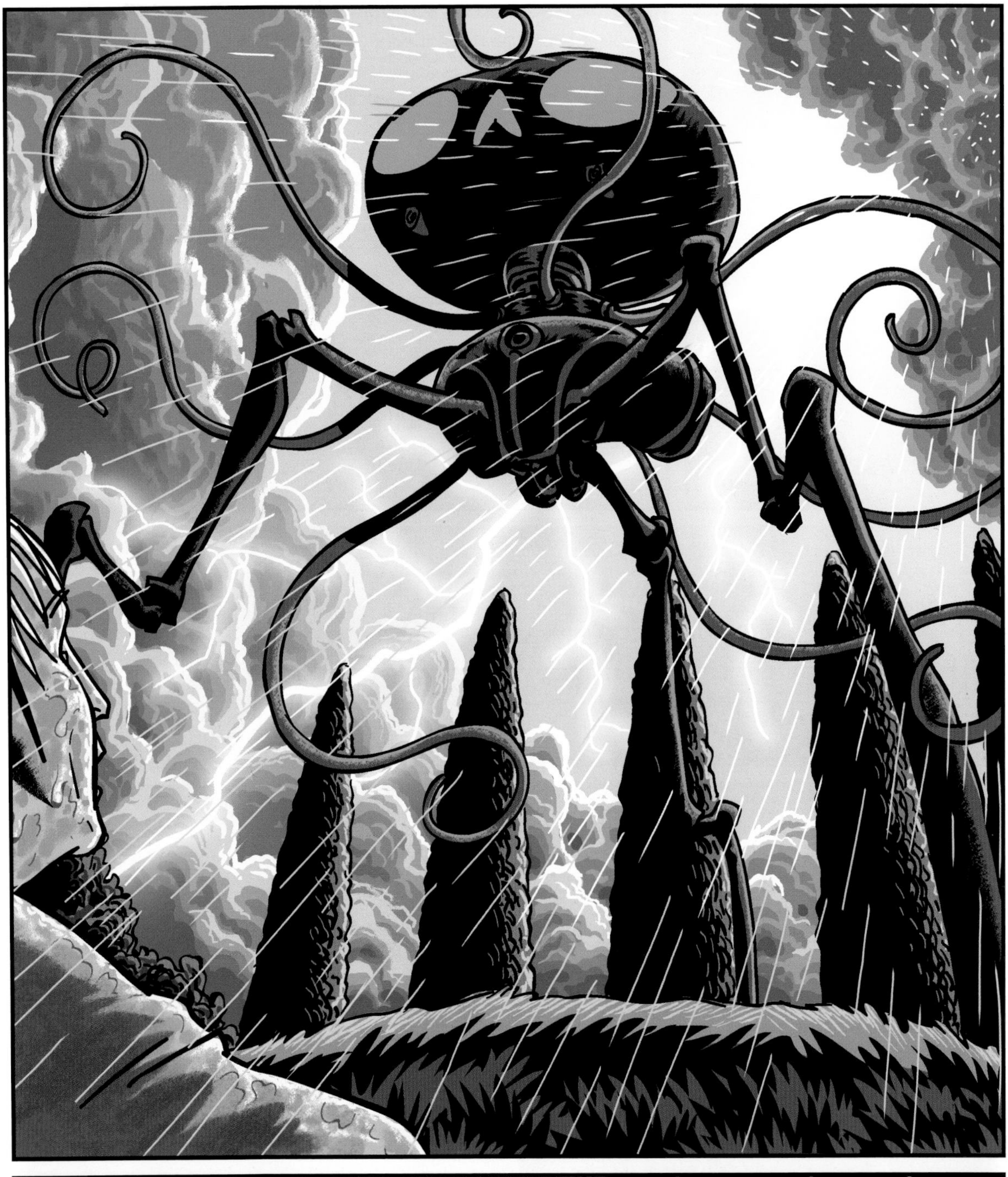

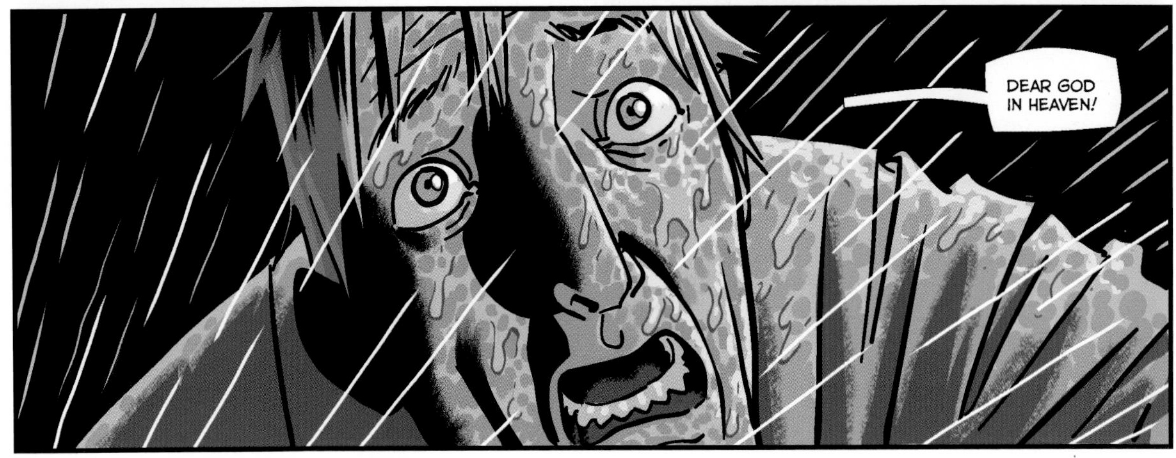
DEAR GOD IN HEAVEN!

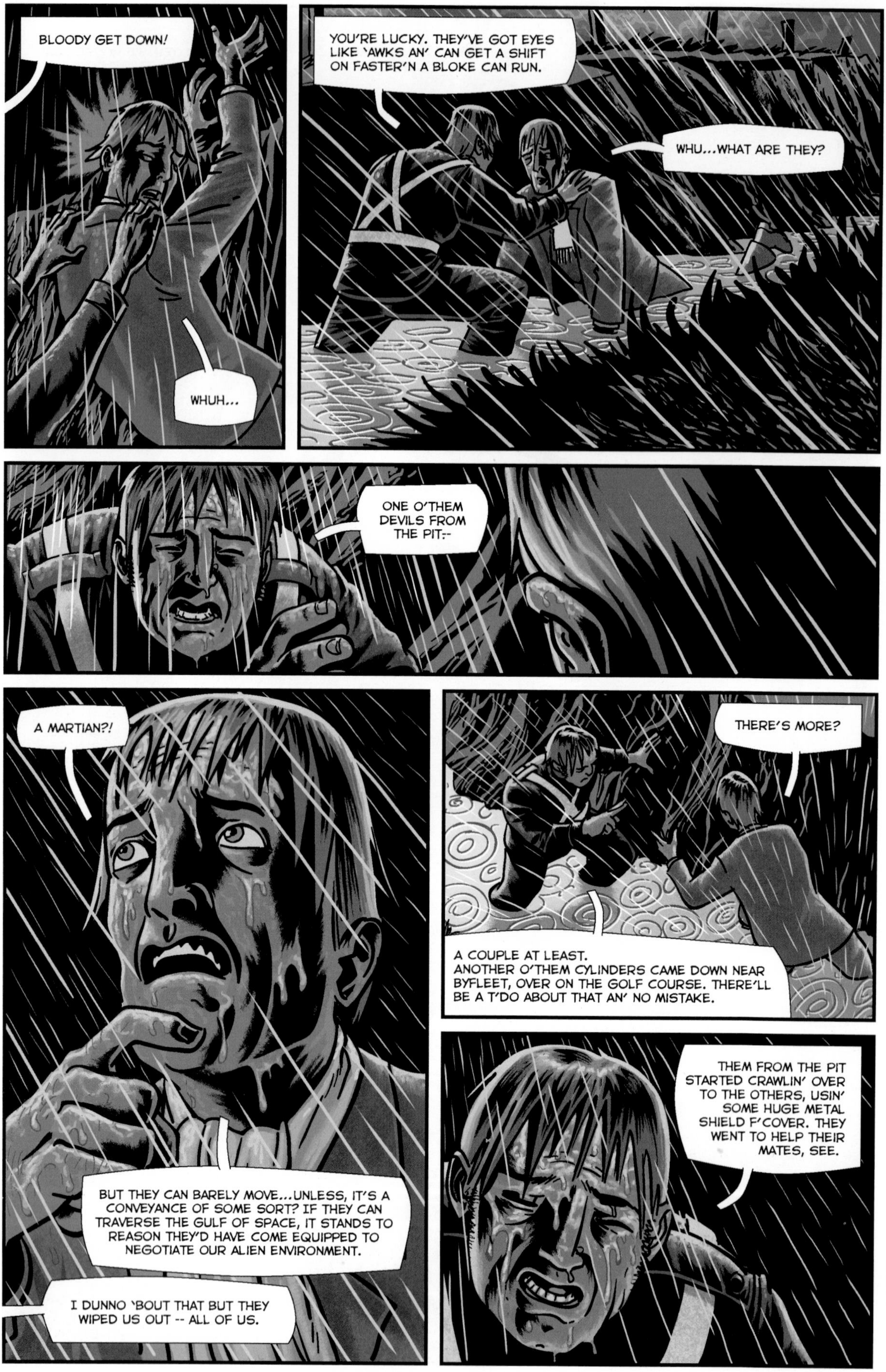

BLOODY GET DOWN!
WHUH...
YOU'RE LUCKY. THEY'VE GOT EYES LIKE 'AWKS AN' CAN GET A SHIFT ON FASTER'N A BLOKE CAN RUN.
WHU...WHAT ARE THEY?
ONE O'THEM DEVILS FROM THE PIT:-
A MARTIAN?!
BUT THEY CAN BARELY MOVE...UNLESS, IT'S A CONVEYANCE OF SOME SORT? IF THEY CAN TRAVERSE THE GULF OF SPACE, IT STANDS TO REASON THEY'D HAVE COME EQUIPPED TO NEGOTIATE OUR ALIEN ENVIRONMENT.
I DUNNO 'BOUT THAT BUT THEY WIPED US OUT -- ALL OF US.
THERE'S MORE?
A COUPLE AT LEAST.
ANOTHER O'THEM CYLINDERS CAME DOWN NEAR BYFLEET, OVER ON THE GOLF COURSE. THERE'LL BE A T'DO ABOUT THAT AN' NO MISTAKE.
THEM FROM THE PIT STARTED CRAWLIN' OVER TO THE OTHERS, USIN' SOME HUGE METAL SHIELD F'COVER. THEY WENT TO HELP THEIR MATES, SEE.

"WE WAS ABOUT TO GIVE 'EM WHAT-FOR...WHEN IT STANDS UP. IT WASN'T A SHIELD BUT THE TOP OF ONE O'THEM MILKIN' STOOLS!

"THE LORD MUST'VE 'AD IS EYE ON ME, I'LL TELL YEH. ME HORSE LOST IT'S FOOTIN' IN A RABBIT HOLE AN' DOWN I WENT... ARSE OVER TIP.

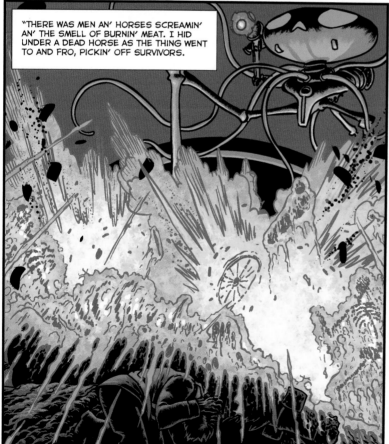

"THERE WAS MEN AN' HORSES SCREAMIN' AN' THE SMELL OF BURNIN' MEAT. I HID UNDER A DEAD HORSE AS THE THING WENT TO AND FRO, PICKIN' OFF SURVIVORS.

"FINALLY IT GAVE UP. IT AN' ANOTHER 'UN THEN WENT OFF T'THE OTHER CYLINDER. WHEN THE COAST WAS CLEAR, I LEGGED IT."

I WAS HEADIN' FOR WEYBRIDGE, WHERE THE REST OF OUR FORCE IS MUSTERED WHEN I SAW THIS 'UN.

WAIT, LOOK...

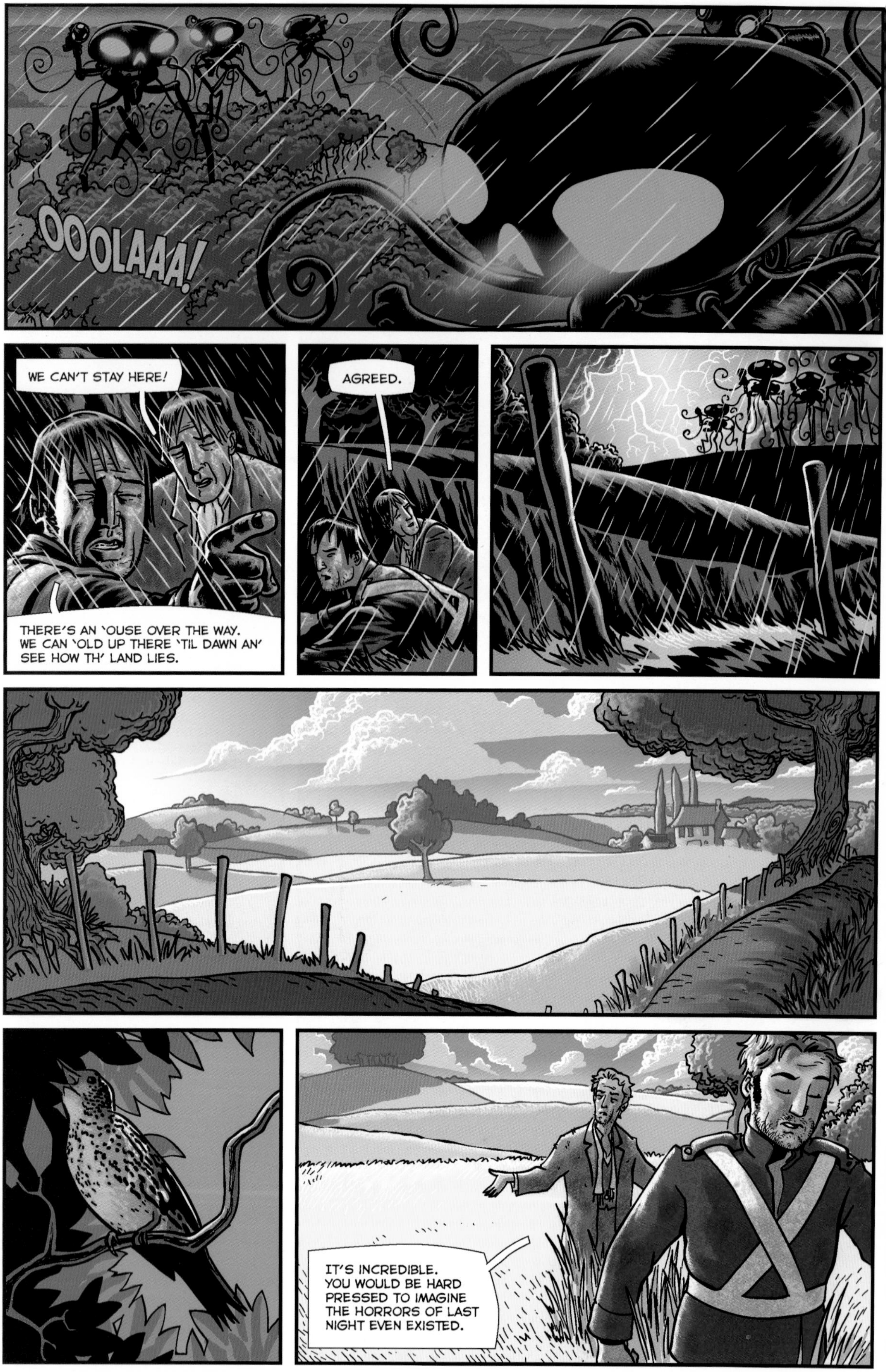
OOOLAAA!
WE CAN'T STAY HERE!
THERE'S AN 'OUSE OVER THE WAY.
WE CAN 'OLD UP THERE 'TIL DAWN AN'
SEE HOW TH' LAND LIES.
AGREED.
IT'S INCREDIBLE.
YOU WOULD BE HARD
PRESSED TO IMAGINE
THE HORRORS OF LAST
NIGHT EVEN EXISTED.

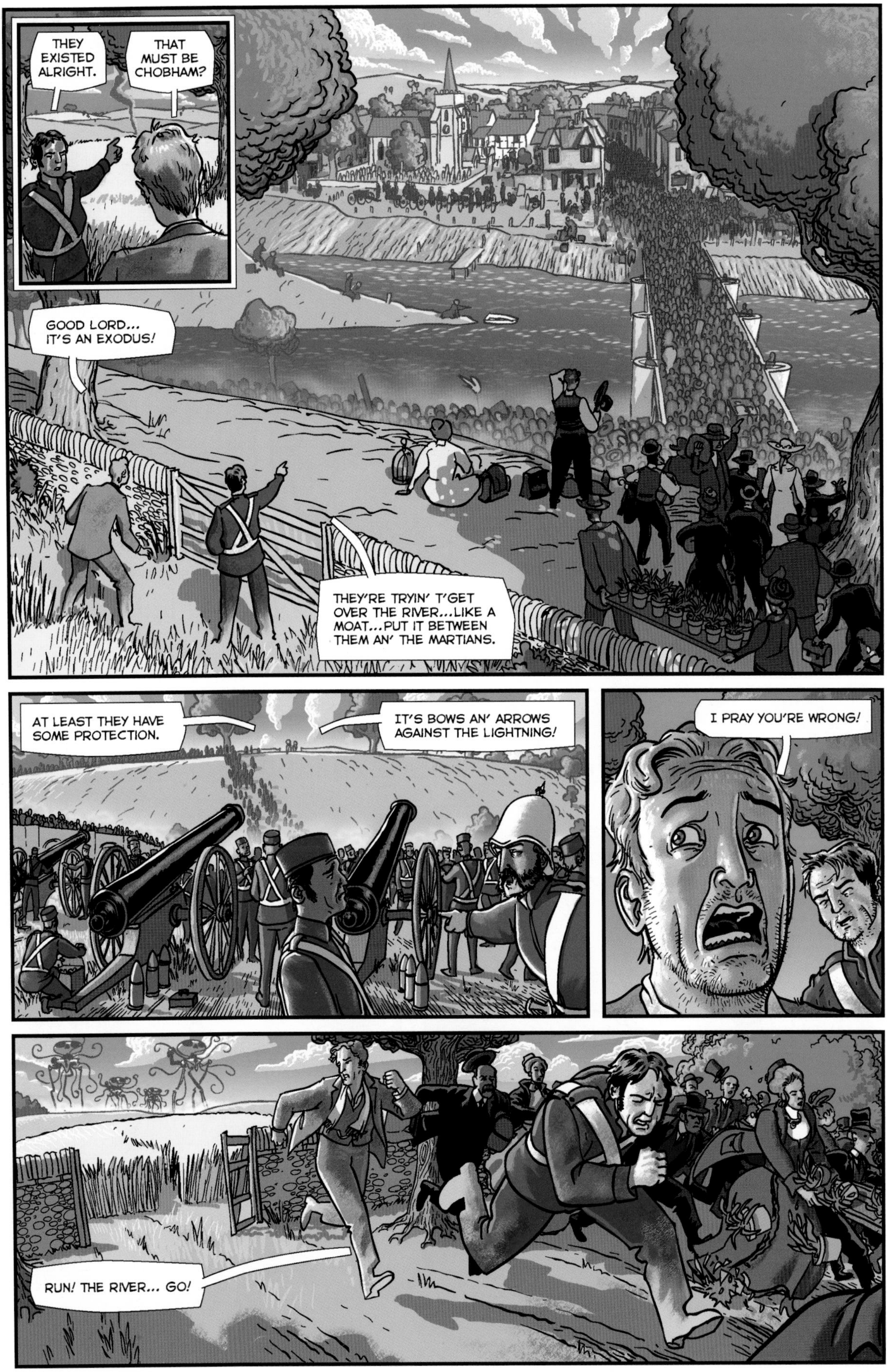
THEY EXISTED ALRIGHT.
THAT MUST BE CHOBHAM?
GOOD LORD... IT'S AN EXODUS!
THEY'RE TRYIN' T'GET OVER THE RIVER...LIKE A MOAT...PUT IT BETWEEN THEM AN' THE MARTIANS.
AT LEAST THEY HAVE SOME PROTECTION.
IT'S BOWS AN' ARROWS AGAINST THE LIGHTNING!
I PRAY YOU'RE WRONG!
RUN! THE RIVER... GO!

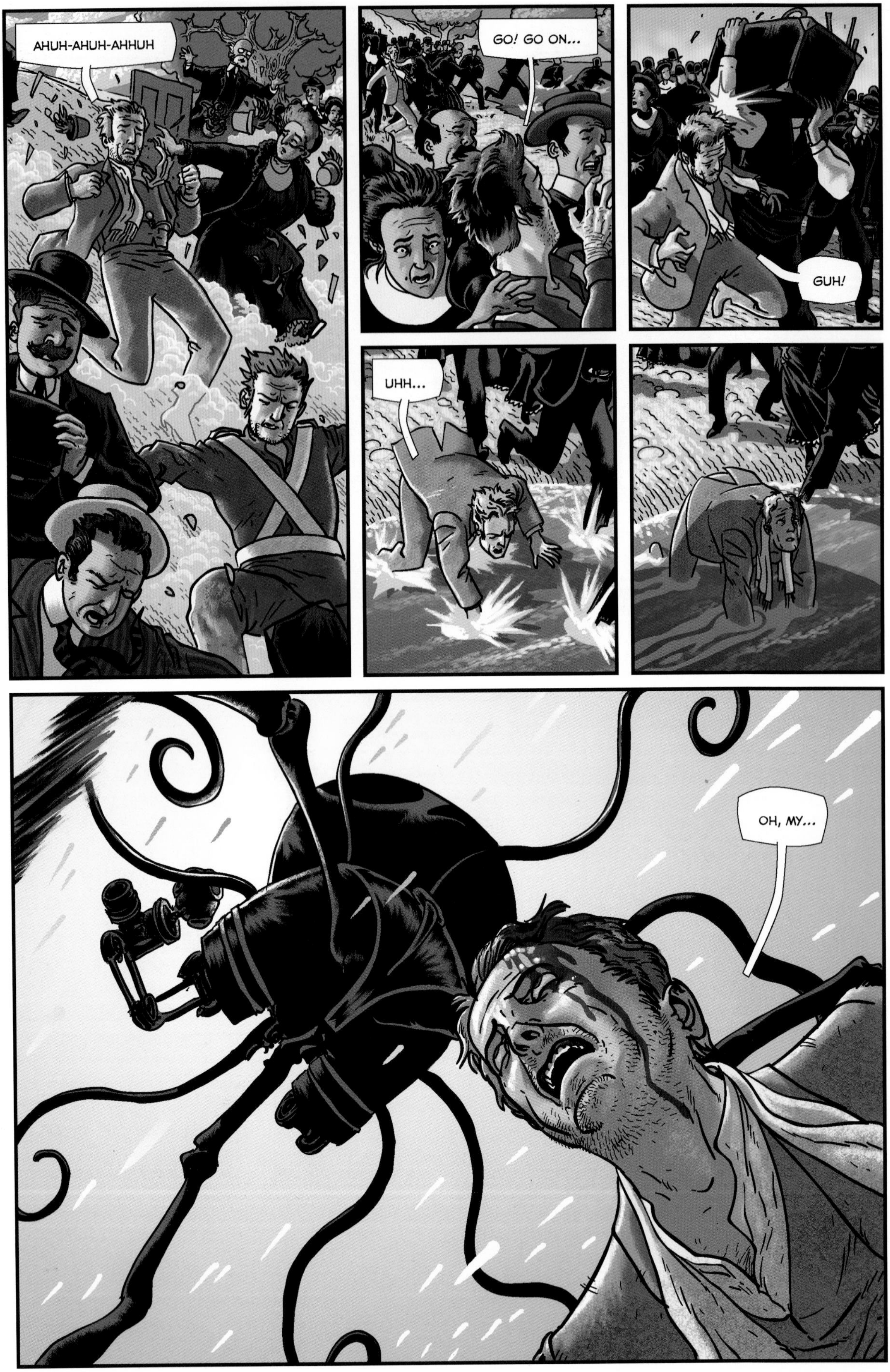
AHUH-AHUH-AHHUH
GO! GO ON...
GUH!
UHH...
OH, MY...

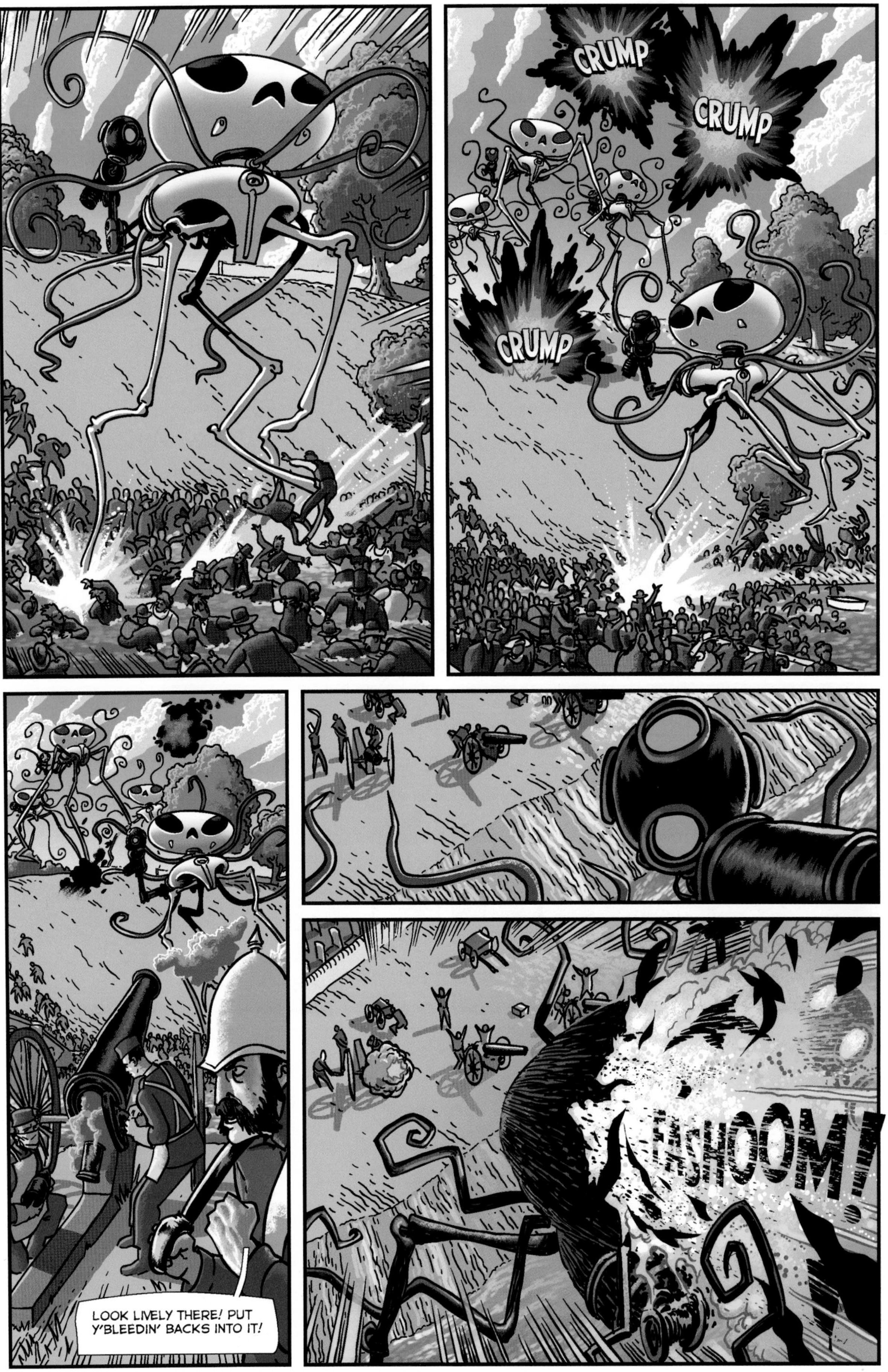
CRUMP
CRUMP
CRUMP
LOOK LIVELY THERE! PUT Y'BLEEDIN' BACKS INTO IT!
FASHOOM!

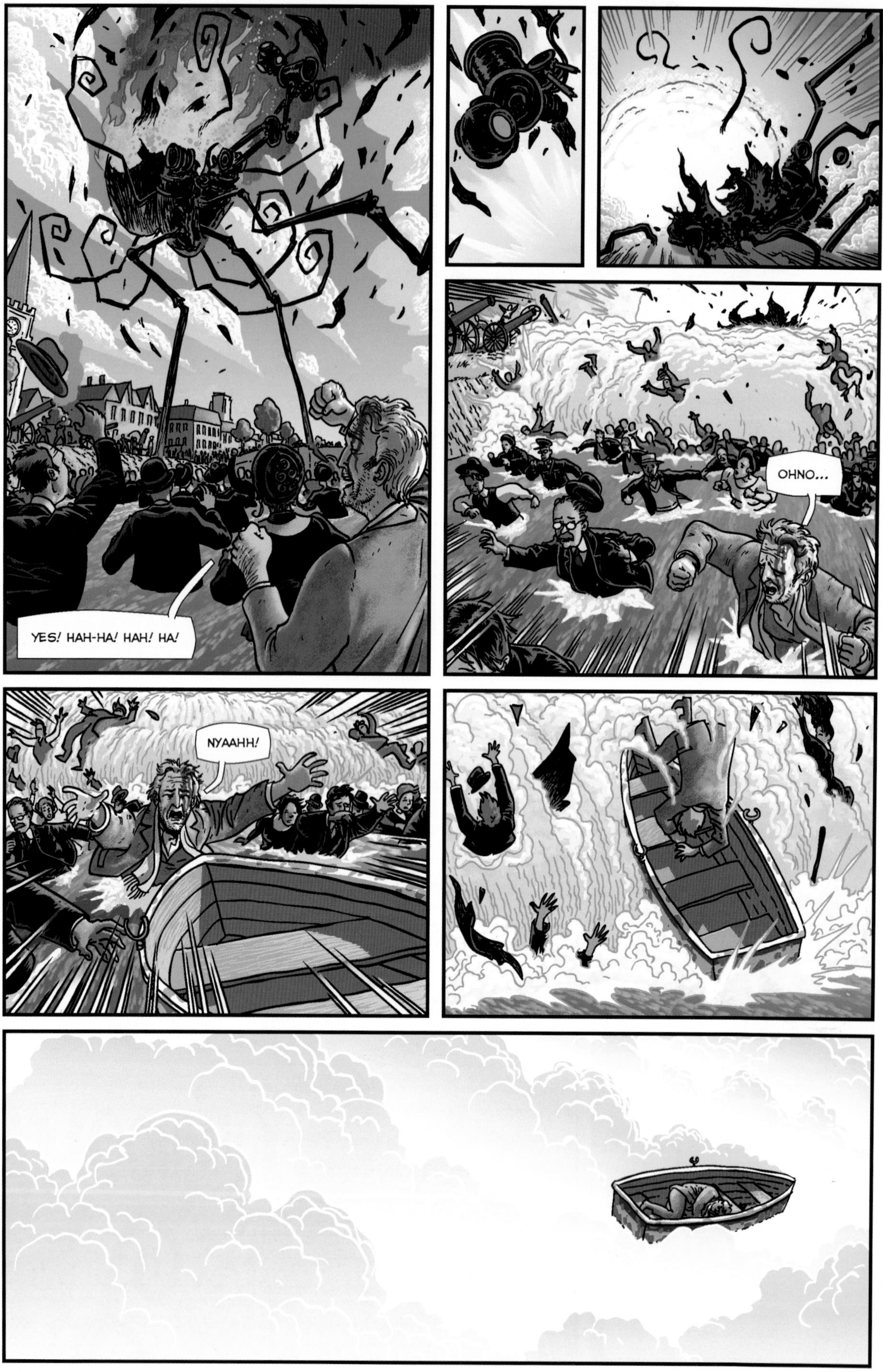
YES! HAH-HA! HAH! HA!
OHNO...
NYAAHH!

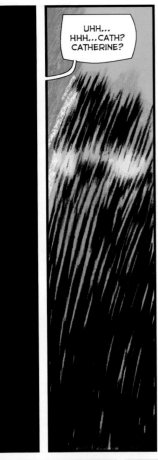

UHH... HHH...CATH? CATHERINE?

NO...NO, I AM NOT SHE. HERE, YOU'D BETTER DRINK THIS.

THANK YOU... UH, VICAR.

NO, I AM ONLY A CURATE, AND YOU ARE SAFE... IF THAT WORD HAS VALUE ANYMORE. I FOUND YOU STAGGERING ALONG THE RIVERBANK NEAR WALTON. YOU WERE DAZED, DELIRIOUS, HAVE BEEN FOR SEVERAL DAYS NOW.

DAYS! WHAT HAS BEEN HAPPENING... WITH THE MARTIANS?

IT IS SODOM AND GOMORRAH! EVERYTHING GONE...DESTROYED! WHAT HAVE WE DONE? WHAT HAS WEYBRIDGE DONE... SWEPT OUT OF EXISTENCE!

THIS MUST BE THE BEGINNING OF THE END. THE GREAT AND TERRIBLE DAY OF THE LORD!

CALM DOWN! YOU'RE SCARED OUT OF YOUR WITS IS ALL. WHAT GOOD IS RELIGION IF IT COLLAPSES UNDER CALAMITY?

THINK WHAT EARTHQUAKES AND FLOODS, WAR, AND VOLCANOES HAVE DONE TO MEN BEFORE. DID YOU THINK GOD HAD EXEMPTED WEYBRIDGE? HE IS NOT AN INSURANCE AGENT!

YOU DO NOT KNOW! YOU HAVE NOT SEEN! NIGHT AFTER NIGHT, THEIR STARS OF ILL OMEN BURN THROUGH THE HEAVENS.

MARTIAN CYLINDERS? HOW MANY?

ENOUGH... ENOUGH TO SEE THE END OF US. LAST I HEARD, LONDON WAS FALLING...

"THE MASS OF MAN IS ON THE MOVE. THE LEGENDARY HOSTS OF GOTHS AND HUNS, THE HUGEST ARMIES ASIA HAS EVER SEEN, ARE BUT A DROP IN THAT CURRENT.

"IT IS NO DISCIPLINED MARCH BUT A STAMPEDE, GIGANTIC AND TERRIBLE, WITHOUT GOAL OR ORDER.

"THE MARTIANS ACT WITHOUT MORALITY OR MERCY. DISCHARGING ENORMOUS CLOUDS OF BLACK, TOXIC VAPOUR BY MEANS OF ROCKETS.

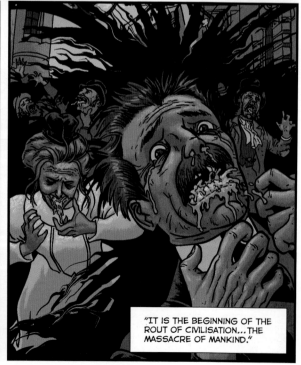

"IT IS THE BEGINNING OF THE ROUT OF CIVILISATION... THE MASSACRE OF MANKIND."

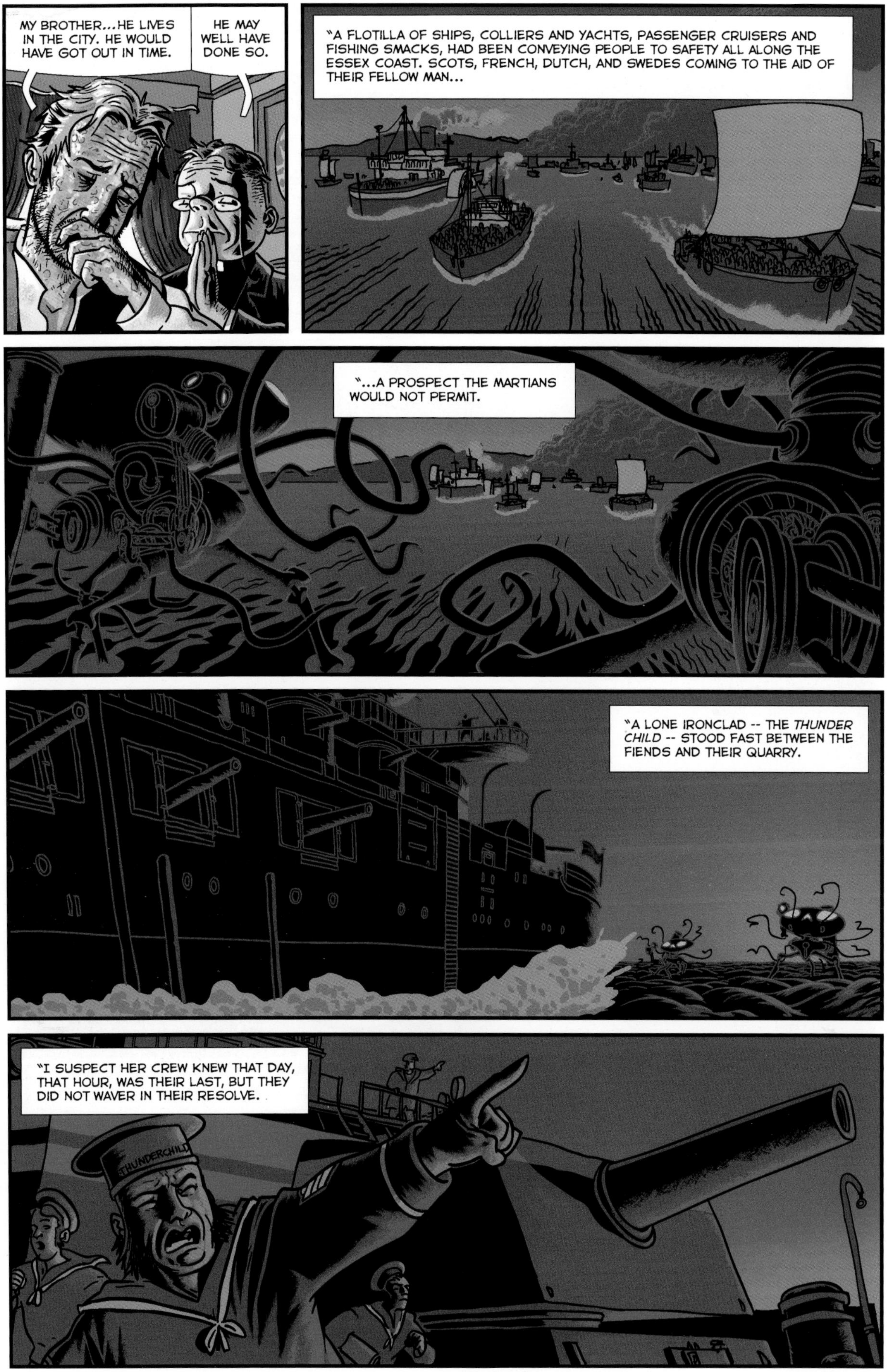
MY BROTHER...HE LIVES IN THE CITY. HE WOULD HAVE GOT OUT IN TIME.
HE MAY WELL HAVE DONE SO.
"A FLOTILLA OF SHIPS, COLLIERS AND YACHTS, PASSENGER CRUISERS AND FISHING SMACKS, HAD BEEN CONVEYING PEOPLE TO SAFETY ALL ALONG THE ESSEX COAST. SCOTS, FRENCH, DUTCH, AND SWEDES COMING TO THE AID OF THEIR FELLOW MAN...
"...A PROSPECT THE MARTIANS WOULD NOT PERMIT.
"A LONE IRONCLAD -- THE *THUNDER CHILD* -- STOOD FAST BETWEEN THE FIENDS AND THEIR QUARRY.
"I SUSPECT HER CREW KNEW THAT DAY, THAT HOUR, WAS THEIR LAST, BUT THEY DID NOT WAVER IN THEIR RESOLVE.
THUNDERCHILD

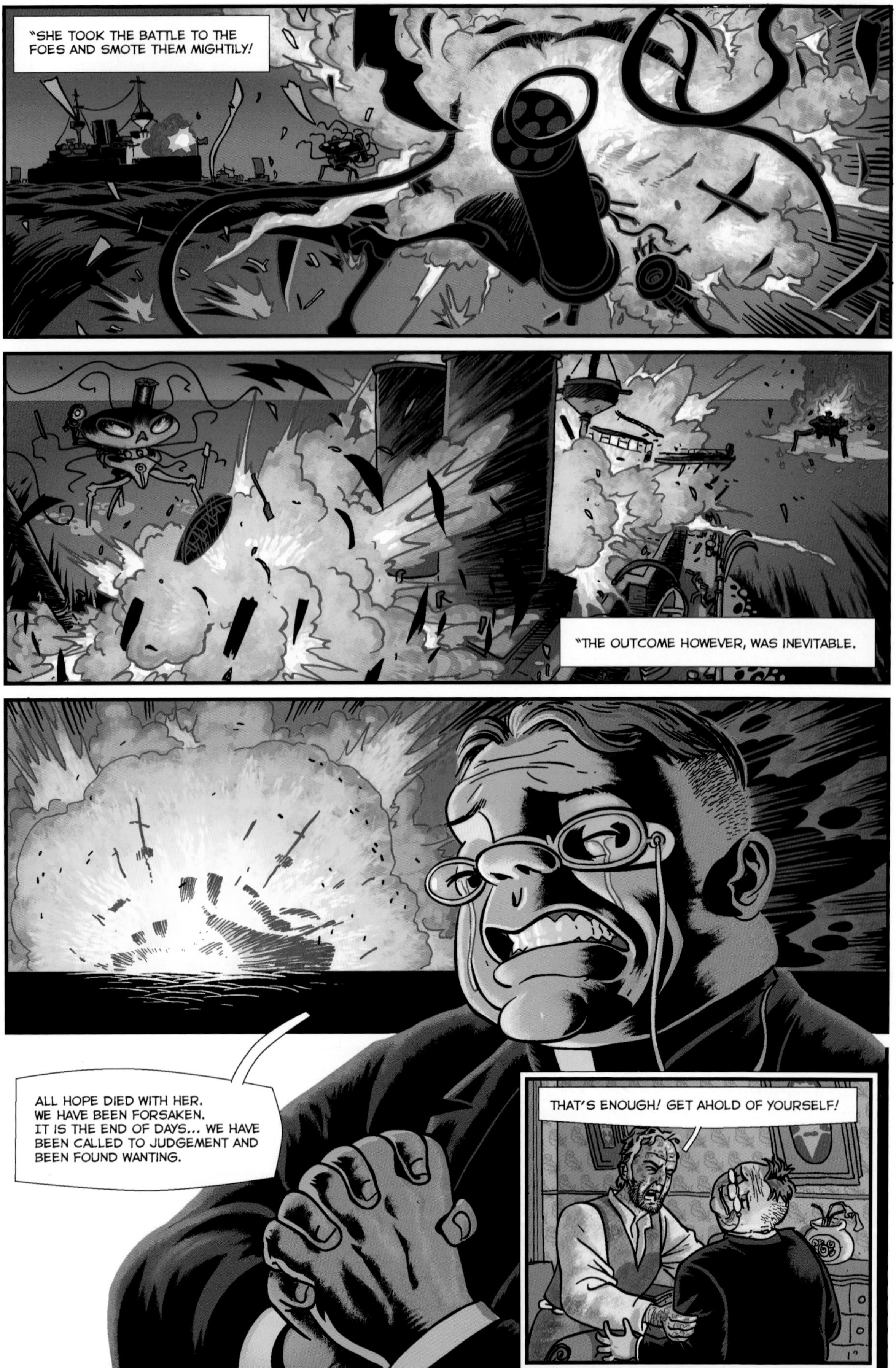
"SHE TOOK THE BATTLE TO THE FOES AND SMOTE THEM MIGHTILY!
"THE OUTCOME HOWEVER, WAS INEVITABLE.
ALL HOPE DIED WITH HER. WE HAVE BEEN FORSAKEN. IT IS THE END OF DAYS... WE HAVE BEEN CALLED TO JUDGEMENT AND BEEN FOUND WANTING.
THAT'S ENOUGH! GET AHOLD OF YOURSELF!

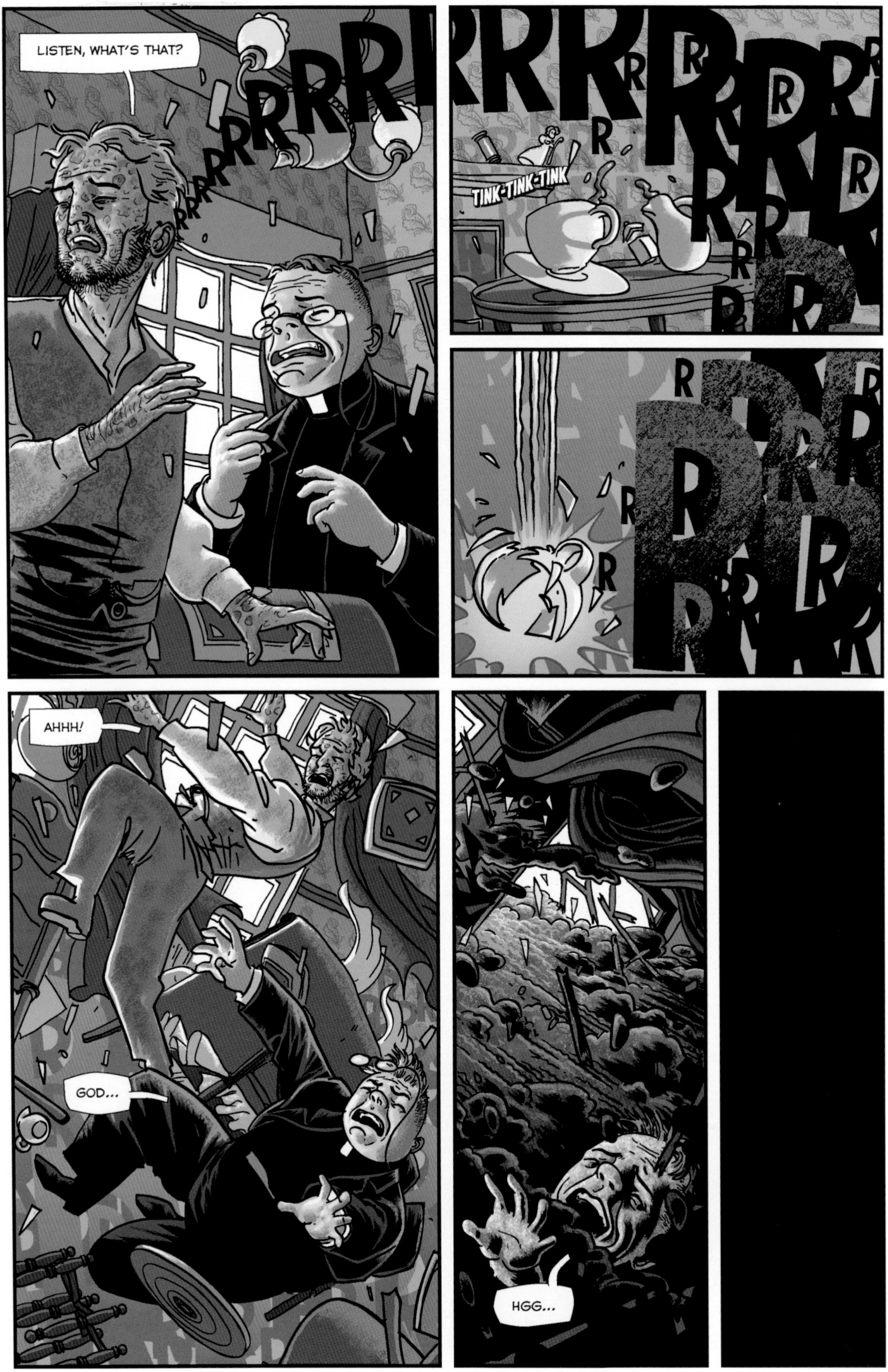
LISTEN, WHAT'S THAT?
RRRRRRRRRRRR
TINK-TINK-TINK
AHHH!
GOD...
HGG...

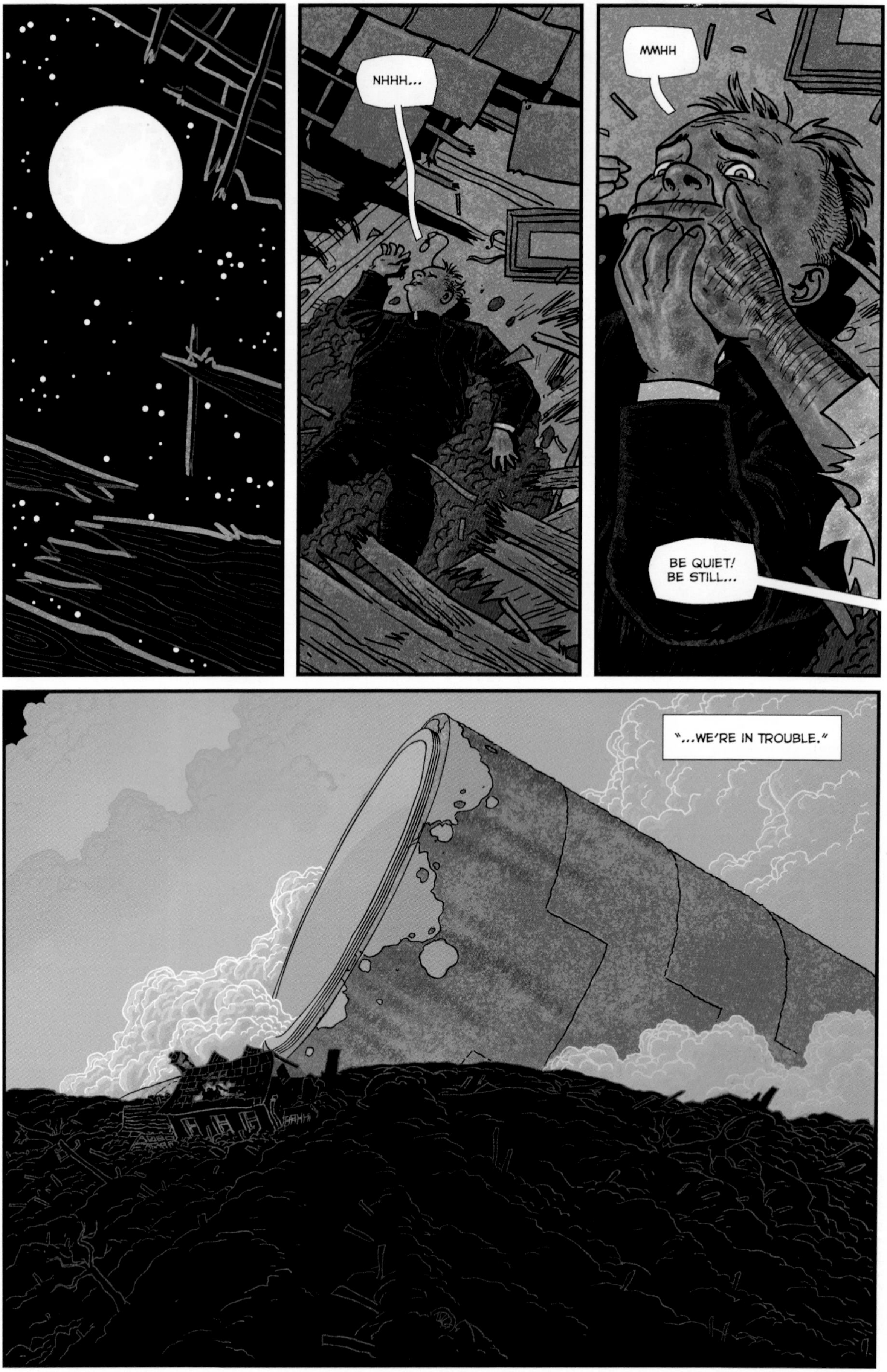
NHHH...
MMHH
BE QUIET! BE STILL...
"...WE'RE IN TROUBLE."

WHAT ARE WE TO DO? ARE THESE CREATURES EVERYWHERE? HAS THE EARTH BEEN GIVEN OVER TO THEM?

YOU MUST TRY TO KEEP YOUR HEAD -- THERE'S A GOOD FELLOW. THERE'S STILL HOPE.

HOPE, INDEED! PERHAPS IT IS YOU, NOT I, WHO IS LOSING THEIR HEAD!

FOOLS RUSH IN, EH?!

WILL YOU LOOK AT THIS!

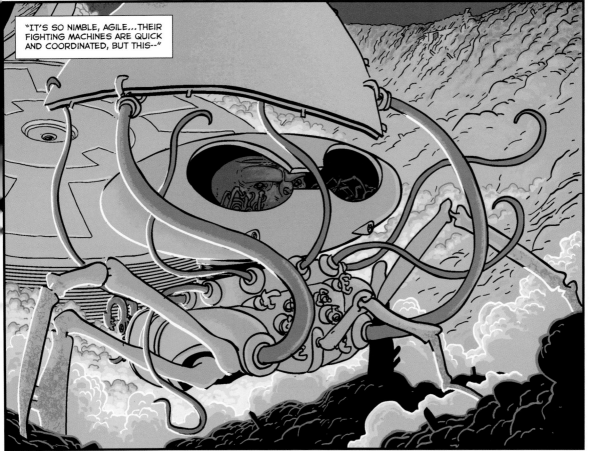

"IT'S SO NIMBLE, AGILE...THEIR FIGHTING MACHINES ARE QUICK AND COORDINATED, BUT THIS--"

"SEE THERE, WE HAVE THE TRUTH OF IT! THE TRIPODS ARRIVE IN SECTIONS. NO WONDER THIS...HANDLING MACHINE...WORKS IN SUCH HASTE. THE MARTIANS ARE AT THEIR MOST VULNERABLE IN THIS STATE."

WHAT'S THAT, DOWN THERE? NEAR THE EDGE.

I CAN'T... YES, I SEE IT!

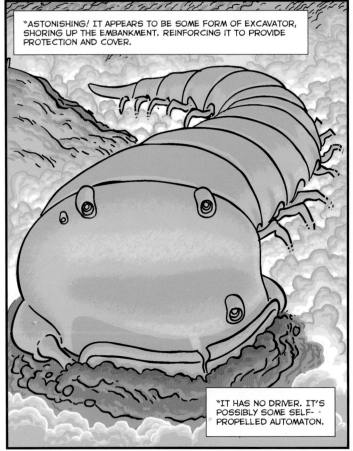

"ASTONISHING! IT APPEARS TO BE SOME FORM OF EXCAVATOR, SHORING UP THE EMBANKMENT. REINFORCING IT TO PROVIDE PROTECTION AND COVER.

"IT HAS NO DRIVER. IT'S POSSIBLY SOME SELF-PROPELLED AUTOMATON.

"THIS IS A RARE SIGHT. THIS KNOWLEDGE WILL BE INVALUABLE IN OUR RESISTING -- OH, OH, MY! DO YOU SEE THEM?"

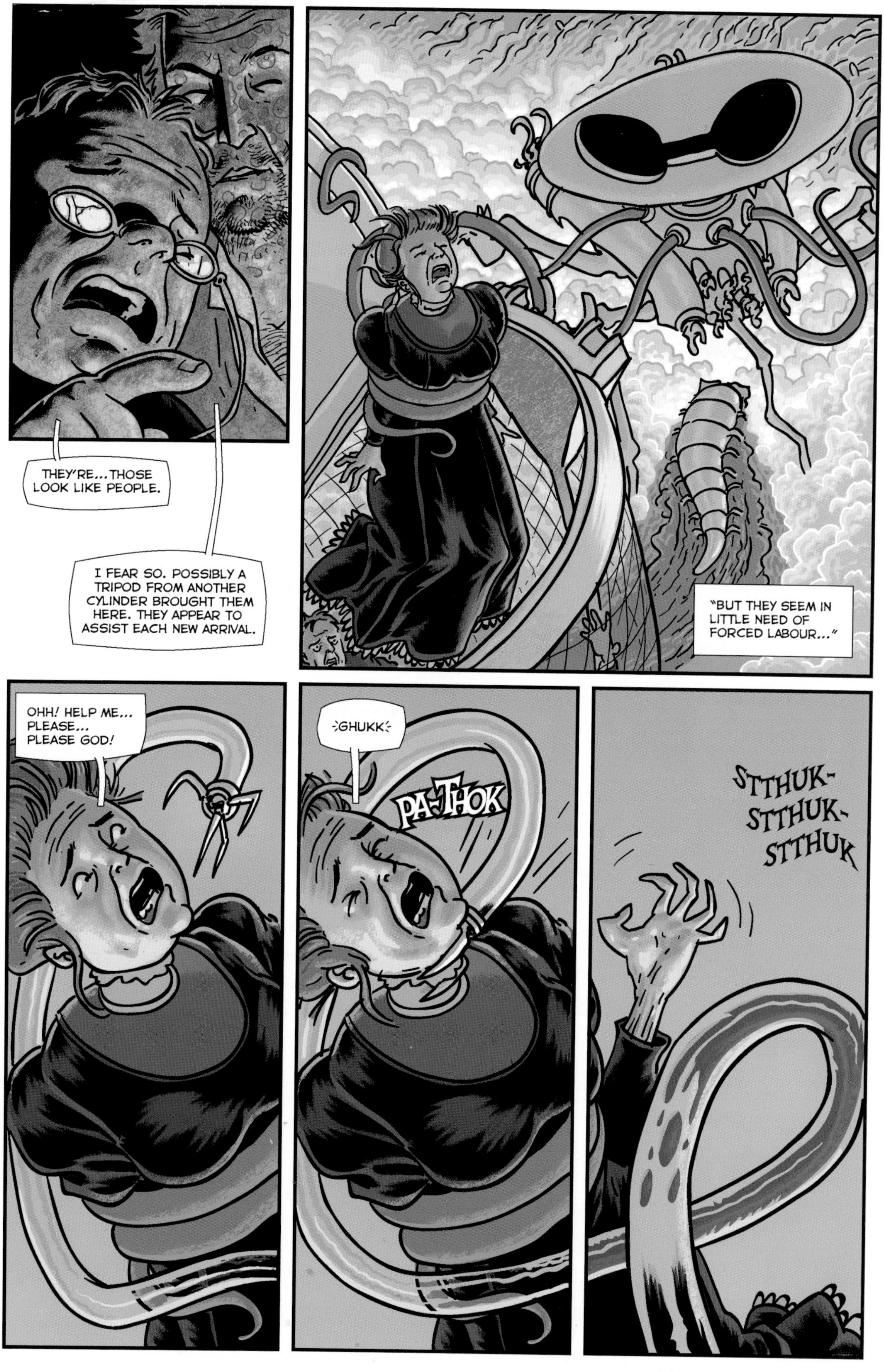
THEY'RE... THOSE LOOK LIKE PEOPLE.
I FEAR SO. POSSIBLY A TRIPOD FROM ANOTHER CYLINDER BROUGHT THEM HERE. THEY APPEAR TO ASSIST EACH NEW ARRIVAL.
"BUT THEY SEEM IN LITTLE NEED OF FORCED LABOUR..."
OHH! HELP ME... PLEASE... PLEASE GOD!
GHUKK
PA-THOK
STTHUK-
STTHUK-
STTHUK

NO...NO...NO! O GOD! IT IS HIS JUSTICE! ON ME AND MINE BE THE PUNISHMENT LAID! WE HAVE SINNED! WE HAVE FALLEN SHORT!

FOR GOD'S SAKE, SHUT UP! YOU'LL HAVE THEM ON US!

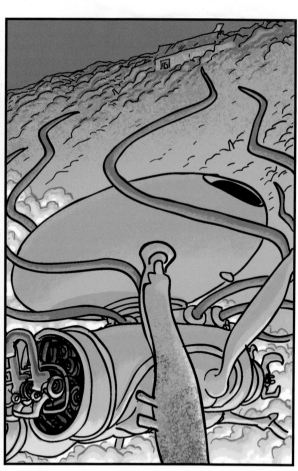

WOE UNTO THIS UNFAITHFUL CITY! WOE! WOE! WOE! TO THE INHABITANTS OF THE EARTH!

SHUT UP, YOU FOOL!

NAY! THE WORD OF THE LORD IS UPON ME! I MUST GO!

I MUST BEAR WITNESS!

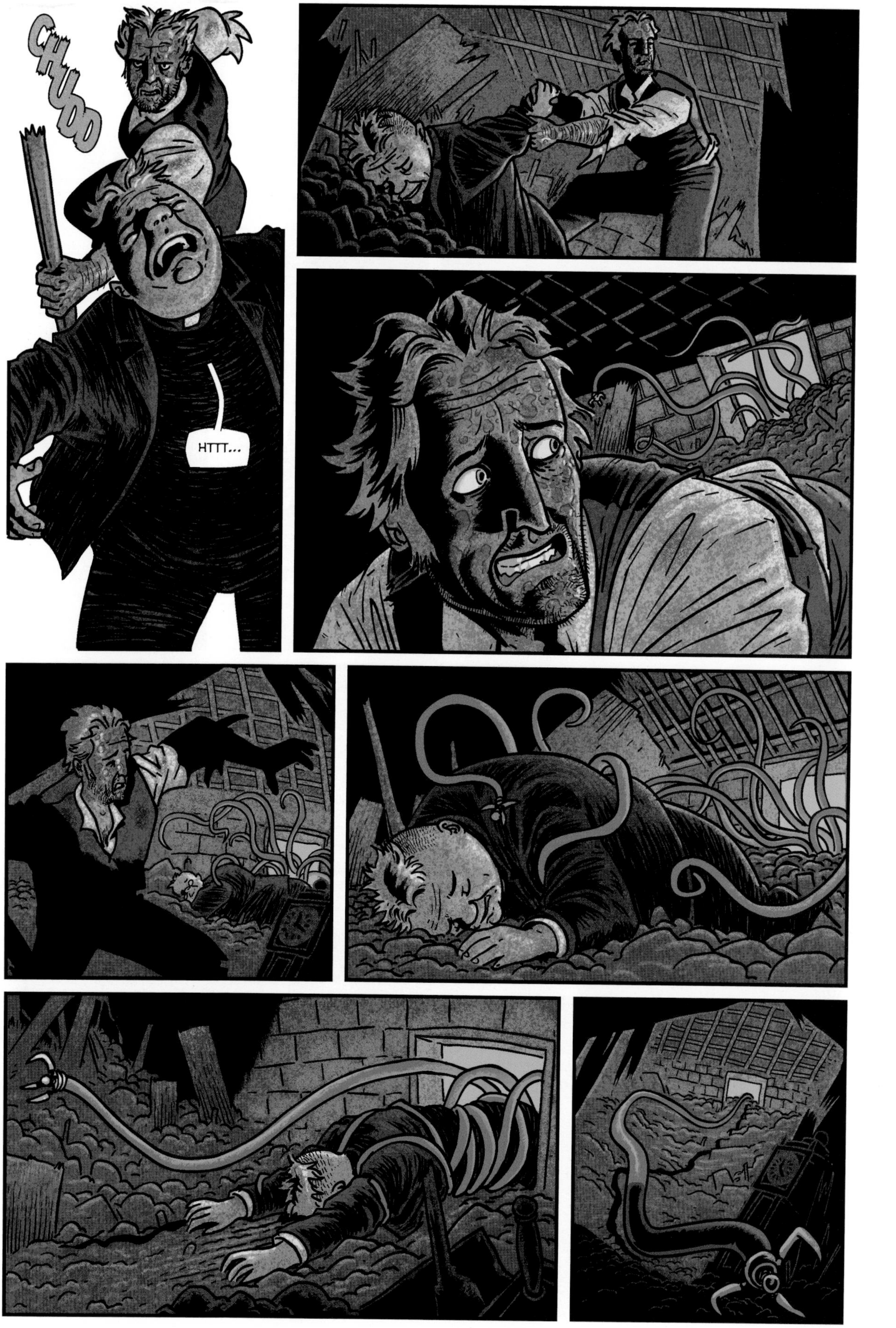
CHUDD
HTTT...

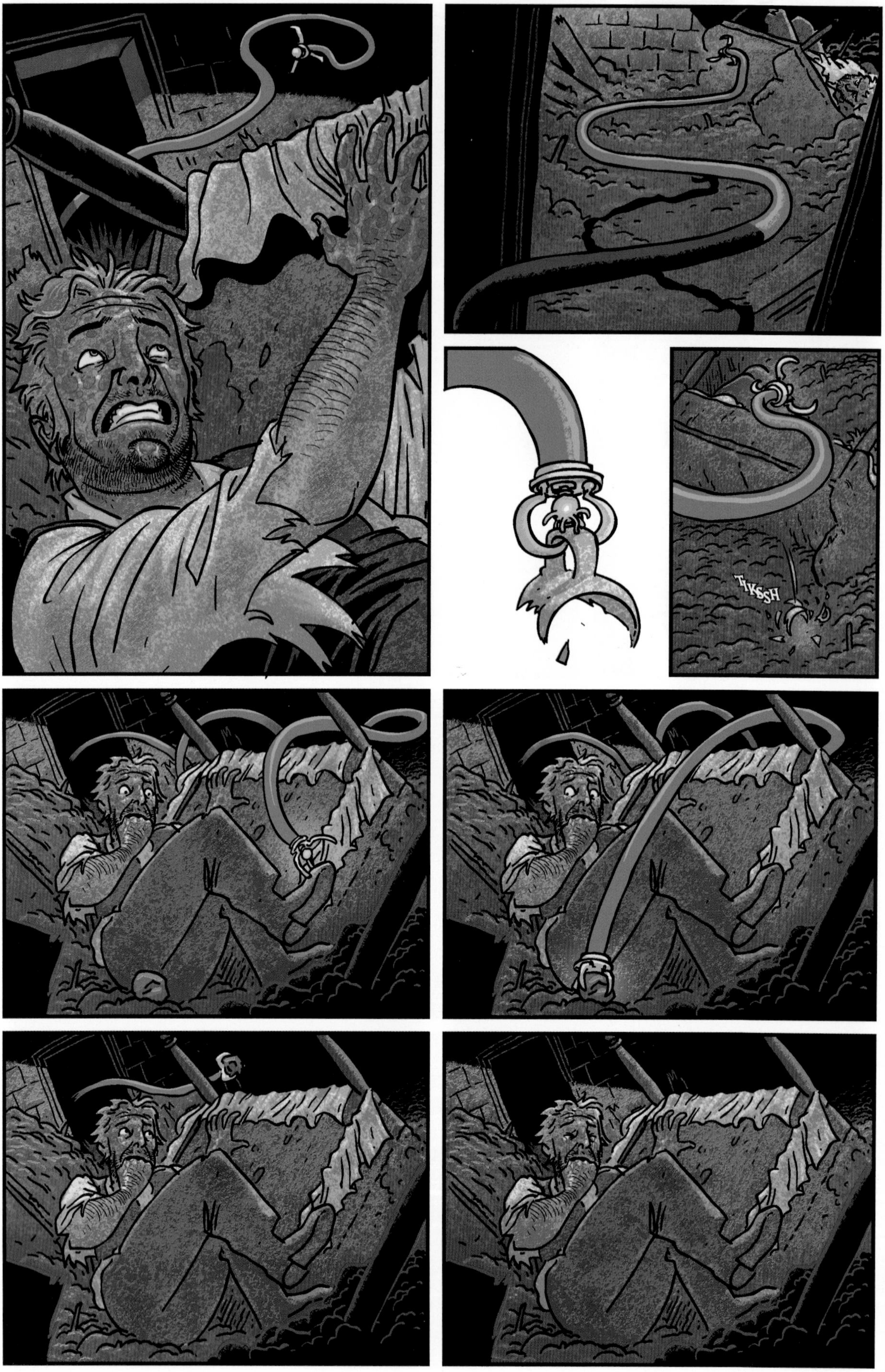
TIKSSH

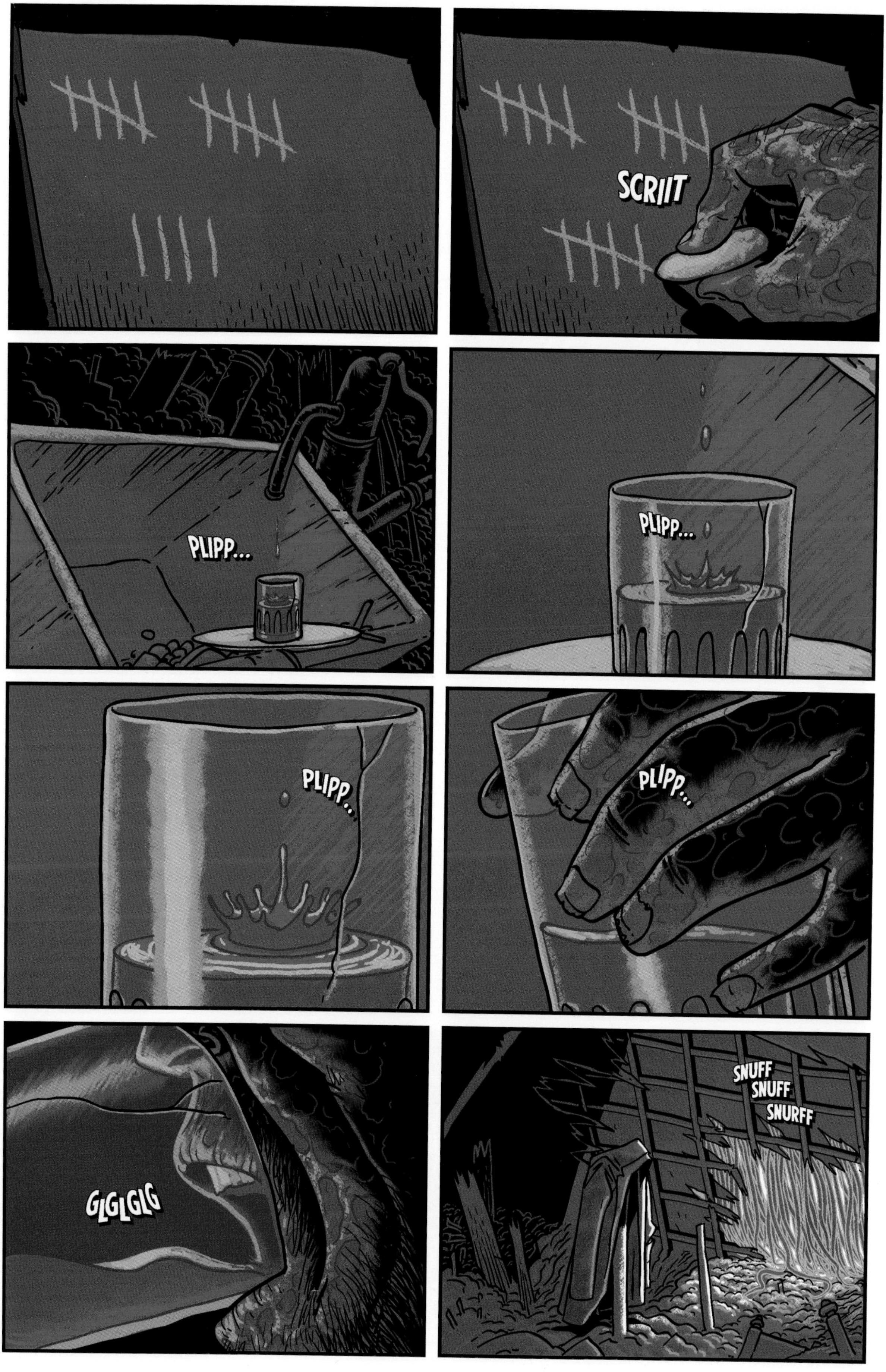
SCRIIT
PLIPP...
PLIPP...
PLIPP...
PLIPP...
GLGLGLG
SNUFF
SNUFF
SNURFF

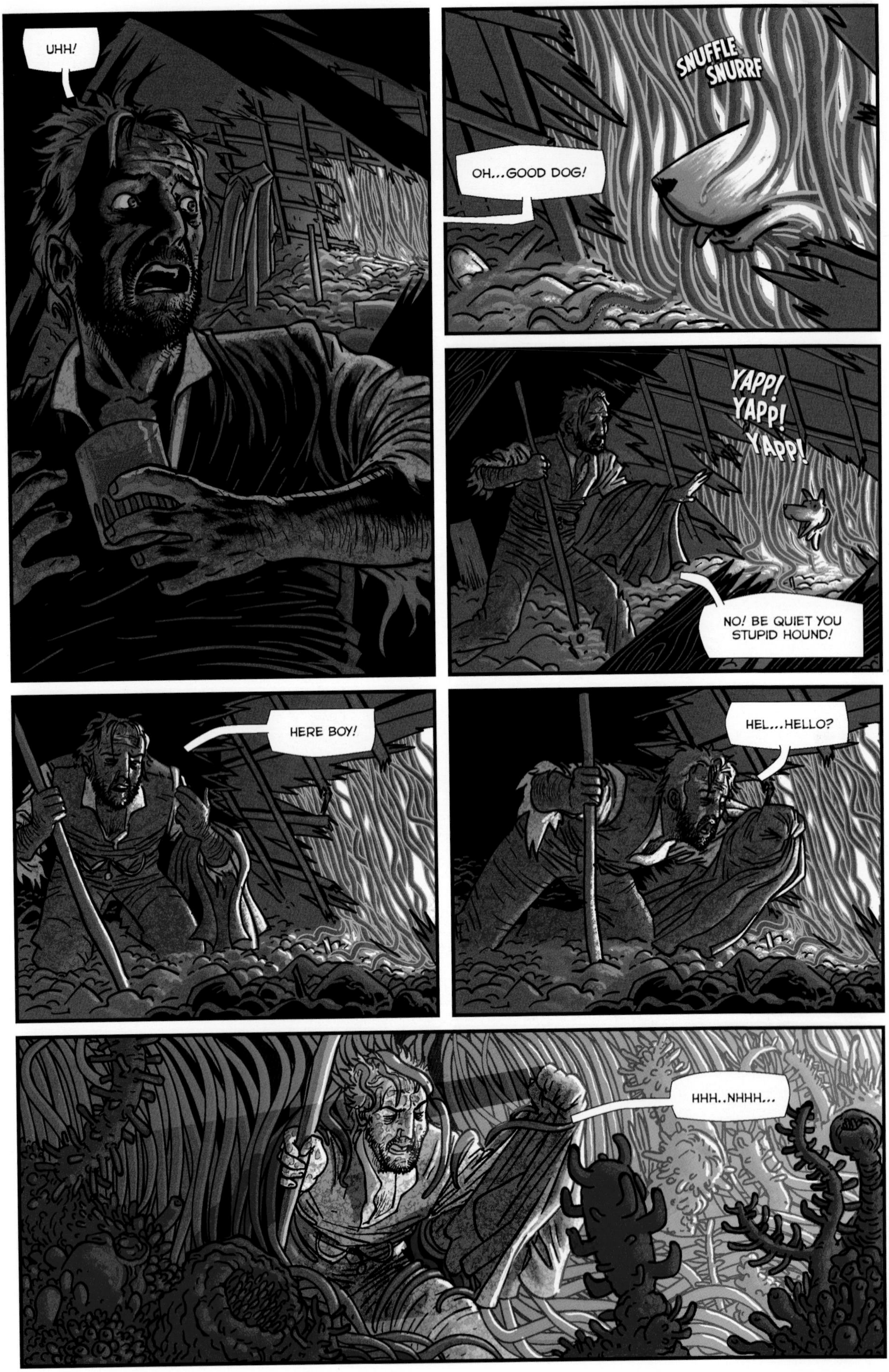
UHH!
SNUFFLE SNURRF
OH...GOOD DOG!
YAPP! YAPP! YAPP!
NO! BE QUIET YOU STUPID HOUND!
HERE BOY!
HEL...HELLO?
HHH..NHHH...

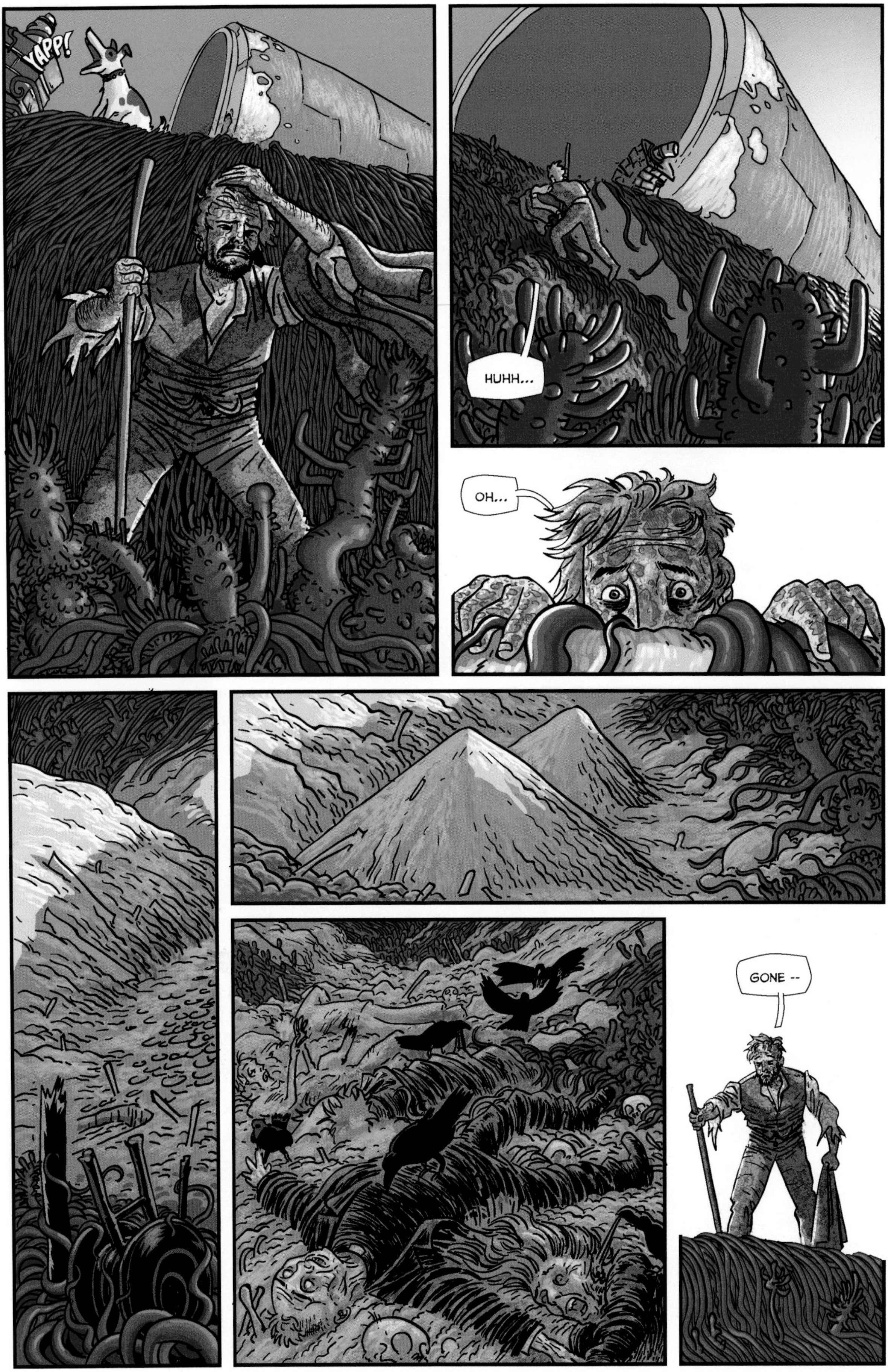
YAPP!
HUHH...
OH...
GONE --

ALL GONE!
OH YES! THANK THE LORD!

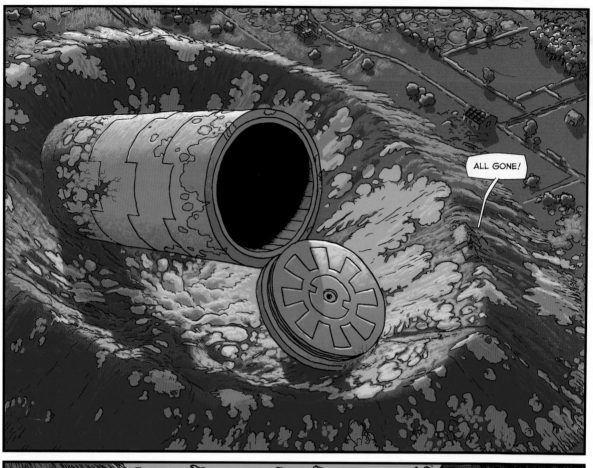

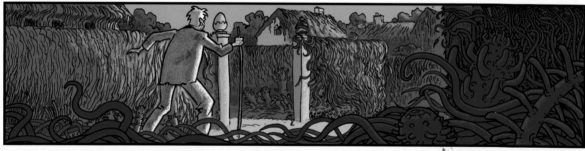

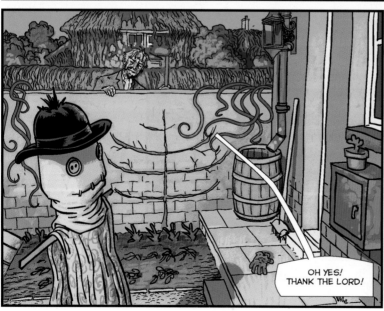

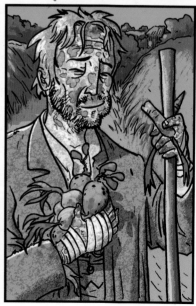

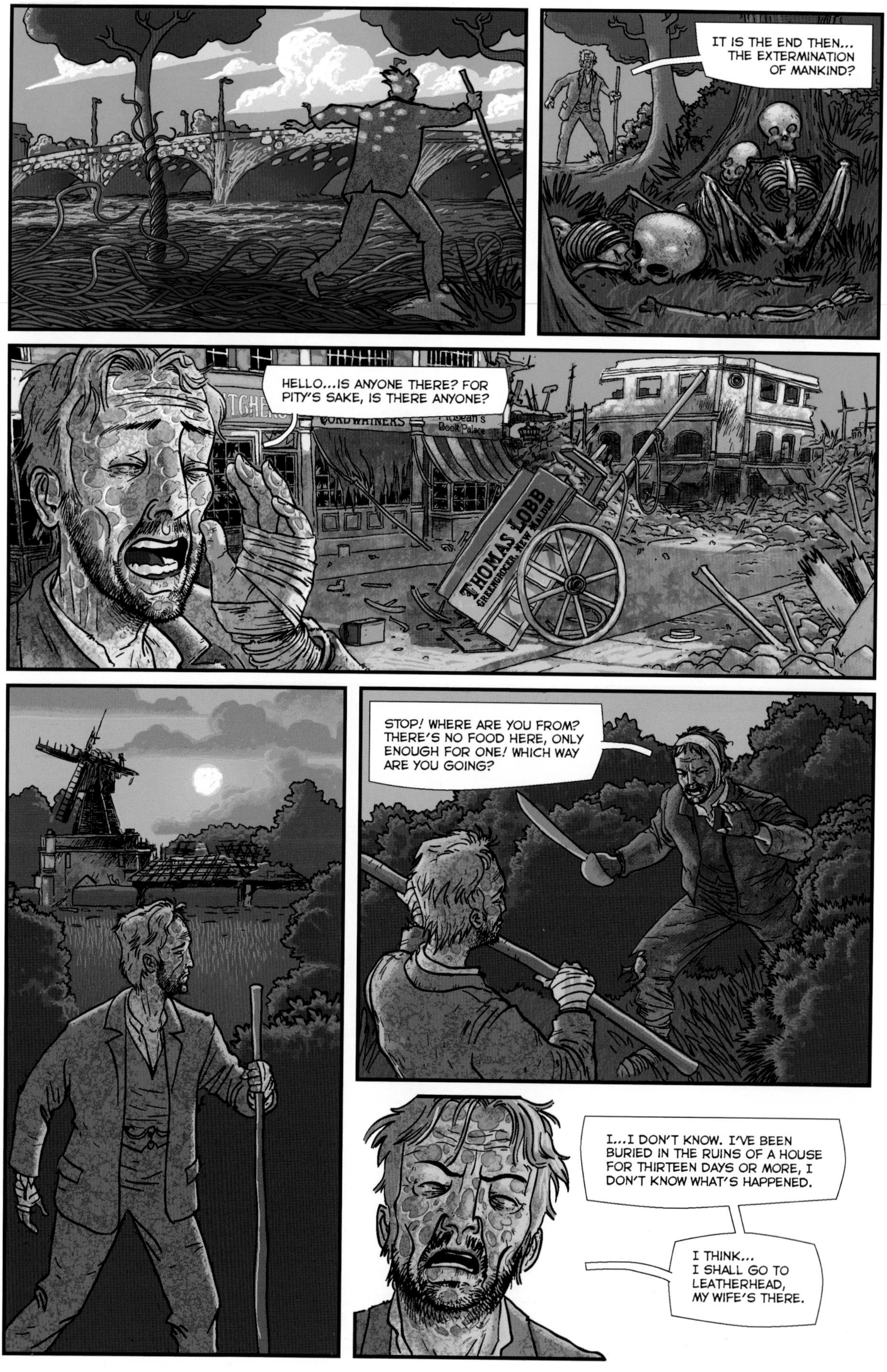
IT IS THE END THEN... THE EXTERMINATION OF MANKIND?
HELLO...IS ANYONE THERE? FOR PITY'S SAKE, IS THERE ANYONE?
CORDWAINERS
Book Palace
THOMAS LOBB
GREENGROCER, NEW MALDEN
STOP! WHERE ARE YOU FROM? THERE'S NO FOOD HERE, ONLY ENOUGH FOR ONE! WHICH WAY ARE YOU GOING?
I...I DON'T KNOW. I'VE BEEN BURIED IN THE RUINS OF A HOUSE FOR THIRTEEN DAYS OR MORE, I DON'T KNOW WHAT'S HAPPENED.
I THINK... I SHALL GO TO LEATHERHEAD, MY WIFE'S THERE.

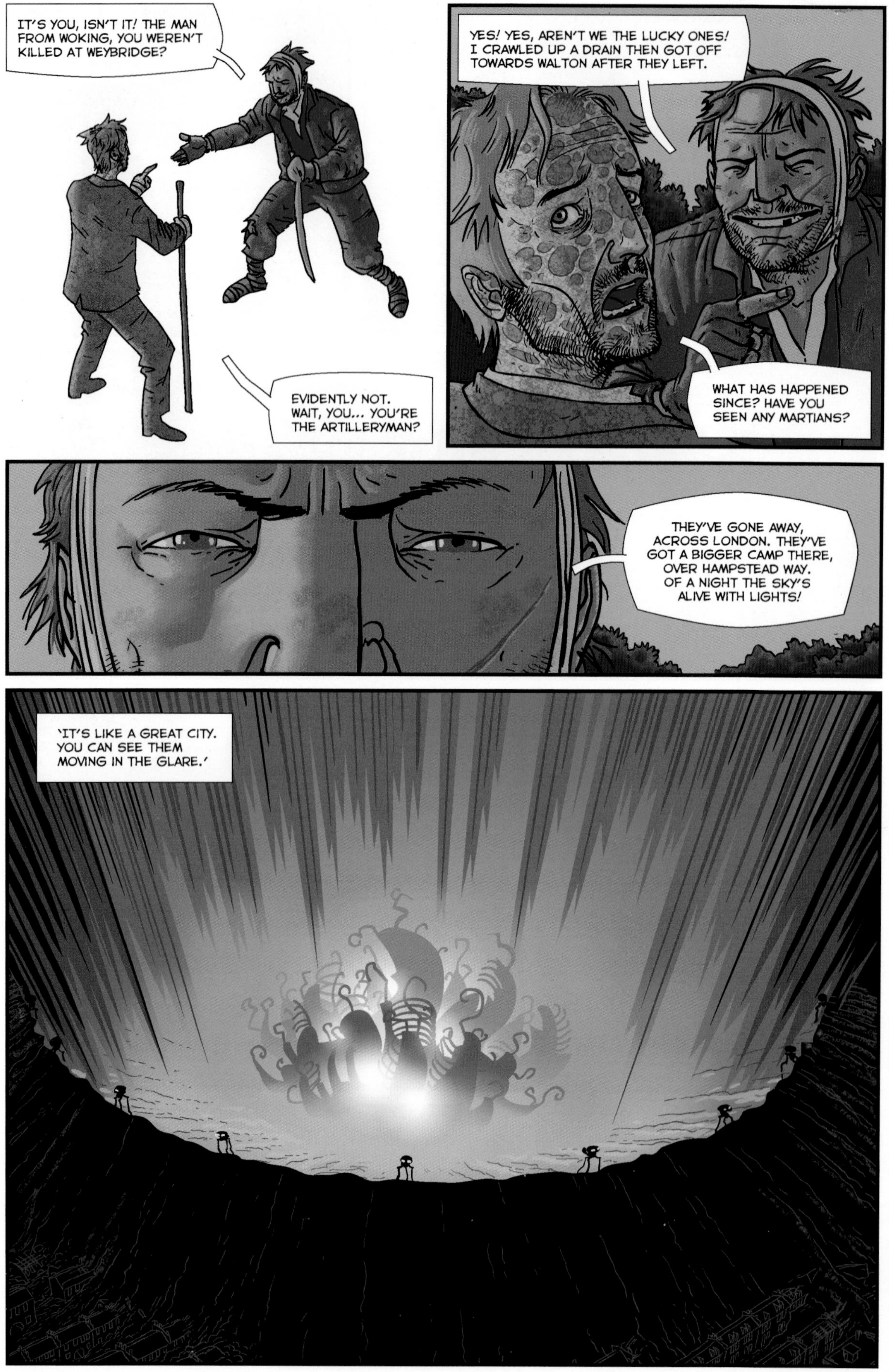
IT'S YOU, ISN'T IT! THE MAN FROM WOKING, YOU WEREN'T KILLED AT WEYBRIDGE?
EVIDENTLY NOT. WAIT, YOU... YOU'RE THE ARTILLERYMAN?
YES! YES, AREN'T WE THE LUCKY ONES! I CRAWLED UP A DRAIN THEN GOT OFF TOWARDS WALTON AFTER THEY LEFT.
WHAT HAS HAPPENED SINCE? HAVE YOU SEEN ANY MARTIANS?
THEY'VE GONE AWAY, ACROSS LONDON. THEY'VE GOT A BIGGER CAMP THERE, OVER HAMPSTEAD WAY. OF A NIGHT THE SKY'S ALIVE WITH LIGHTS!
'IT'S LIKE A GREAT CITY. YOU CAN SEE THEM MOVING IN THE GLARE.'

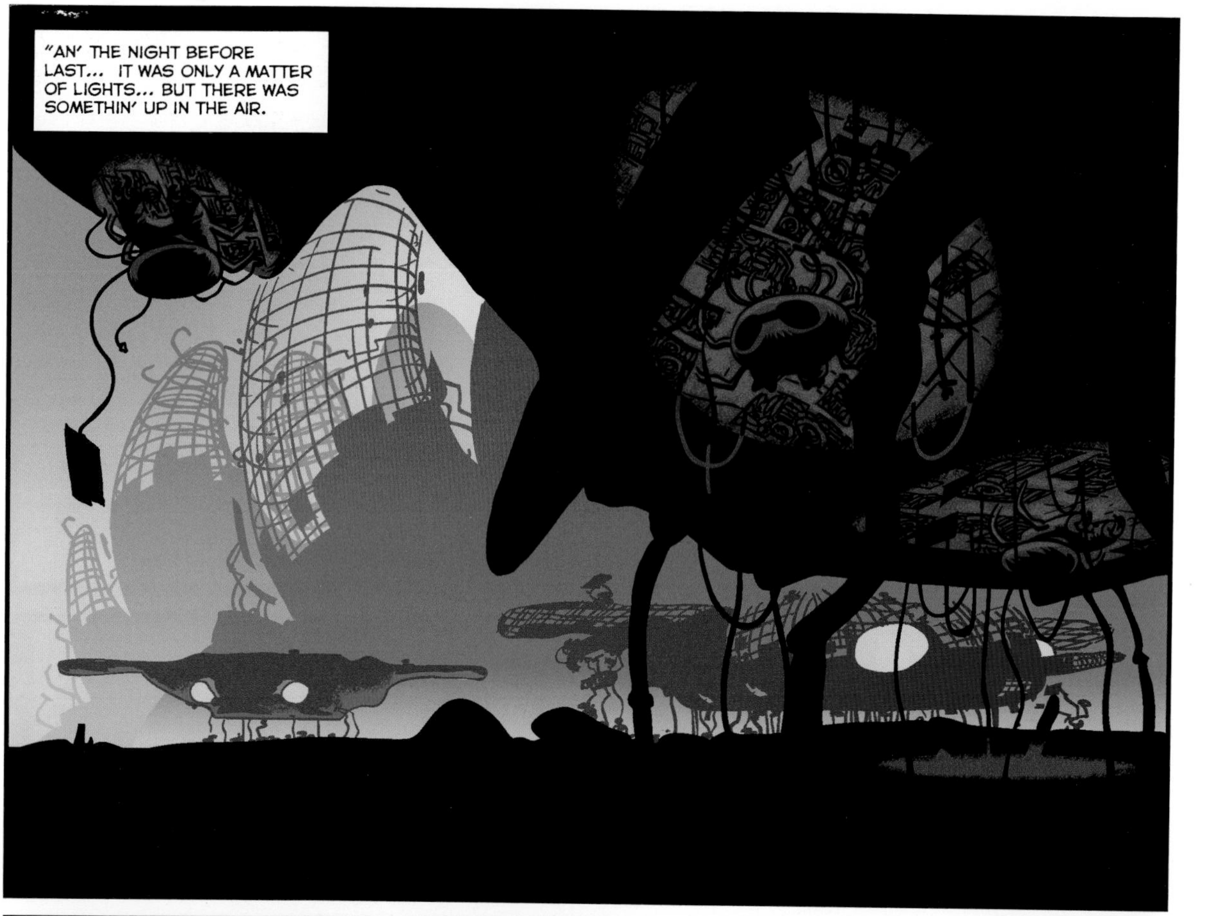
"AN' THE NIGHT BEFORE LAST... IT WAS ONLY A MATTER OF LIGHTS... BUT THERE WAS SOMETHIN' UP IN THE AIR.

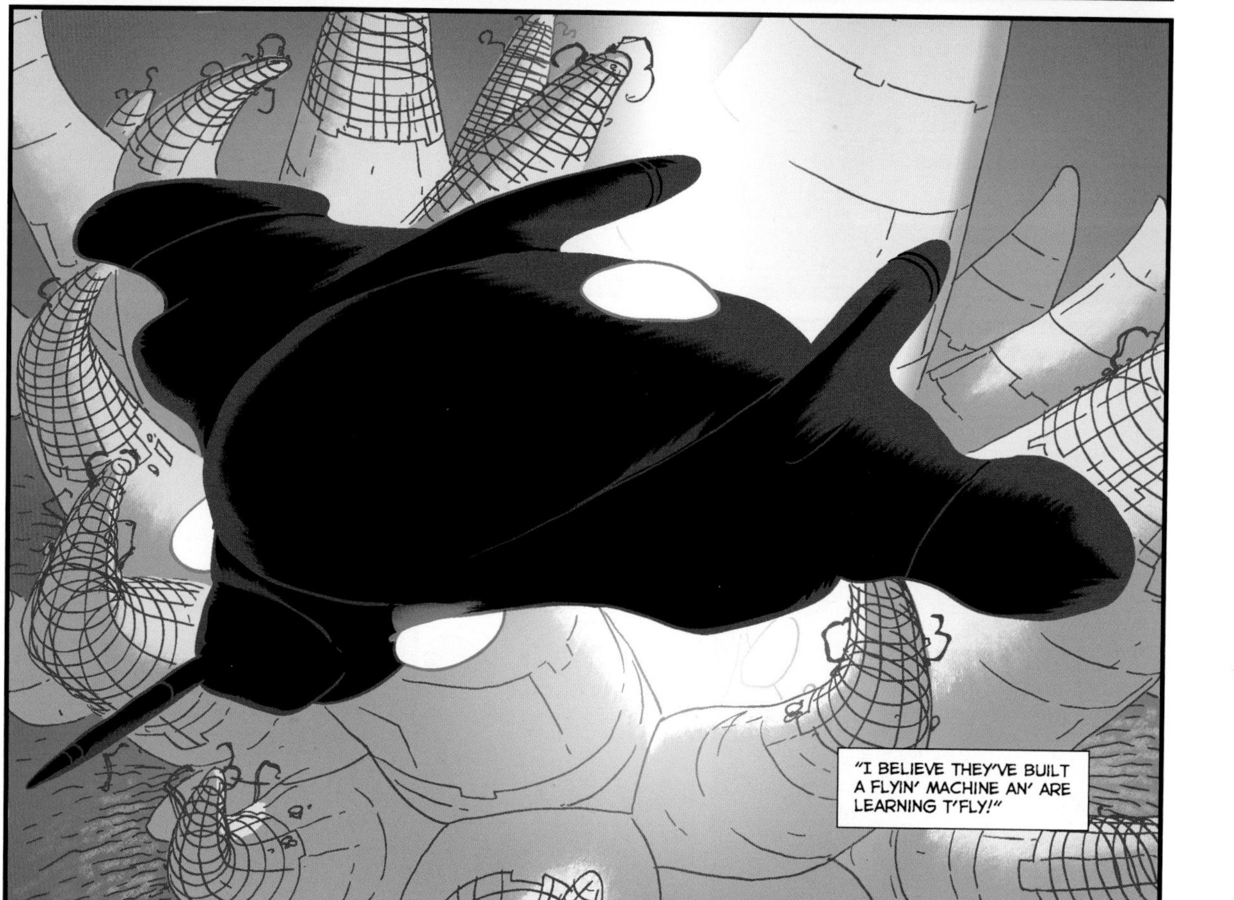
"I BELIEVE THEY'VE BUILT A FLYIN' MACHINE AN' ARE LEARNING T'FLY!"

FLY! THEN IT'S OVER FOR HUMANITY. THEIR WAR WILL GO AROUND THE WORLD!

THIS ISN'T WAR, IT NEVER WAS, ANY MORE THAN THERE'S WAR BETWEEN MEN AND ANTS!

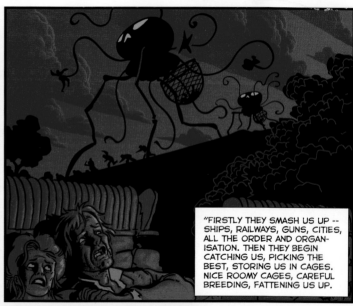

"FIRSTLY THEY SMASH US UP -- SHIPS, RAILWAYS, GUNS, CITIES, ALL THE ORDER AND ORGANISATION. THEN THEY BEGIN CATCHING US, PICKING THE BEST, STORING US IN CAGES. NICE ROOMY CAGES, CAREFUL BREEDING, FATTENING US UP.

"THERE'S PLENTY THAT'D TAKE TO IT, TOO. I'VE SEEN 'EM, ALL THOSE LITTLE CLERKS THAT HAVEN'T ANY SPIRIT IN 'EM. NO PROUD DREAMS OR LUSTS. A MAN WHO HASN'T HAD ONE OR THE OTHER IS JUST FUNK AND PRECAUTIONS!

"SKEDADDLING OFF TO WORK, SEASON TICKET IN HAND, FEARFUL OF BEING DISMISSED. SKEDADDLING BACK HOME, FEARFUL OF THE WIFE AN' MISSIN' THEIR DINNER.

"AN' ON SUNDAYS -- FEAR OF THE HEREAFTER! AS IF HELL WAS BUILT FOR RABBITS! THEY'LL COME AN' BE CAUGHT CHEERFUL LIKE. THEY'LL WONDER WHAT PEOPLE DID BEFORE THERE WERE MARTIANS TO TAKE CARE OF 'EM!"

LIKELY THE MARTIANS WILL MAKE PETS OF SOME. TEACH 'EM TRICKS... AN' SOME, MAYBE, THEY'LL TRAIN TO HUNT US!

NO, NO HUMAN BEING WOULD --

THERE'S MEN WHO'D DO IT CHEERFULLY. IT'S NONSENSE TO PRETEND THERE ISN'T. THAT'S WHY WE'VE GOT TO PREPARE AN' PLAN.

FOLLOW ME.

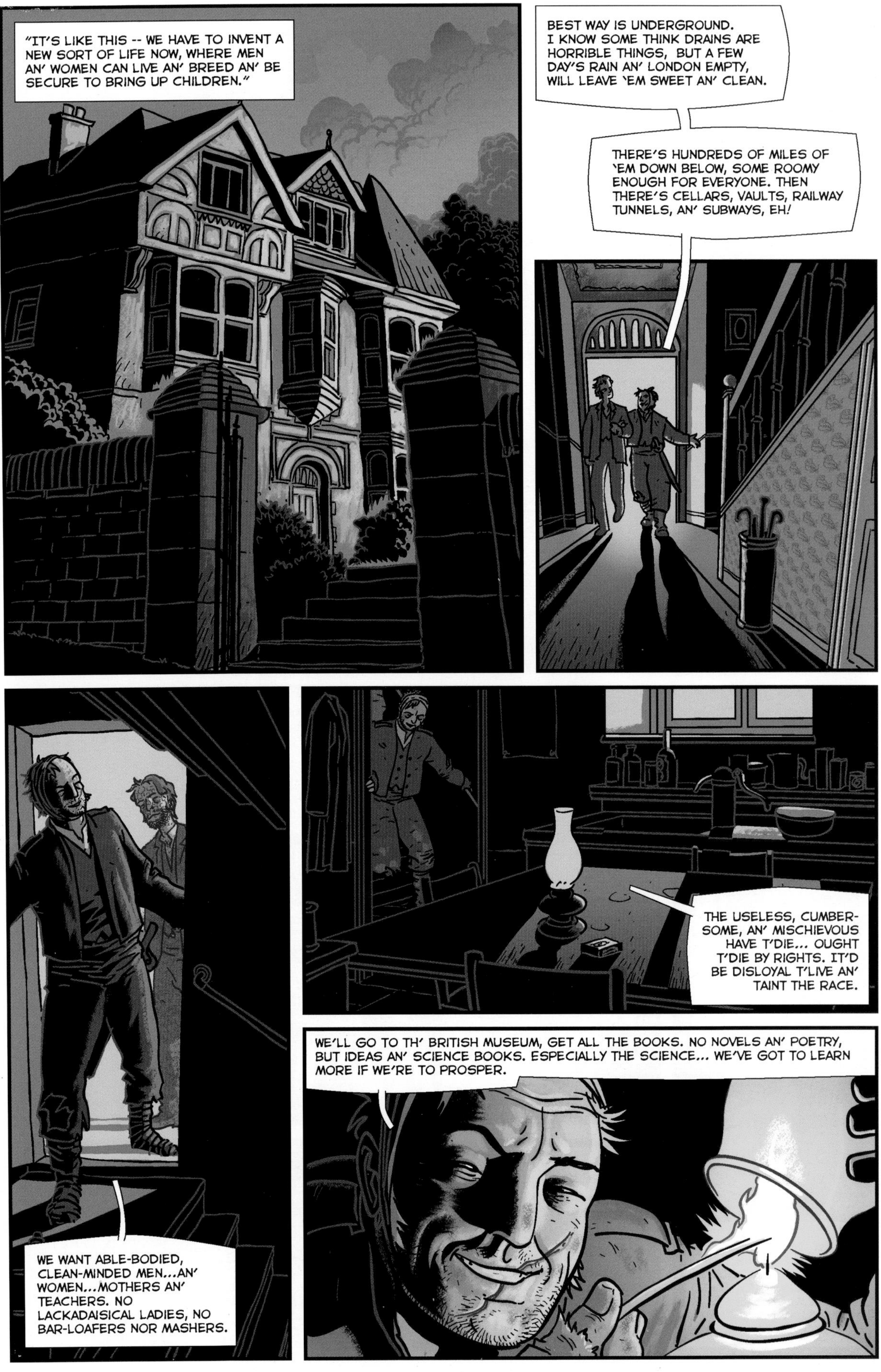
"IT'S LIKE THIS -- WE HAVE TO INVENT A NEW SORT OF LIFE NOW, WHERE MEN AN' WOMEN CAN LIVE AN' BREED AN' BE SECURE TO BRING UP CHILDREN."
BEST WAY IS UNDERGROUND. I KNOW SOME THINK DRAINS ARE HORRIBLE THINGS, BUT A FEW DAY'S RAIN AN' LONDON EMPTY, WILL LEAVE 'EM SWEET AN' CLEAN.
THERE'S HUNDREDS OF MILES OF 'EM DOWN BELOW, SOME ROOMY ENOUGH FOR EVERYONE. THEN THERE'S CELLARS, VAULTS, RAILWAY TUNNELS, AN' SUBWAYS, EH!
WE WANT ABLE-BODIED, CLEAN-MINDED MEN...AN' WOMEN...MOTHERS AN' TEACHERS. NO LACKADAISICAL LADIES, NO BAR-LOAFERS NOR MASHERS.
THE USELESS, CUMBERSOME, AN' MISCHIEVOUS HAVE T'DIE... OUGHT T'DIE BY RIGHTS. IT'D BE DISLOYAL T'LIVE AN' TAINT THE RACE.
WE'LL GO TO TH' BRITISH MUSEUM, GET ALL THE BOOKS. NO NOVELS AN' POETRY, BUT IDEAS AN' SCIENCE BOOKS. ESPECIALLY THE SCIENCE... WE'VE GOT TO LEARN MORE IF WE'RE TO PROSPER.

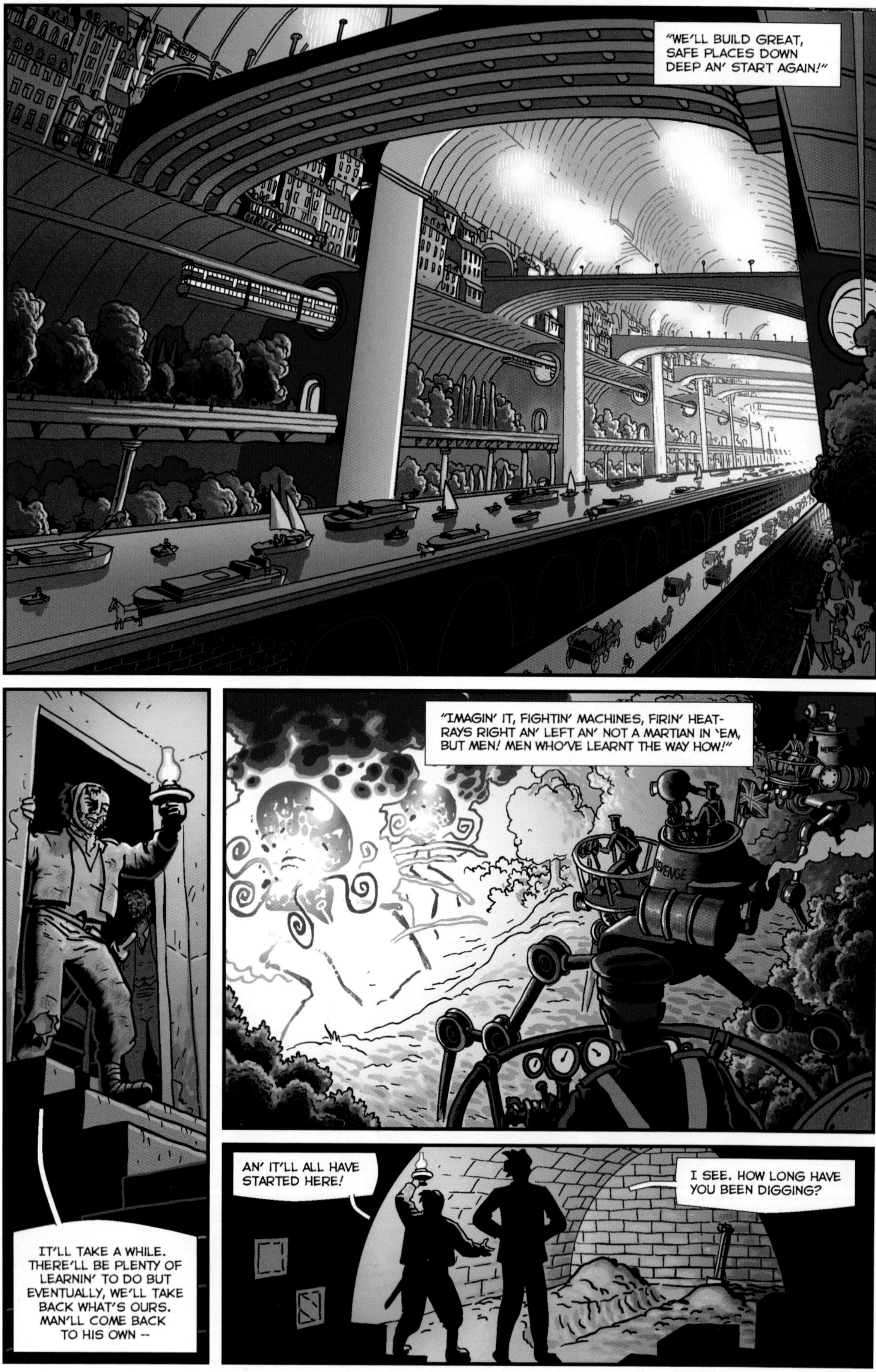
"WE'LL BUILD GREAT, SAFE PLACES DOWN DEEP AN' START AGAIN!"
"IMAGIN' IT, FIGHTIN' MACHINES, FIRIN' HEAT-RAYS RIGHT AN' LEFT AN' NOT A MARTIAN IN 'EM, BUT MEN! MEN WHO'VE LEARNT THE WAY HOW!"
IT'LL TAKE A WHILE. THERE'LL BE PLENTY OF LEARNIN' TO DO BUT EVENTUALLY, WE'LL TAKE BACK WHAT'S OURS. MAN'LL COME BACK TO HIS OWN --
AN' IT'LL ALL HAVE STARTED HERE!
I SEE. HOW LONG HAVE YOU BEEN DIGGING?

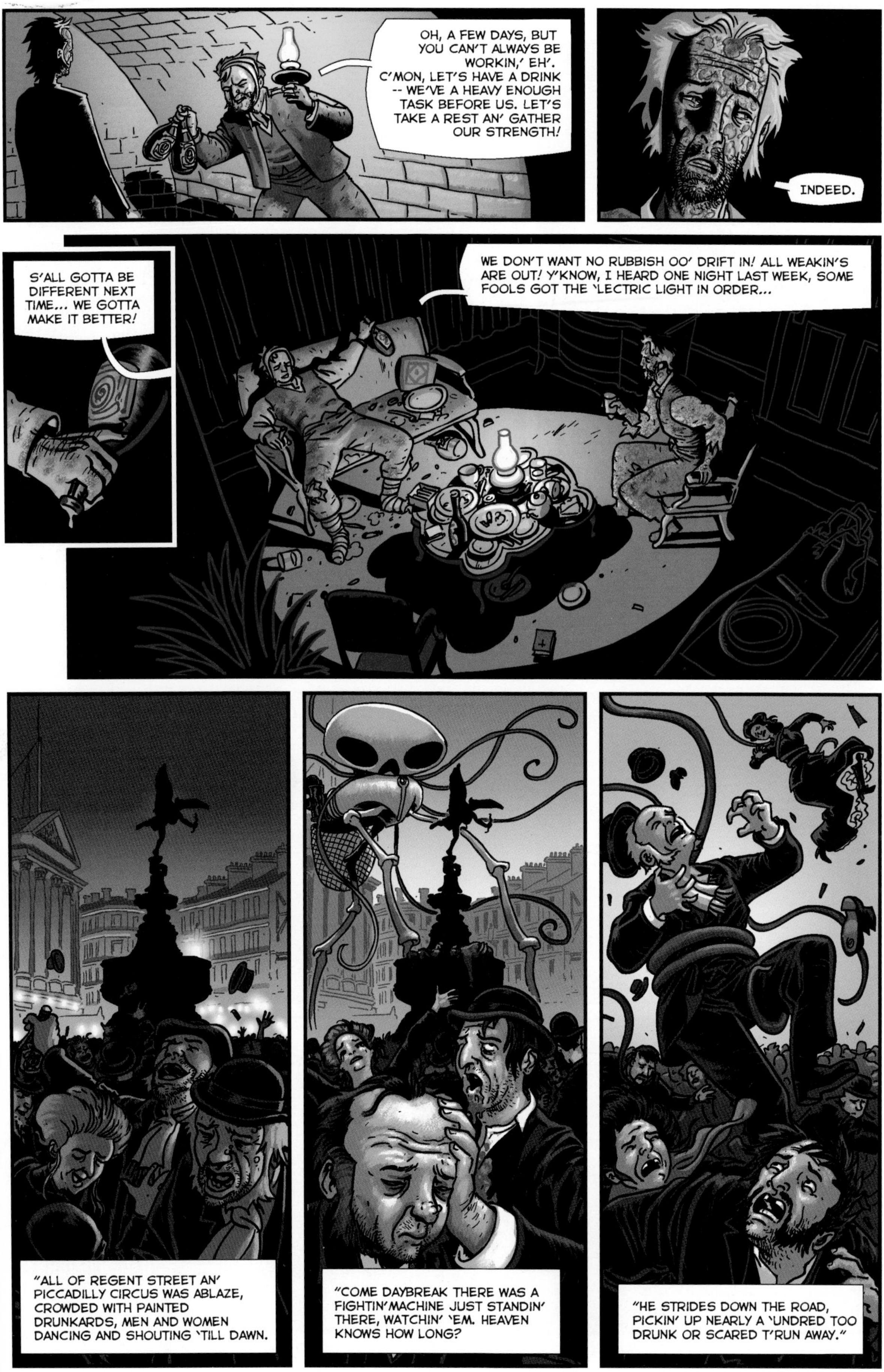
OH, A FEW DAYS, BUT YOU CAN'T ALWAYS BE WORKIN,' EH'. C'MON, LET'S HAVE A DRINK -- WE'VE A HEAVY ENOUGH TASK BEFORE US. LET'S TAKE A REST AN' GATHER OUR STRENGTH!
INDEED.
S'ALL GOTTA BE DIFFERENT NEXT TIME... WE GOTTA MAKE IT BETTER!
WE DON'T WANT NO RUBBISH OO' DRIFT IN! ALL WEAKIN'S ARE OUT! Y'KNOW, I HEARD ONE NIGHT LAST WEEK, SOME FOOLS GOT THE 'LECTRIC LIGHT IN ORDER...
"ALL OF REGENT STREET AN' PICCADILLY CIRCUS WAS ABLAZE, CROWDED WITH PAINTED DRUNKARDS, MEN AND WOMEN DANCING AND SHOUTING 'TILL DAWN.
"COME DAYBREAK THERE WAS A FIGHTIN'MACHINE JUST STANDIN' THERE, WATCHIN' 'EM. HEAVEN KNOWS HOW LONG?
"HE STRIDES DOWN THE ROAD, PICKIN' UP NEARLY A 'UNDRED TOO DRUNK OR SCARED T'RUN AWAY."

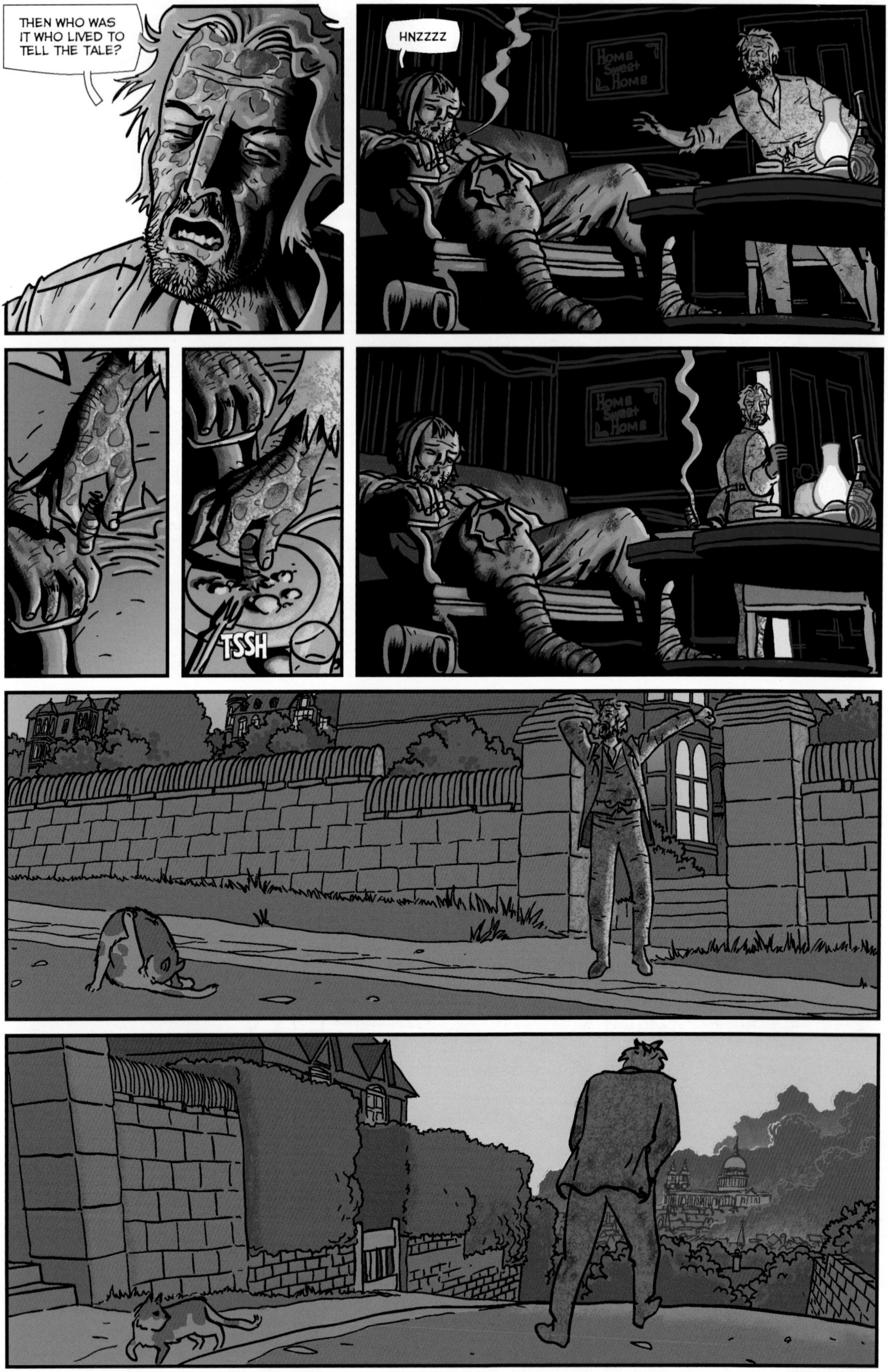
THEN WHO WAS IT WHO LIVED TO TELL THE TALE?
HNZZZZ
HOME SWEET HOME
TSSH
HOME SWEET HOME

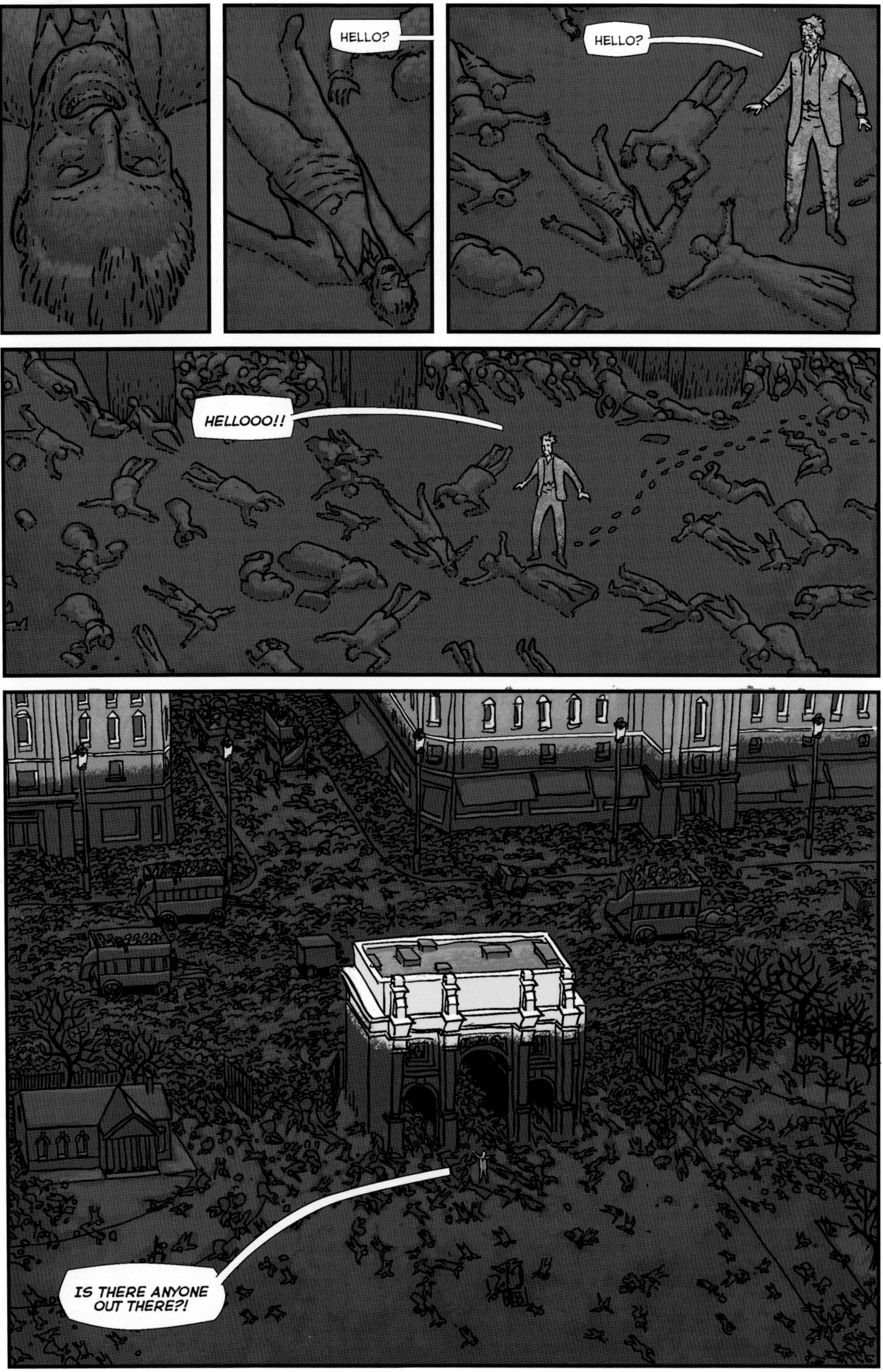
HELLO?
HELLO?
HELLOOO!!
IS THERE ANYONE OUT THERE?!

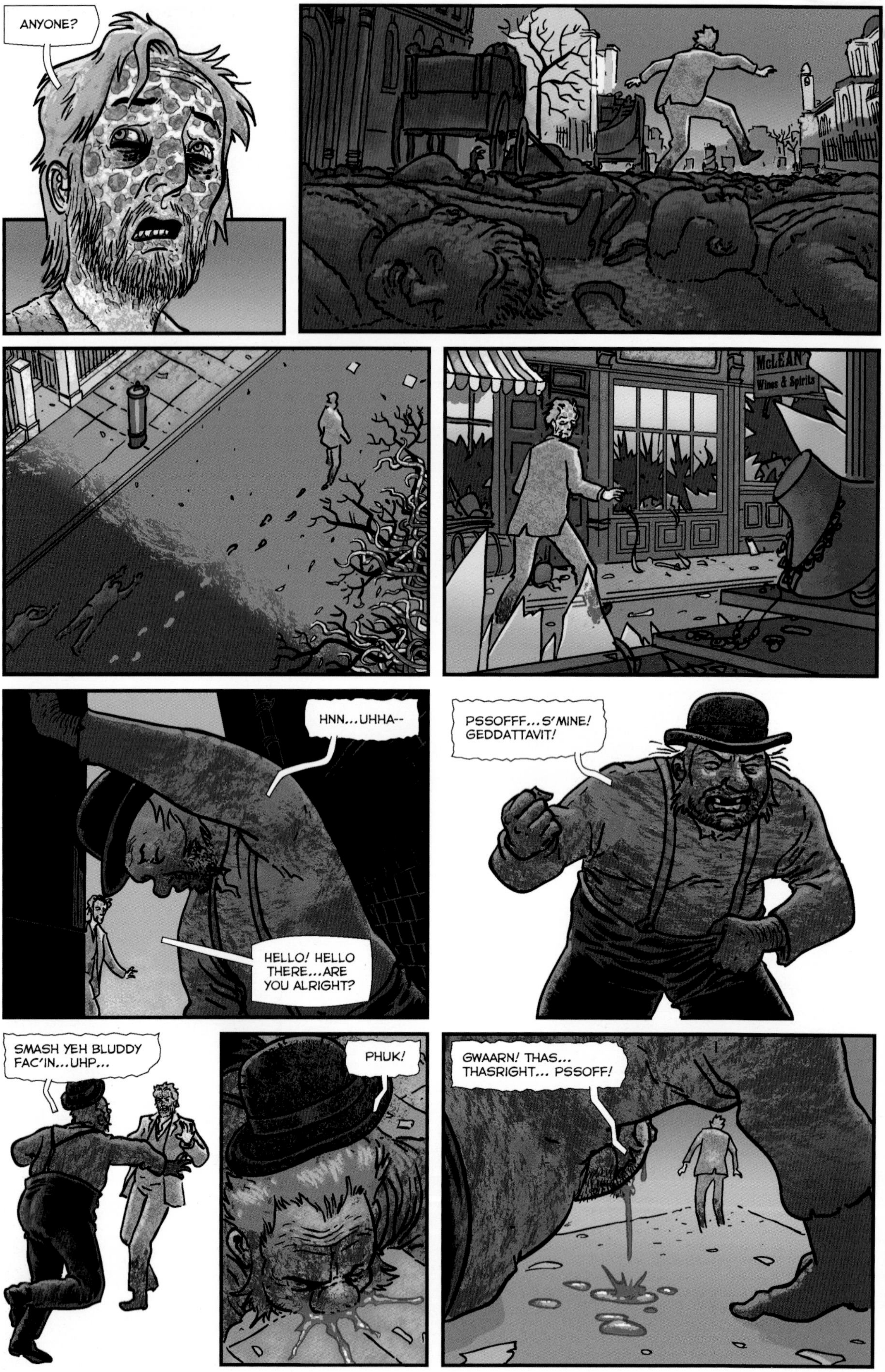
ANYONE?
McLEAN
Wines & Spirits
HNN...UHHA--
HELLO! HELLO THERE...ARE YOU ALRIGHT?
PSSOFFF...S'MINE! GEDDATTAVIT!
SMASH YEH BLUDDY FAC'IN...UHP...
PHUK!
GWAARN! THAS... THASRIGHT... PSSOFF!

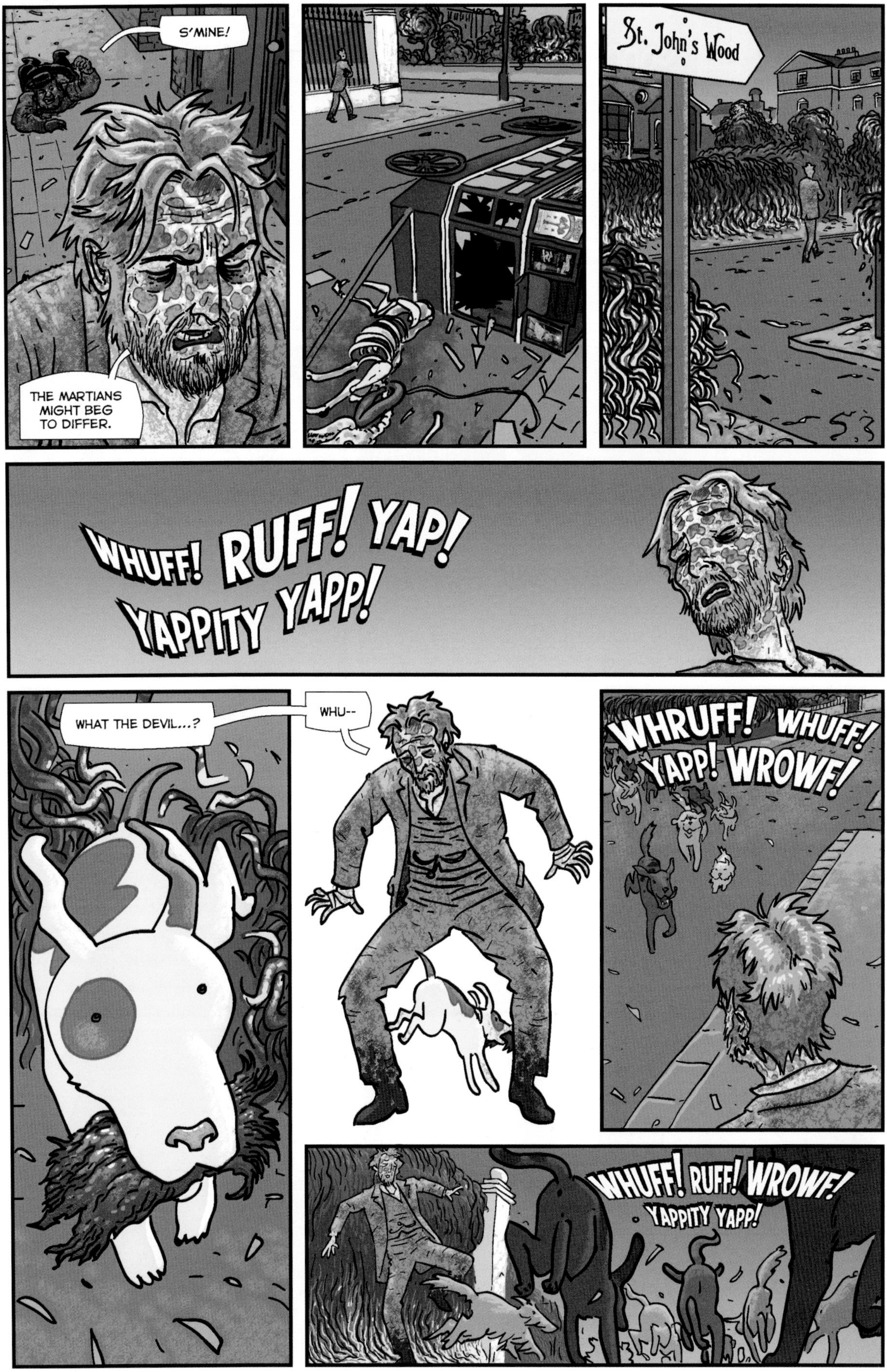
S'MINE!
THE MARTIANS MIGHT BEG TO DIFFER.
St. John's Wood
WHUFF! RUFF! YAP!
YAPPITY YAPP!
WHAT THE DEVIL...?
WHU--
WHRUFF! WHUFF!
YAPP! WROWF!
WHUFF! RUFF! WROWF!
YAPPITY YAPP!

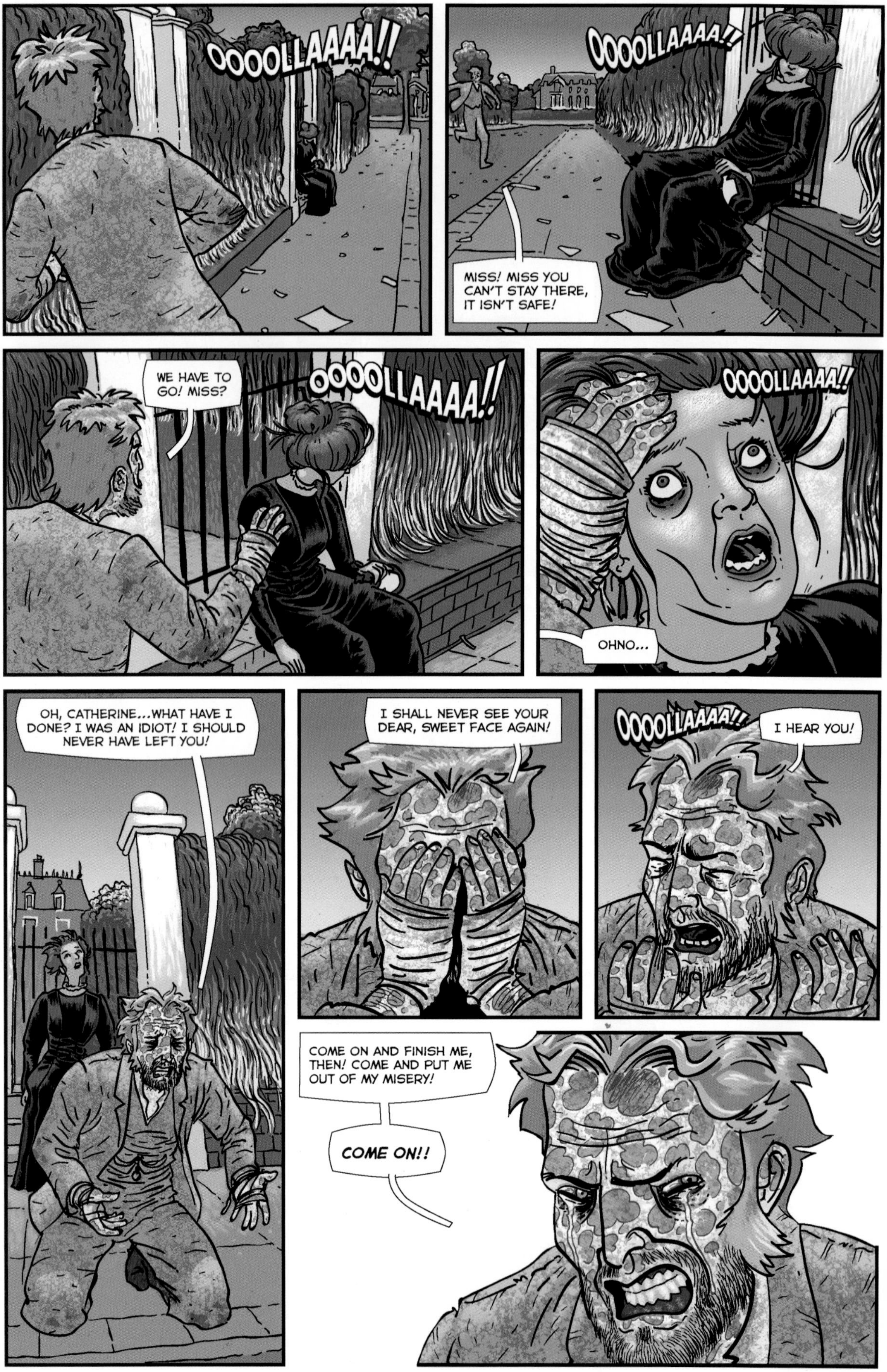
OOOOLLAAAA!!
OOOOLLAAAA!!
MISS! MISS YOU CAN'T STAY THERE, IT ISN'T SAFE!
WE HAVE TO GO! MISS?
OOOOLLAAAA!!
OOOOLLAAAA!!
OHNO...
OH, CATHERINE...WHAT HAVE I DONE? I WAS AN IDIOT! I SHOULD NEVER HAVE LEFT YOU!
I SHALL NEVER SEE YOUR DEAR, SWEET FACE AGAIN!
OOOOLLAAAA!!
I HEAR YOU!
COME ON AND FINISH ME, THEN! COME AND PUT ME OUT OF MY MISERY!
COME ON!!

OOOOLLAAAA!!

VERY WELL, I SHALL COME TO YOU!

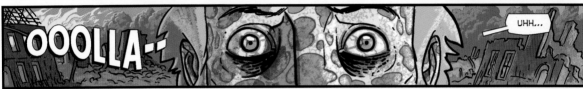

OOOLLA--

UHH...

WELL, WHAT ARE YOU WAITING FOR? HERE I AM! FINISH ME!

END IT! SAVE ME THE TROUBLE OF KILLING MYSELF!

IS THAT... BLOOD? THAT LOOKS LIKE BLOOD?

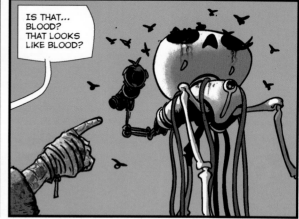

IT'S DEAD!

IT'S DEAD!

UFF HUFF HFF

GOOD GOD!

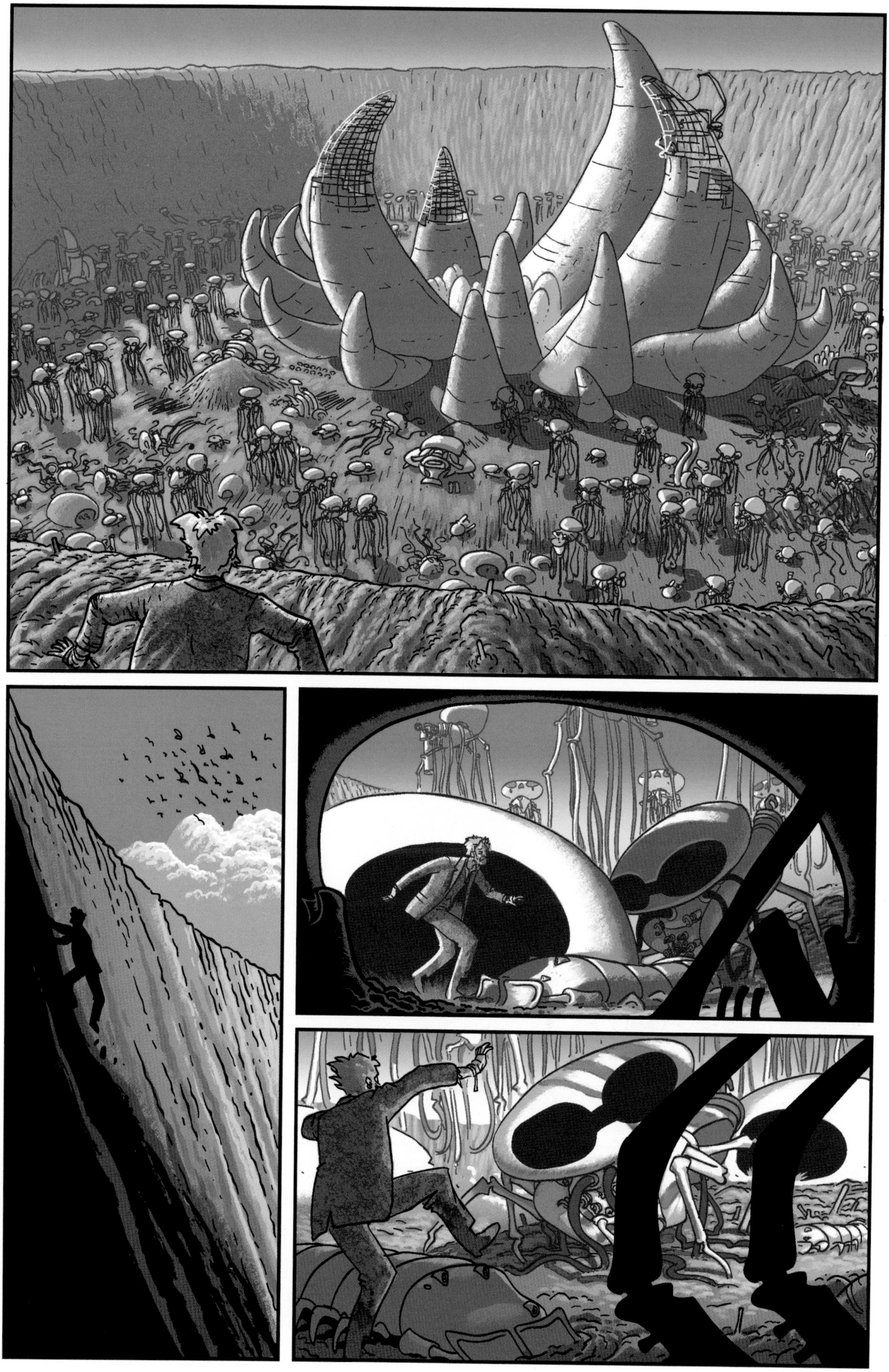

INCREDIBLE...

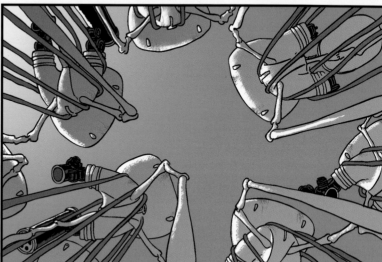

OH...

SURELY THAT CAN ONLY BE... A FLYING MACHINE?

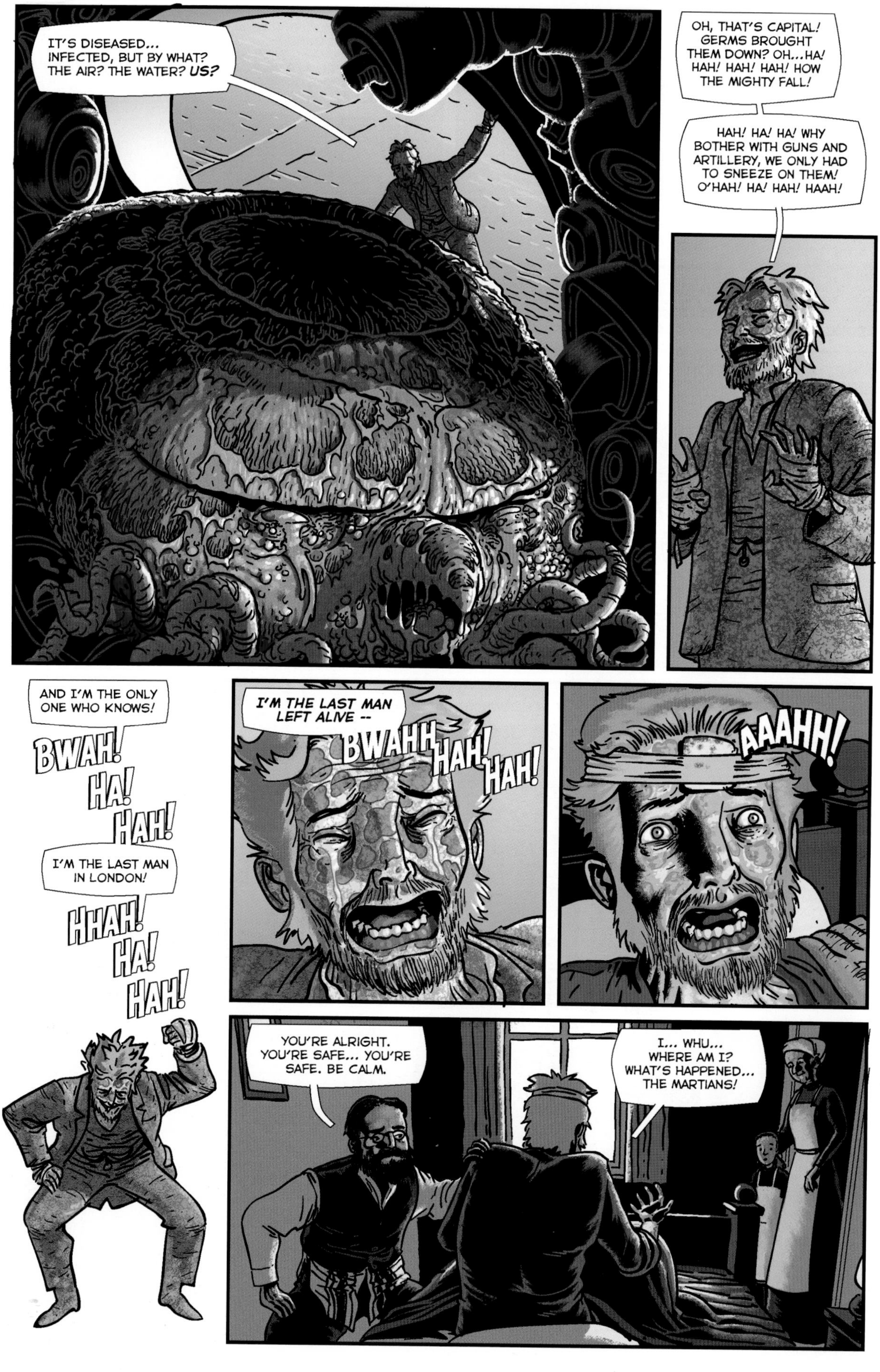
IT'S DISEASED... INFECTED, BUT BY WHAT? THE AIR? THE WATER? US?
OH, THAT'S CAPITAL! GERMS BROUGHT THEM DOWN? OH...HA! HAH! HAH! HAH! HOW THE MIGHTY FALL!
HAH! HA! HA! WHY BOTHER WITH GUNS AND ARTILLERY, WE ONLY HAD TO SNEEZE ON THEM! O'HAH! HA! HAH! HAAH!
AND I'M THE ONLY ONE WHO KNOWS!
BWAH! HA! HAH!
I'M THE LAST MAN IN LONDON!
HHAH! HA! HAH!
I'M THE LAST MAN LEFT ALIVE --
BWAHH HAH! HAH!
AAAHH!
YOU'RE ALRIGHT. YOU'RE SAFE... YOU'RE SAFE. BE CALM.
I... WHU... WHERE AM I? WHAT'S HAPPENED... THE MARTIANS!

...ARE ALL DEAD. WE FOUND YOU FOUR DAYS AGO, WANDERING, WEEPING IN THE RUINS. YOUR GRIEF HAS BEEN HARD ON YOU, BUT GOD WILLING, YOU ARE WELL AGAIN.

IS IT REALLY OVER?

YES! THE BELLS WERE RINGING EVERYWHERE! SOMEONE TELEGRAPHED PARIS THEN SOME SHIPS CAME FROM FRANCE AND IRELAND! THEY'RE COMING FROM AMERICA, TOO!

SHUSH NOW, RACHEL. LET THE MAN REST.

NO...THANK YOU. I FEEL A LOT BETTER THAN I HAVE OF LATE. MY WIFE IS AT MY COUSIN'S IN LEATHERHEAD. I HAVE TO FIND HER.

COME ON, RACHEL. HELP ME WITH THE BREAKFAST.

BUT MOTHER...

WHAT IS IT? WHAT'S WRONG?

LEATHERHEAD IS GONE, DESTROYED ABOUT TEN DAYS AGO. HARDLY ANYONE ESCAPED.

AH...I SEE. THEN I SHALL RETURN HOME... TO WOKING AND WHATEVER'S LEFT THERE.

I WILL COME WITH YOU.

BLESS YOU, BUT NO. YOUR PLACE IS HERE, WITH YOUR FAMILY...

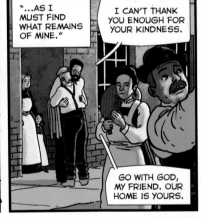

"...AS I MUST FIND WHAT REMAINS OF MINE."

I CAN'T THANK YOU ENOUGH FOR YOUR KINDNESS.

GO WITH GOD, MY FRIEND. OUR HOME IS YOURS.

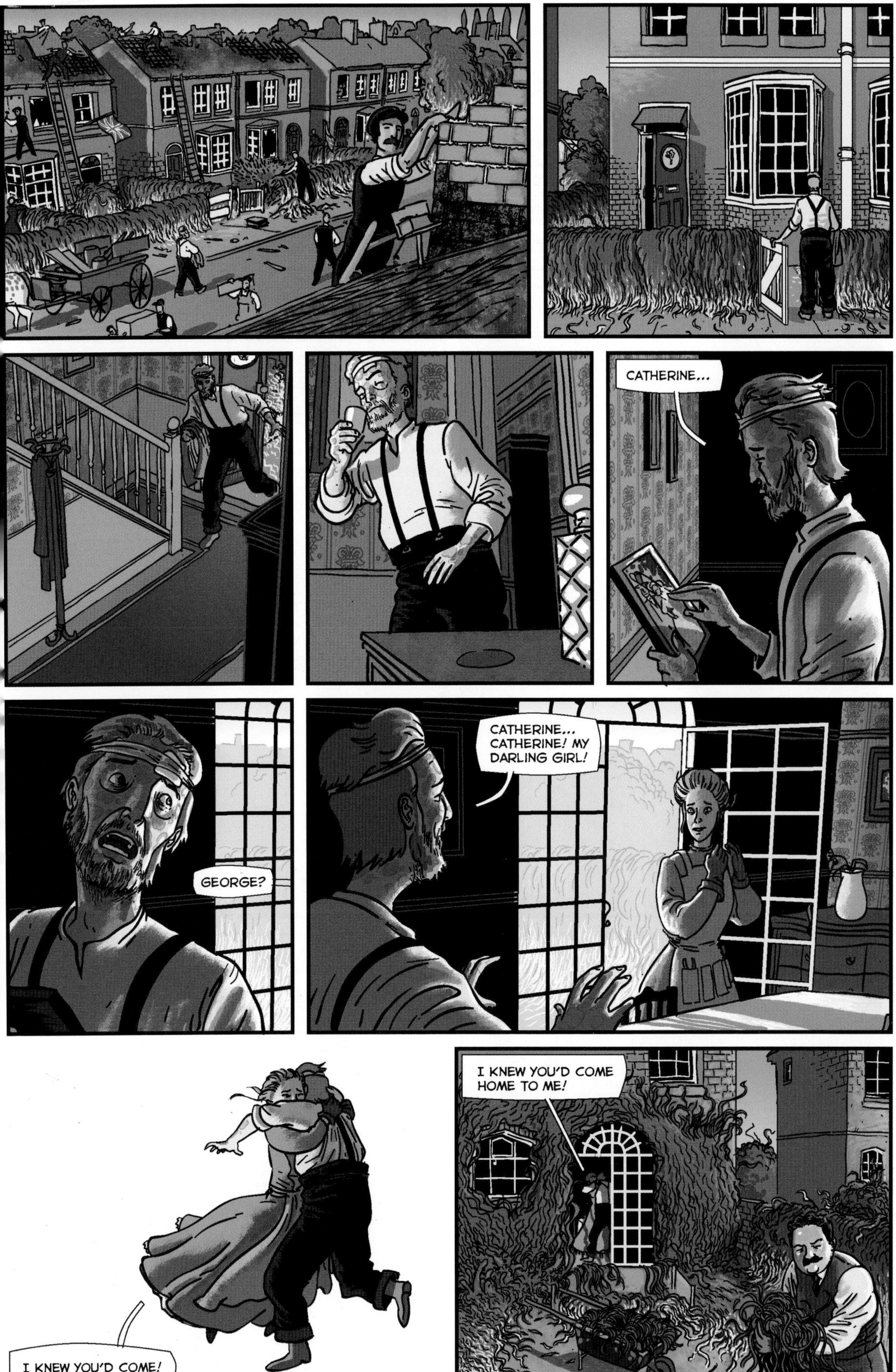
CATHERINE...
GEORGE?
CATHERINE... CATHERINE! MY DARLING GIRL!
I KNEW YOU'D COME!
I KNEW YOU'D COME HOME TO ME!

AFTER ALL MEN'S DEVICES HAD FAILED, THE MARTIANS WERE SLAIN BY THE HUMBLEST THINGS THAT GOD IN HIS WISDOM HAD PUT UPON THIS EARTH.

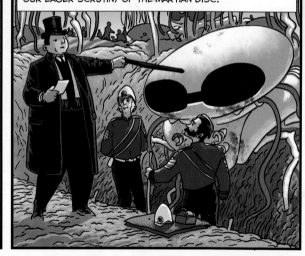

YET WE CAN NO LONGER REGARD THIS PLANET AS A SECURE, ABIDING PLACE FOR MAN. WHILE THE GIFTS TO HUMAN SCIENCE ARE ENORMOUS, THERE WILL BE NO RELAXATION OF OUR EAGER SCRUTINY OF THE MARTIAN DISC.

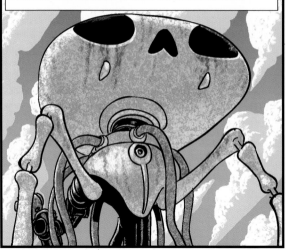

SEVEN MONTHS AGO, WITH VENUS IN OPPOSITION, LUMINOUS MARKINGS SCORED THE FACE OF MARS ONCE MORE. THEY MAY HAVE OBSERVED THE FATE OF THEIR EARTHLY PIONEERS AND DECIDED VENUS A SAFER SETTLEMENT?

THE STRESS AND DANGER OF THAT TIME HAUNTS ME STILL. THE WRITHING FLAMES, THE BLACK POWDER, THE SHROUDED, CONTORTED BODIES, TATTERED AND DOG-BITTEN.

THEN TO HOLD MY WIFE'S HAND AGAIN, THEY ARE DISPELLED. PHANTOMS OF A ONCE DEAD CITY. YET FROM ALL OF THIS I HAVE CONJURED A DIM BUT WONDERFUL VISION.

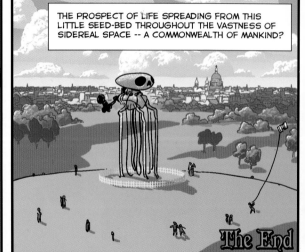

IF THE MARTIANS CAN INDEED REACH VENUS, MIGHT SUCH A THING BE POSSIBLE FOR MEN?

THE PROSPECT OF LIFE SPREADING FROM THIS LITTLE SEED-BED THROUGHOUT THE VASTNESS OF SIDEREAL SPACE -- A COMMONWEALTH OF MANKIND?

The End

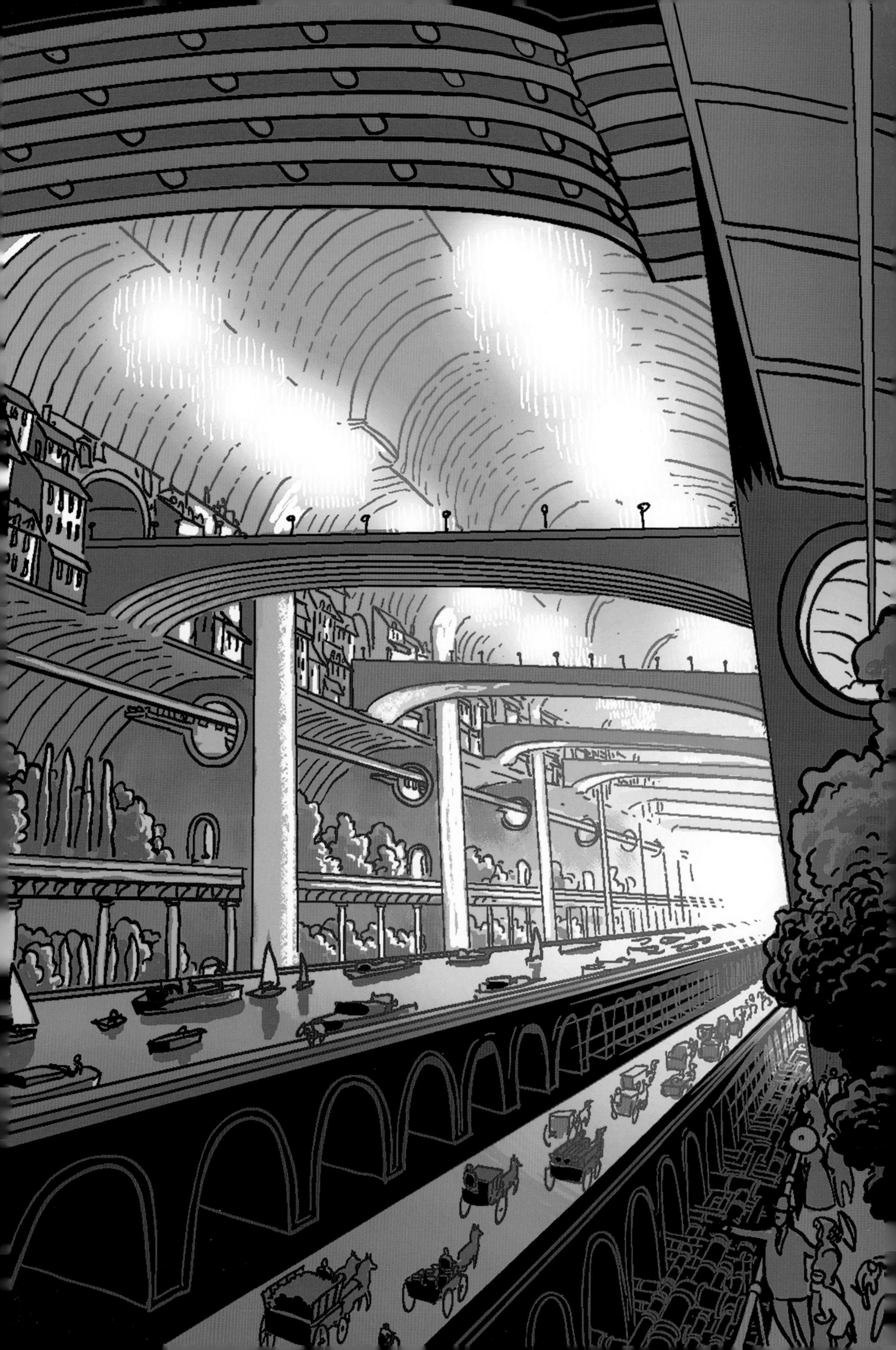

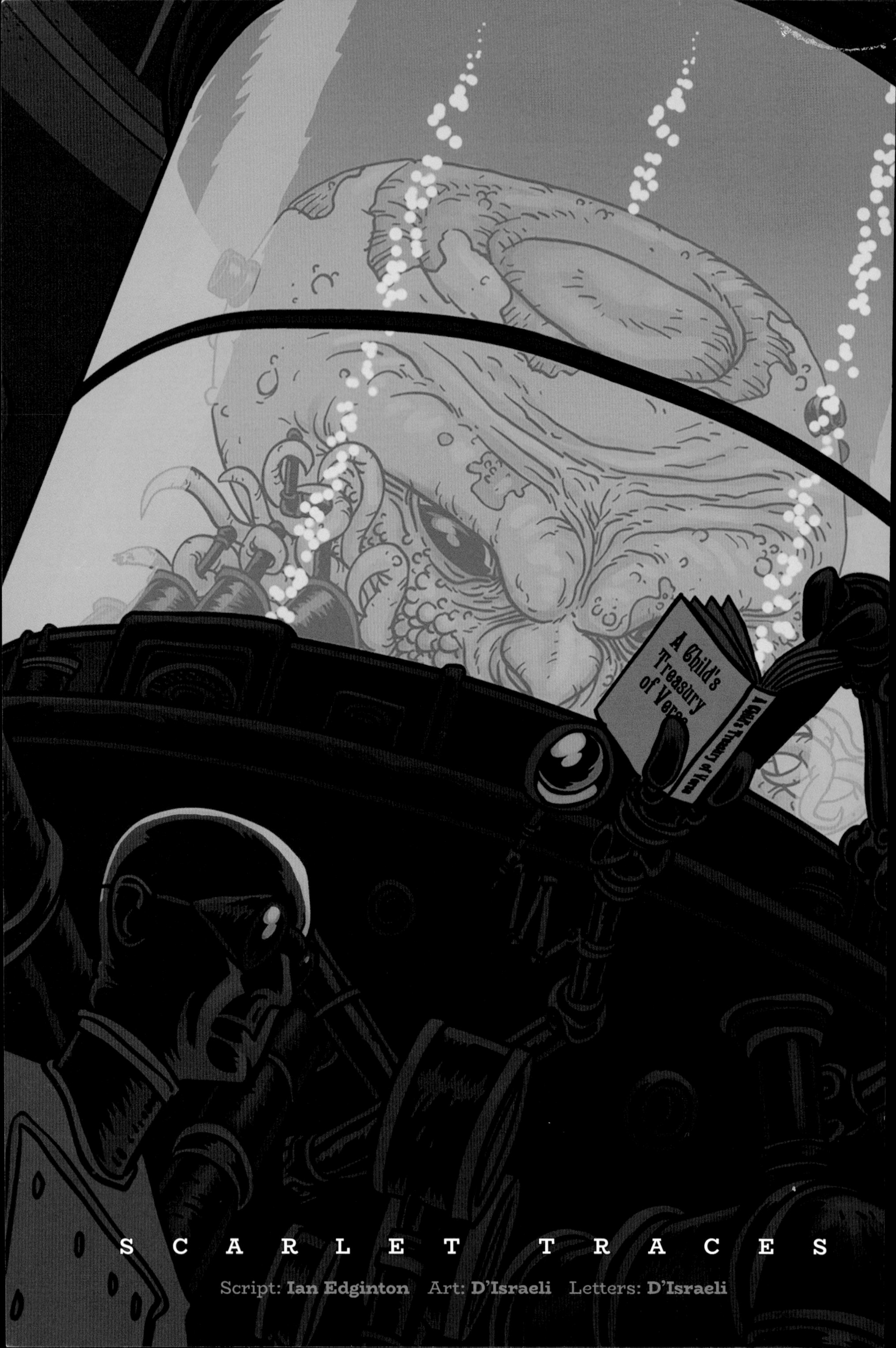
A Child's Treasury of Verse

S C A R L E T   T R A C E S

Script: **Ian Edginton** Art: **D'Israeli** Letters: **D'Israeli**

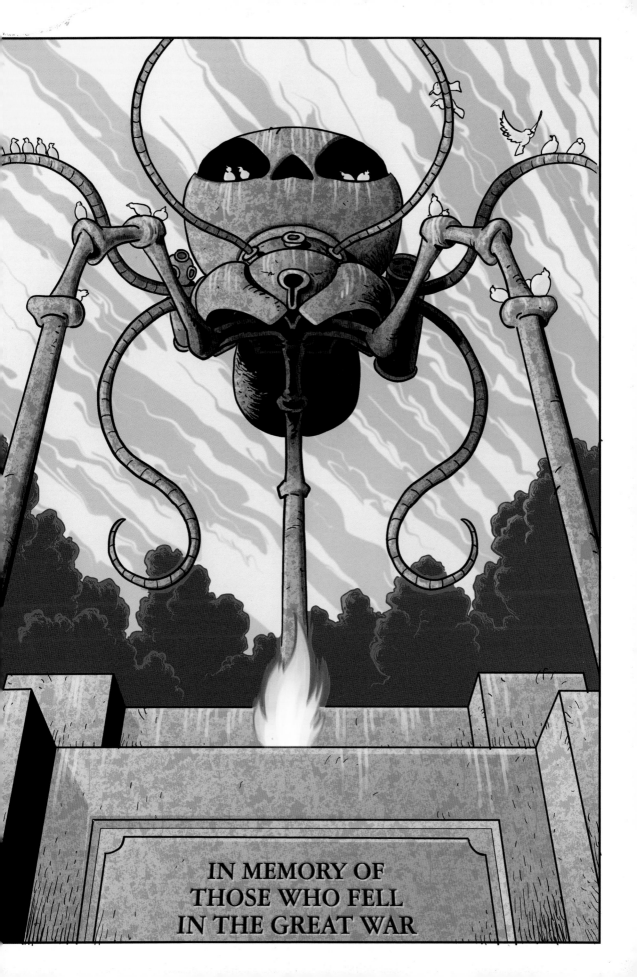

IN MEMORY OF
THOSE WHO FELL
IN THE GREAT WAR

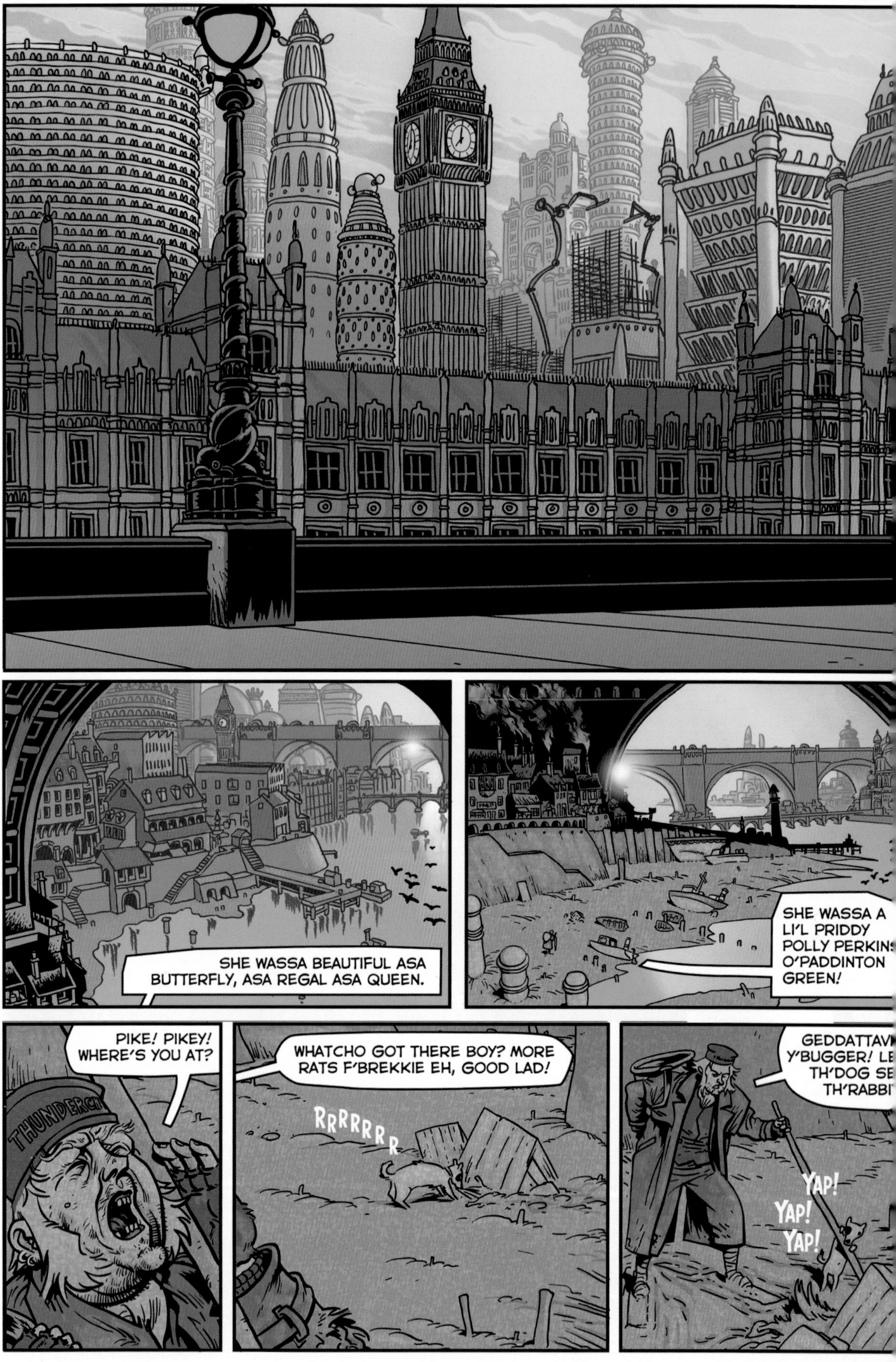
SHE WASSA BEAUTIFUL ASA BUTTERFLY, ASA REGAL ASA QUEEN.
SHE WASSA A LI'L PRIDDY POLLY PERKIN O'PADDINTON GREEN!
PIKE! PIKEY! WHERE'S YOU AT?
THUNDERCH
WHATCHO GOT THERE BOY? MORE RATS F'BREKKIE EH, GOOD LAD!
RRRRRRR
GEDDATTAV Y'BUGGER! LE TH'DOG SE TH'RABBI
YAP!
YAP!
YAP!

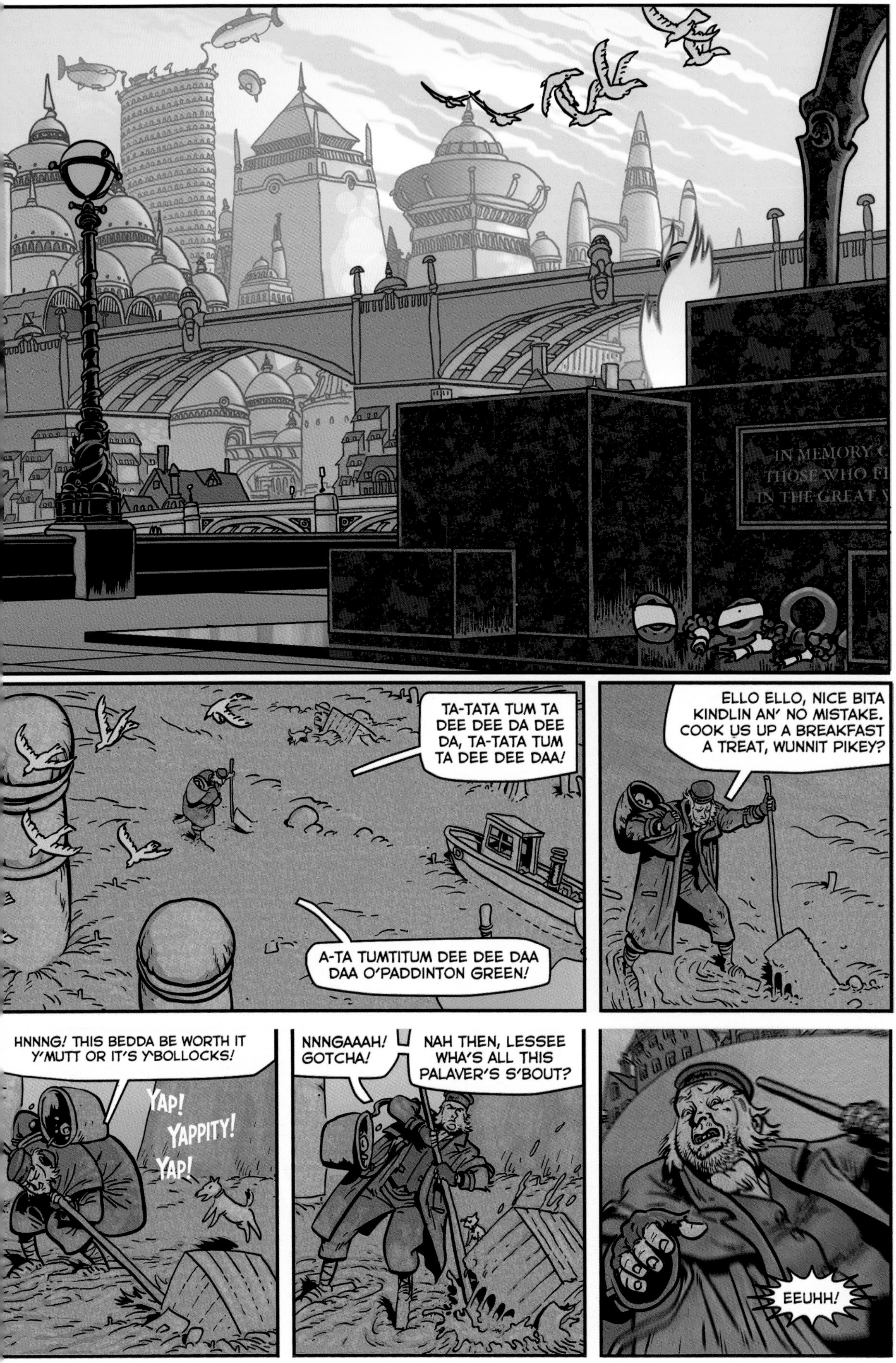
IN MEMORY O
THOSE WHO FI
IN THE GREAT W
TA-TATA TUM TA DEE DEE DA DEE DA, TA-TATA TUM TA DEE DEE DAA!
A-TA TUMTITUM DEE DEE DAA DAA O'PADDINTON GREEN!
ELLO ELLO, NICE BITA KINDLIN AN' NO MISTAKE. COOK US UP A BREAKFAST A TREAT, WUNNIT PIKEY?
HNNNG! THIS BEDDA BE WORTH IT Y'MUTT OR IT'S Y'BOLLOCKS!
YAP!
YAPPITY!
YAP!
NNNGAAAH! GOTCHA!
NAH THEN, LESSEE WHA'S ALL THIS PALAVER'S S'BOUT?
EEUHH!

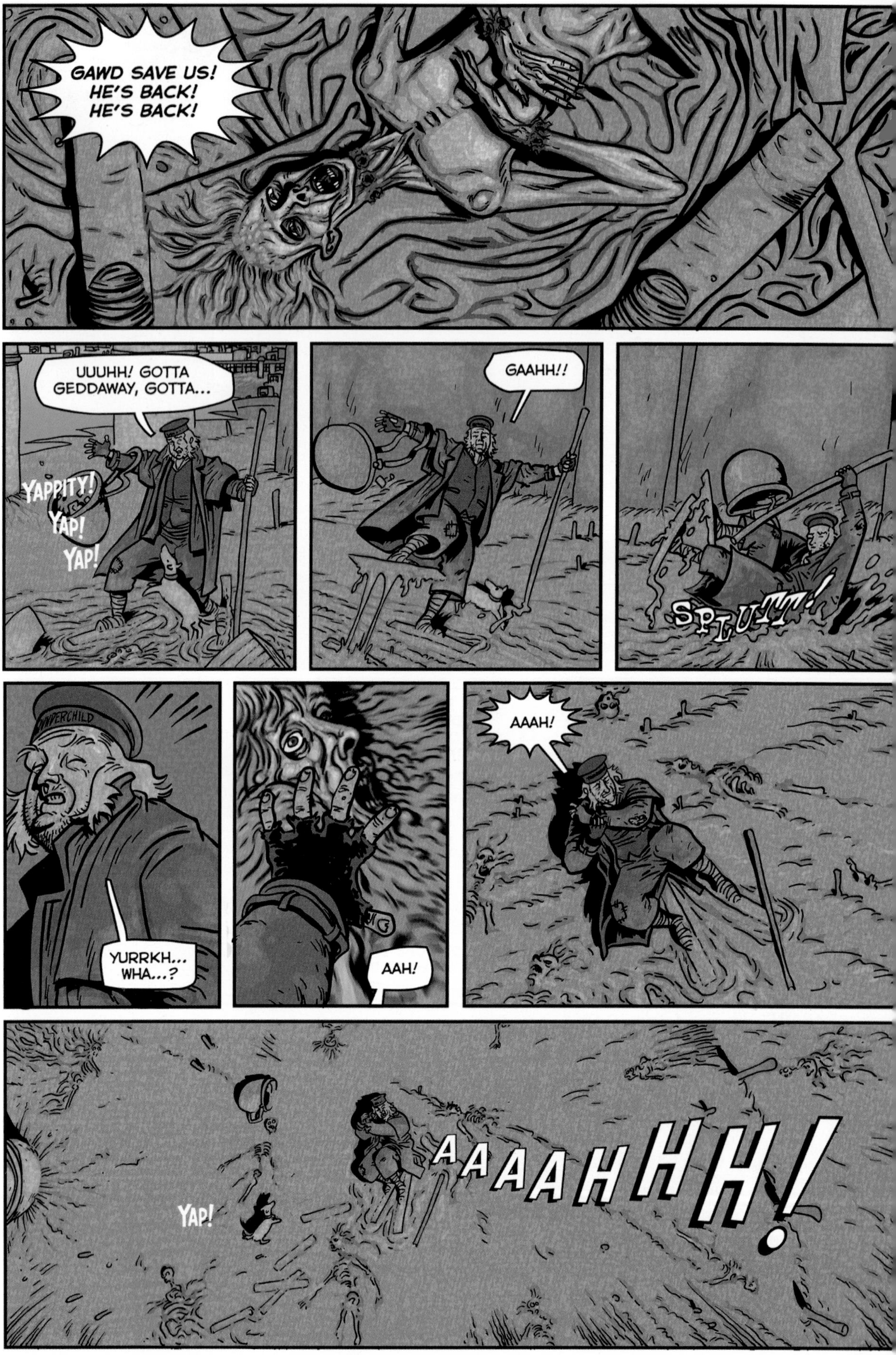
GAWD SAVE US! HE'S BACK! HE'S BACK!
UUUHH! GOTTA GEDDAWAY, GOTTA...
YAPPITY! YAP! YAP!
GAAHH!!
SPLUTT!
DUNDERCHILD
YURRKH... WHA...?
AAH!
AAAH!
AAAAHHHH!
YAP!

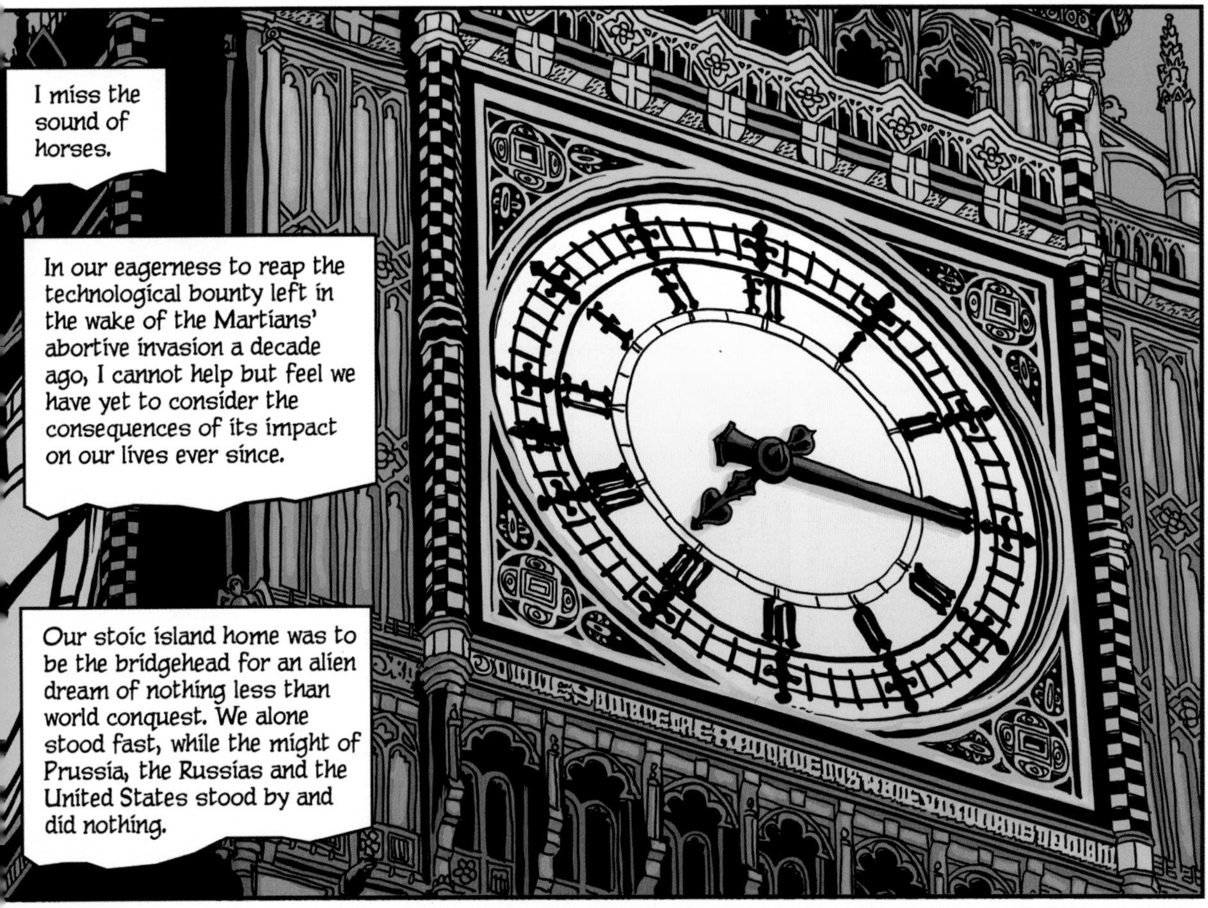
I miss the sound of horses.
In our eagerness to reap the technological bounty left in the wake of the Martians' abortive invasion a decade ago, I cannot help but feel we have yet to consider the consequences of its impact on our lives ever since.
Our stoic island home was to be the bridgehead for an alien dream of nothing less than world conquest. We alone stood fast, while the might of Prussia, the Russias and the United States stood by and did nothing.

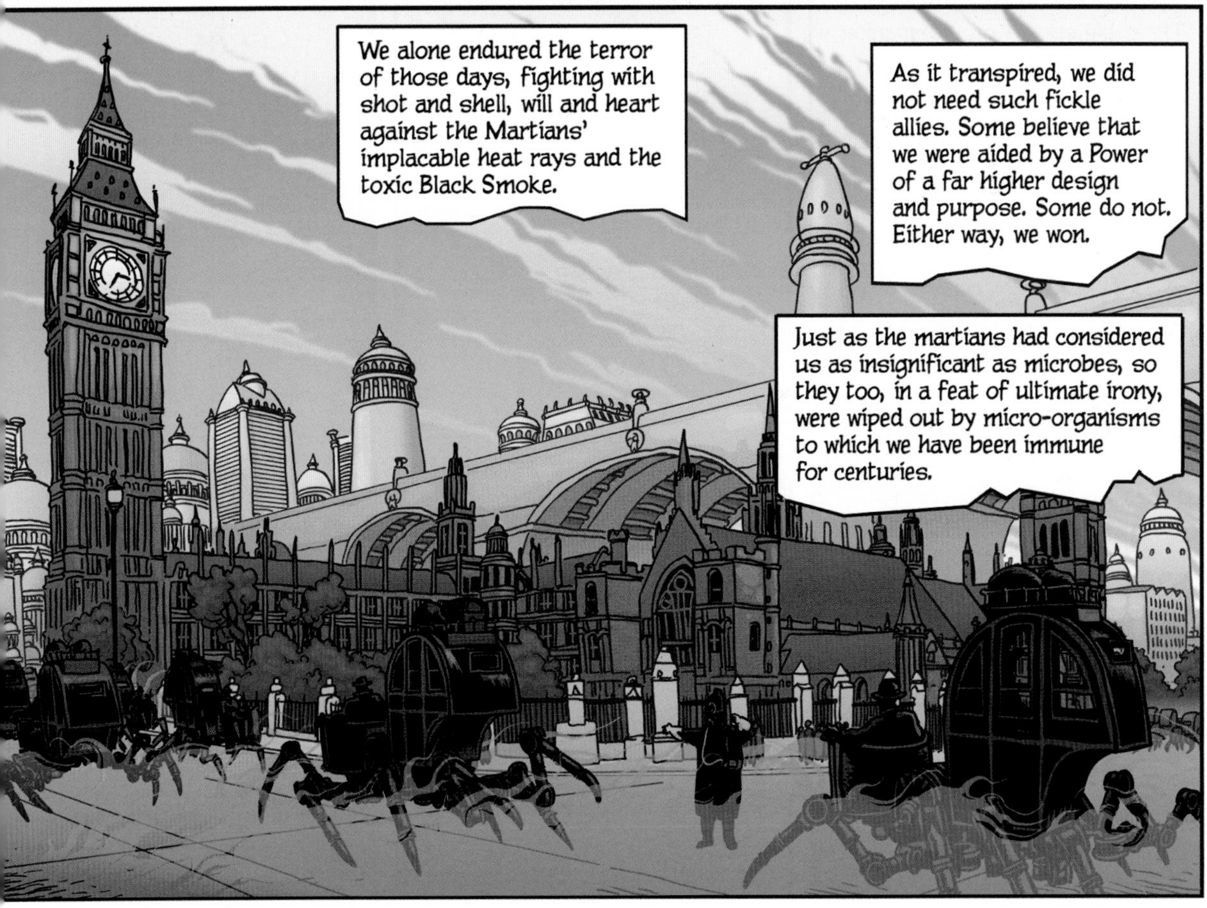
We alone endured the terror of those days, fighting with shot and shell, will and heart against the Martians' implacable heat rays and the toxic Black Smoke.
As it transpired, we did not need such fickle allies. Some believe that we were aided by a Power of a far higher design and purpose. Some do not. Either way, we won.
Just as the martians had considered us as insignificant as microbes, so they too, in a feat of ultimate irony, were wiped out by micro-organisms to which we have been immune for centuries.

The Martians' unwitting bequest to their would-be slaves was a form of technology as then undreamt of by mankind.
OXFORD STREET
OVERGROUND
ST. GILES CIRCUS
EXIT
OXFORD CIRCUS
HMS THUNDERCHILD
Within a decade our brightest minds had unravelled its secrets, their machineries of war and subjugation adapted and assimilated into our everyday usage.
The noble steed - our companion and carriage for millennia is replaced by a clockwork toy! Homes are heated and lit by a version of the once-dreaded heat ray. The great mills and factories of the North are now vast, mechanised estates.
To The Continent
To The Midlands
TENTH ANNIVERSARY INVASION SPECIAL
The British Empire is now truly a world power without peer, but I cannot help but wonder if we have not lost something in the process.
We have saved the world and become the envy of it... or rather feared by it.

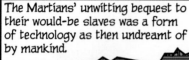

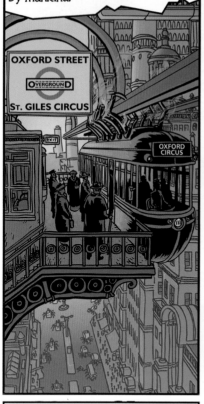

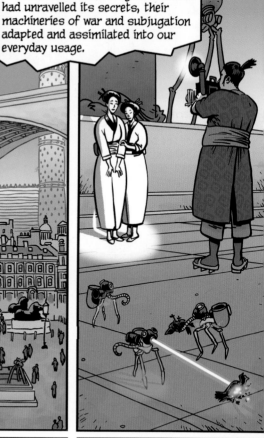

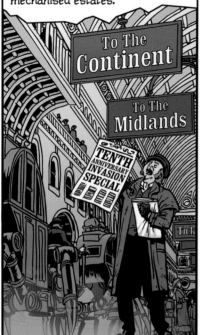

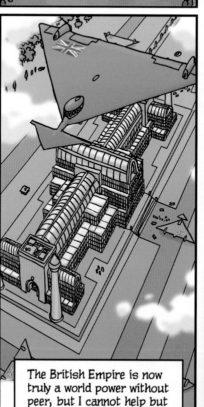

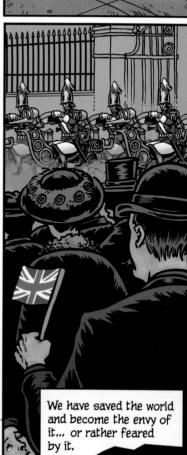

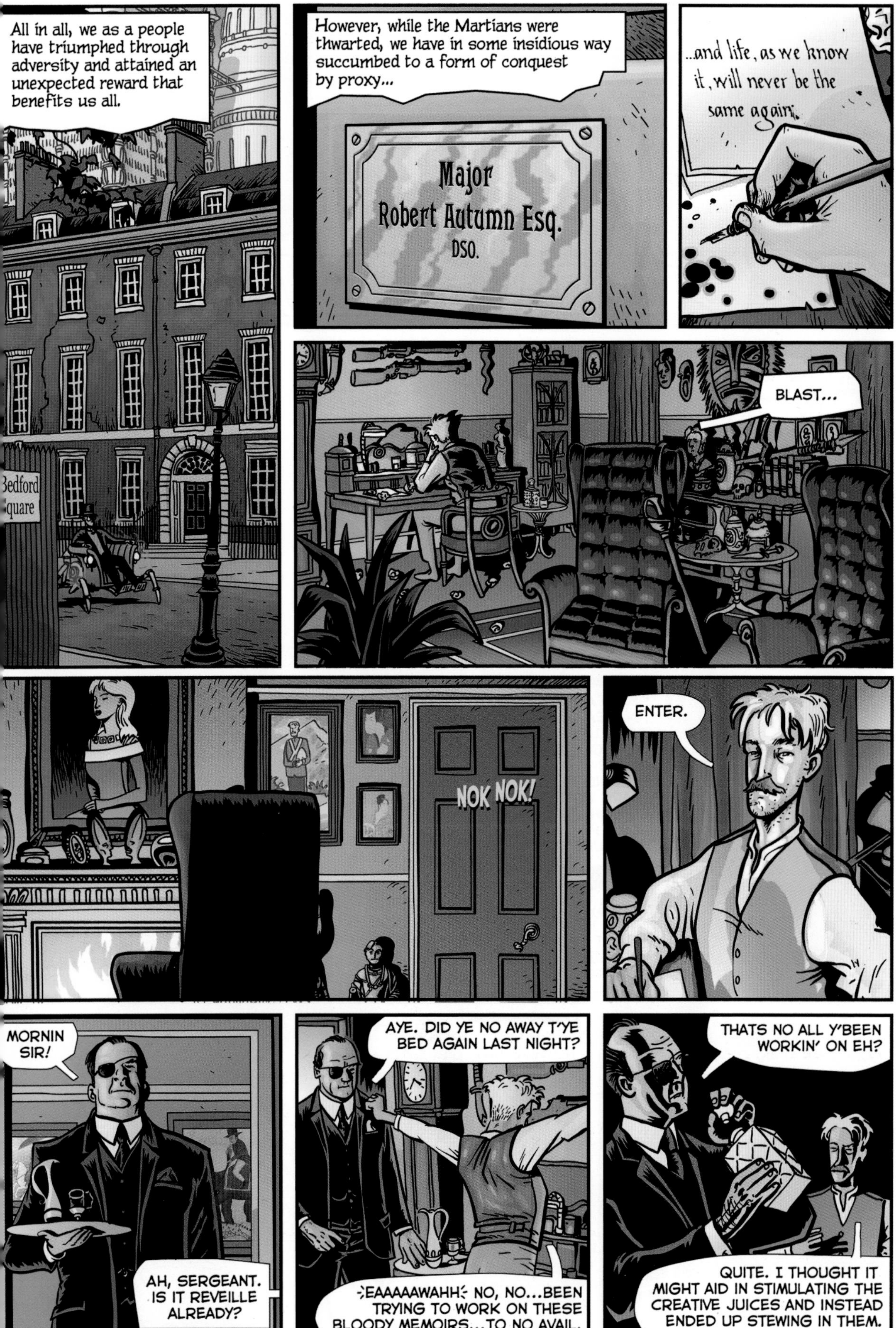
All in all, we as a people have triumphed through adversity and attained an unexpected reward that benefits us all.
Bedford Square
However, while the Martians were thwarted, we have in some insidious way succumbed to a form of conquest by proxy...
Major Robert Autumn Esq. DSO.
...and life, as we know it, will never be the same again.
BLAST...
NOK NOK!
ENTER.
MORNIN SIR!
AH, SERGEANT. IS IT REVEILLE ALREADY?
AYE. DID YE NO AWAY T'YE BED AGAIN LAST NIGHT?
EAAAAAWAHH NO, NO...BEEN TRYING TO WORK ON THESE BLOODY MEMOIRS...TO NO AVAIL.
THATS NO ALL Y'BEEN WORKIN' ON EH?
QUITE. I THOUGHT IT MIGHT AID IN STIMULATING THE CREATIVE JUICES AND INSTEAD ENDED UP STEWING IN THEM.

AH MADE A POT O'THE TURKISH, JUST TAE BE ON THE SAFE SIDE.

GOOD MAN!

SIR, WI' RESPECT. MEBBE Y'SHOULD GI' THE WRITIN' REST A WHILE. Y'BEIN' AT IT FER WEEKS NOW AN'...WELL, Y'NO GETTIN' ANYWHERE ARE YE?

REALLY?

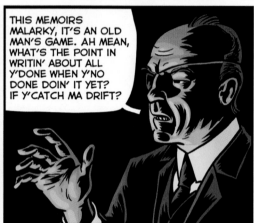

THIS MEMOIRS MALARKY, IT'S AN OLD MAN'S GAME. AH MEAN, WHAT'S THE POINT IN WRITIN' ABOUT ALL Y'DONE WHEN Y'NO DONE DOIN' IT YET? IF Y'CATCH MA DRIFT?

INDEED?

SERGEANT, I ONCE SAW YOU BEAT A BENGAL TIGER UNCONSCIOUS WITH YOUR BARE HANDS. REDUCE A HULKING COSSACK TO TEARS WITH NOTHING BUT A HEARTY LAUGH AND A PAIR OF MANICURE SCISSORS.

HOWEVER, THE THING THAT IMPRESSES ME MOST ABOUT YOU , IS YOUR IRREFUTABLE SCOTS LOGIC.

YE'D NO BE TAKIN THE PISS WOULD YE SIR?

PERISH THE THOUGHT! TRUTH IS, I'VE REACHED A SIMILAR CONCLUSION MYSELF.

IN THE SMALL HOURS OF THE MORNING, A MAN IS APT TO SEARCH HIS SOUL MORE THAN AT ANY OTHER TIME.

I ASKED MYSELF, WHY AM I DOING THIS? WRITING ABOUT A LIFE HALF LIVED? I FOUND I DID NOT LIKE THE ANSWER.

IT'S FOR NOTHING BUT VANITY AND VALIDATION.

SIR?

YOU AND I HAVE SERVED QUEEN AND COUNTRY WITH UNSTINTING LOYALTY. BOTH ON THE BATTLE-FIELD AND IN CLOAK AND DAGGER GAMES BEHIND THE SCENES.

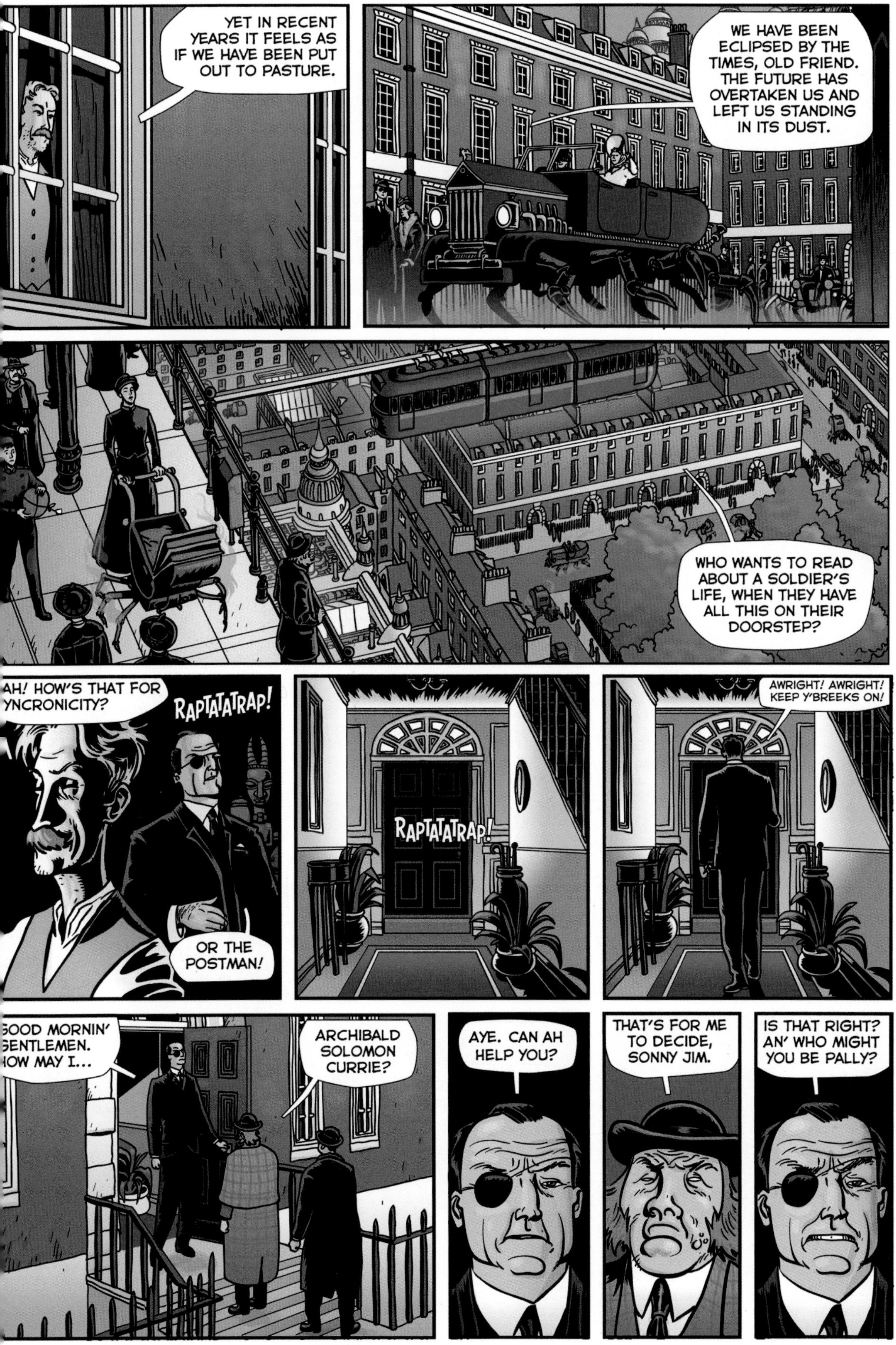

YET IN RECENT YEARS IT FEELS AS IF WE HAVE BEEN PUT OUT TO PASTURE.
WE HAVE BEEN ECLIPSED BY THE TIMES, OLD FRIEND. THE FUTURE HAS OVERTAKEN US AND LEFT US STANDING IN ITS DUST.
WHO WANTS TO READ ABOUT A SOLDIER'S LIFE, WHEN THEY HAVE ALL THIS ON THEIR DOORSTEP?
AH! HOW'S THAT FOR YNCRONICITY?
RAPTATATRAP!
OR THE POSTMAN!
RAPTATATRAP!
AWRIGHT! AWRIGHT! KEEP Y'BREEKS ON!
GOOD MORNIN' GENTLEMEN. HOW MAY I...
ARCHIBALD SOLOMON CURRIE?
AYE. CAN AH HELP YOU?
THAT'S FOR ME TO DECIDE, SONNY JIM.
IS THAT RIGHT? AN' WHO MIGHT YOU BE PALLY?

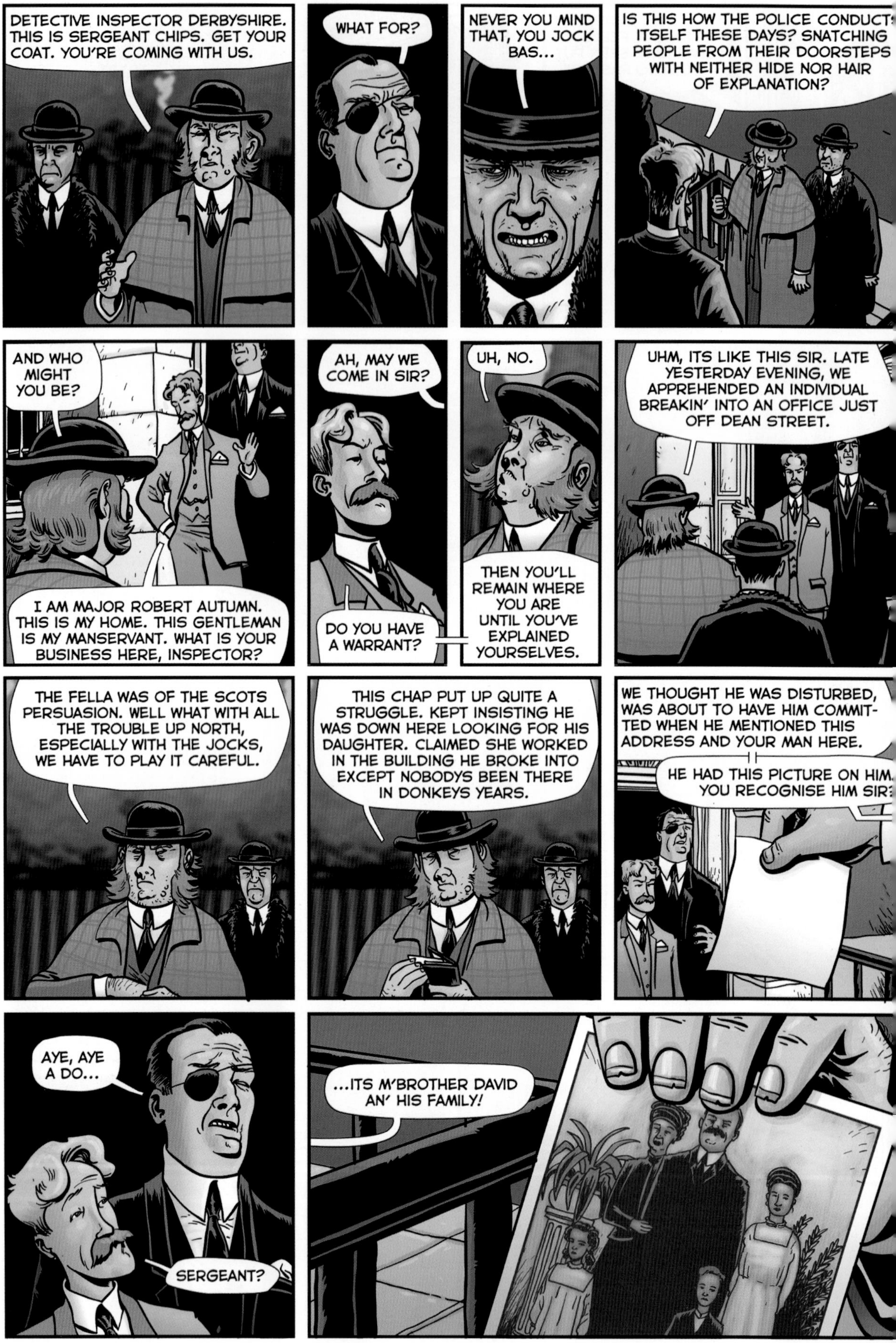
DETECTIVE INSPECTOR DERBYSHIRE. THIS IS SERGEANT CHIPS. GET YOUR COAT. YOU'RE COMING WITH US.
WHAT FOR?
NEVER YOU MIND THAT, YOU JOCK BAS...
IS THIS HOW THE POLICE CONDUCTS ITSELF THESE DAYS? SNATCHING PEOPLE FROM THEIR DOORSTEPS WITH NEITHER HIDE NOR HAIR OF EXPLANATION?
AND WHO MIGHT YOU BE?
I AM MAJOR ROBERT AUTUMN. THIS IS MY HOME. THIS GENTLEMAN IS MY MANSERVANT. WHAT IS YOUR BUSINESS HERE, INSPECTOR?
AH, MAY WE COME IN SIR?
UH, NO.
DO YOU HAVE A WARRANT?
THEN YOU'LL REMAIN WHERE YOU ARE UNTIL YOU'VE EXPLAINED YOURSELVES.
UHM, ITS LIKE THIS SIR. LATE YESTERDAY EVENING, WE APPREHENDED AN INDIVIDUAL BREAKIN' INTO AN OFFICE JUST OFF DEAN STREET.
THE FELLA WAS OF THE SCOTS PERSUASION. WELL WHAT WITH ALL THE TROUBLE UP NORTH, ESPECIALLY WITH THE JOCKS, WE HAVE TO PLAY IT CAREFUL.
THIS CHAP PUT UP QUITE A STRUGGLE. KEPT INSISTING HE WAS DOWN HERE LOOKING FOR HIS DAUGHTER. CLAIMED SHE WORKED IN THE BUILDING HE BROKE INTO EXCEPT NOBODYS BEEN THERE IN DONKEYS YEARS.
WE THOUGHT HE WAS DISTURBED, WAS ABOUT TO HAVE HIM COMMITTED WHEN HE MENTIONED THIS ADDRESS AND YOUR MAN HERE.
HE HAD THIS PICTURE ON HIM. YOU RECOGNISE HIM SIR?
AYE, AYE A DO...
SERGEANT?
...ITS M'BROTHER DAVID AN' HIS FAMILY!

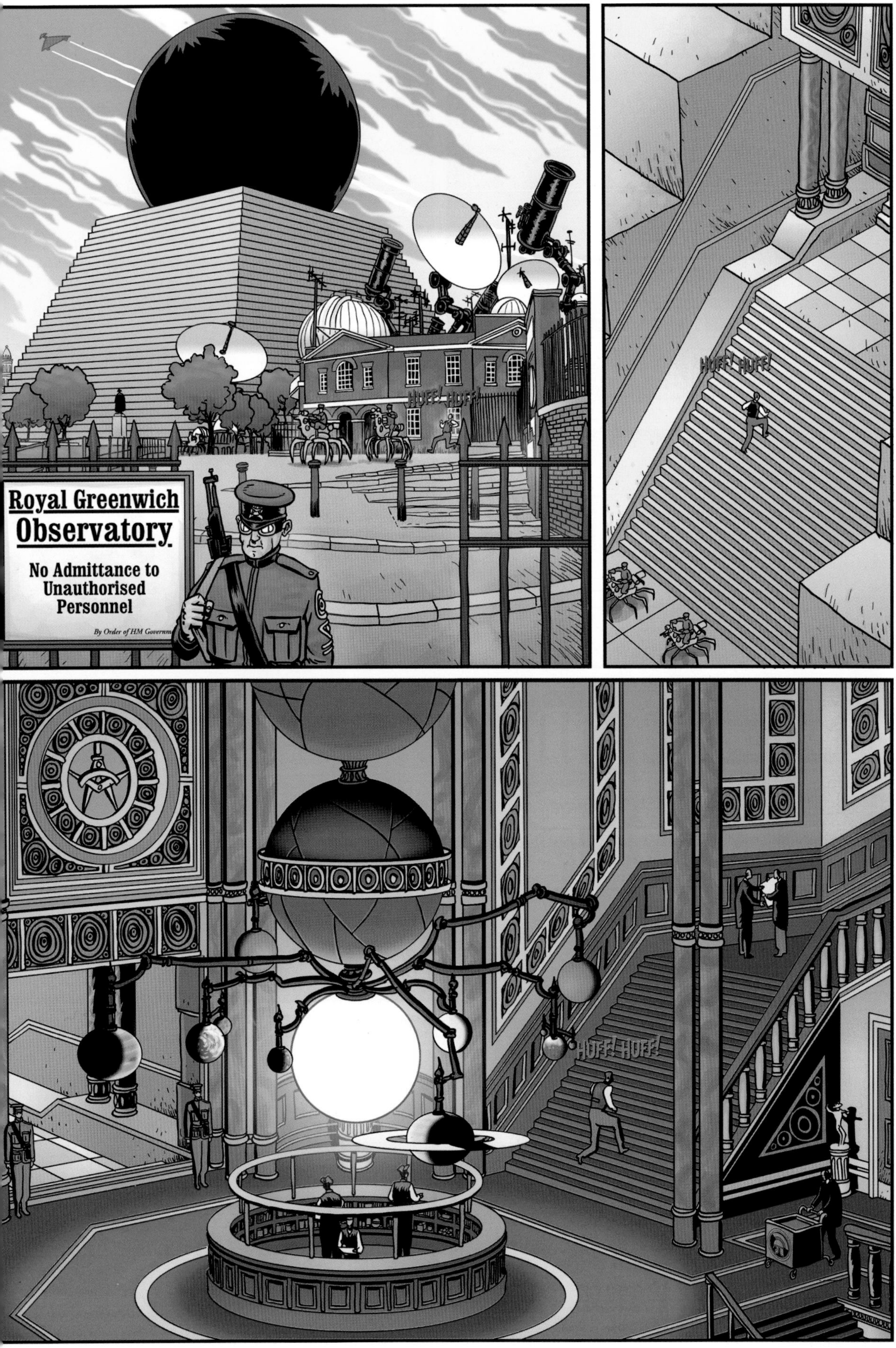
Royal Greenwich Observatory
No Admittance to Unauthorised Personnel
By Order of HM Governm
HUFF! HUFF!
HUFF! HUFF!
HUFF! HUFF!

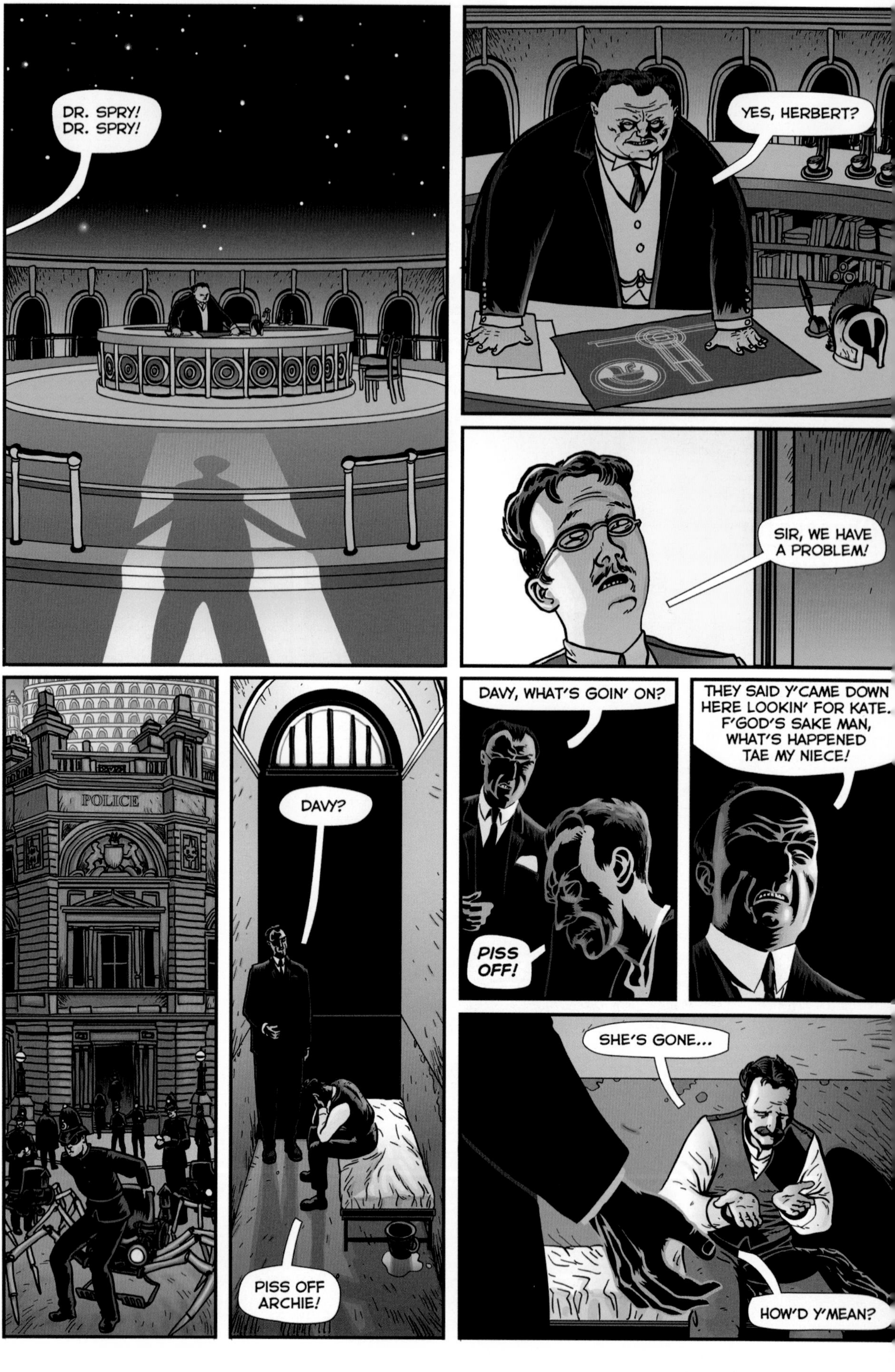
DR. SPRY!
DR. SPRY!
YES, HERBERT?
SIR, WE HAVE A PROBLEM!
POLICE
DAVY?
PISS OFF ARCHIE!
DAVY, WHAT'S GOIN' ON?
PISS OFF!
THEY SAID Y'CAME DOWN HERE LOOKIN' FOR KATE. F'GOD'S SAKE MAN, WHAT'S HAPPENED TAE MY NIECE!
SHE'S GONE...
HOW'D Y'MEAN?

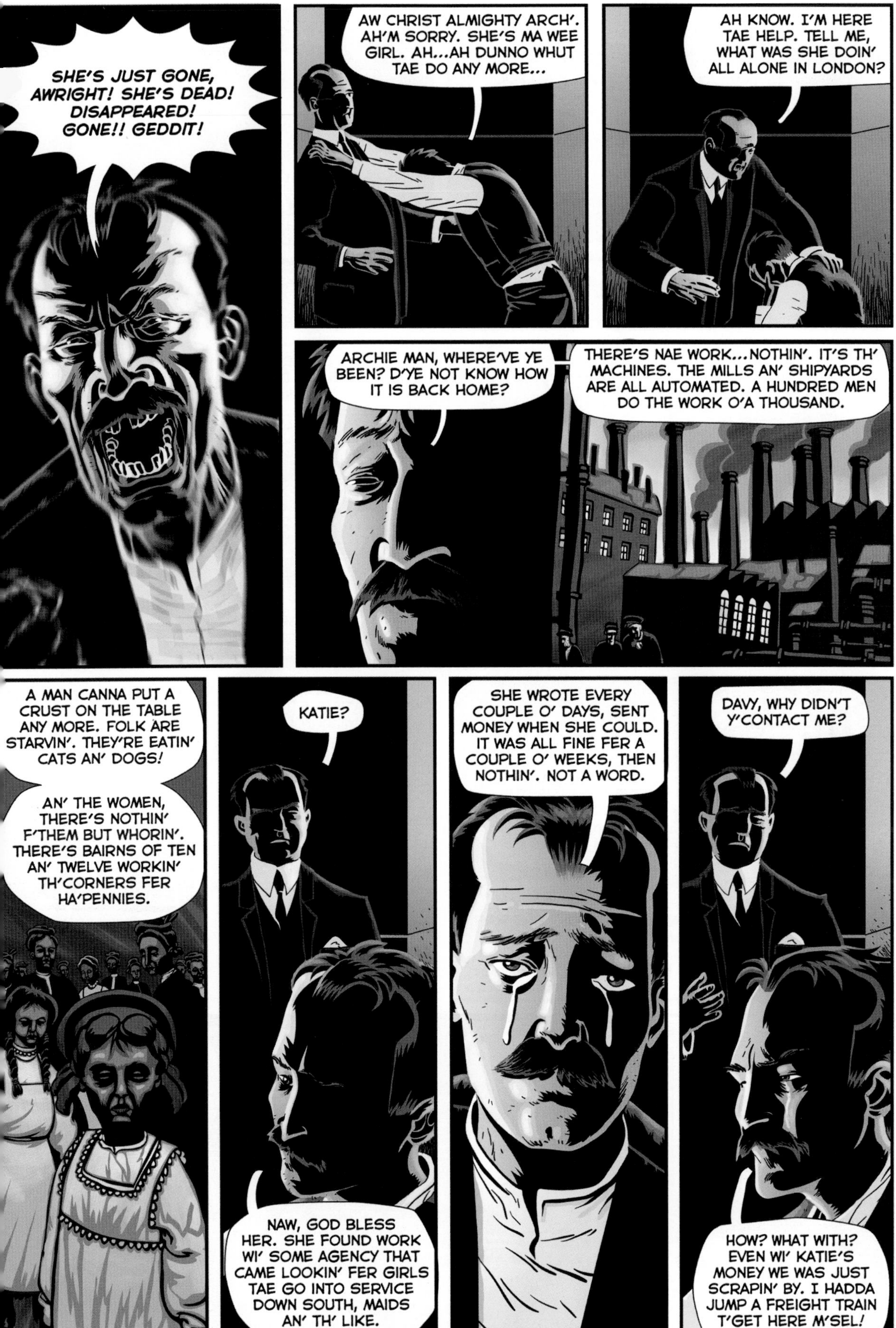
SHE'S JUST GONE, AWRIGHT! SHE'S DEAD! DISAPPEARED! GONE!! GEDDIT!
AW CHRIST ALMIGHTY ARCH'. AH'M SORRY. SHE'S MA WEE GIRL. AH...AH DUNNO WHUT TAE DO ANY MORE...
AH KNOW. I'M HERE TAE HELP. TELL ME, WHAT WAS SHE DOIN' ALL ALONE IN LONDON?
ARCHIE MAN, WHERE'VE YE BEEN? D'YE NOT KNOW HOW IT IS BACK HOME?
THERE'S NAE WORK...NOTHIN'. IT'S TH' MACHINES. THE MILLS AN' SHIPYARDS ARE ALL AUTOMATED. A HUNDRED MEN DO THE WORK O'A THOUSAND.
A MAN CANNA PUT A CRUST ON THE TABLE ANY MORE. FOLK ARE STARVIN'. THEY'RE EATIN' CATS AN' DOGS!
AN' THE WOMEN, THERE'S NOTHIN' F'THEM BUT WHORIN'. THERE'S BAIRNS OF TEN AN' TWELVE WORKIN' TH'CORNERS FER HA'PENNIES.
KATIE?
NAW, GOD BLESS HER. SHE FOUND WORK WI' SOME AGENCY THAT CAME LOOKIN' FER GIRLS TAE GO INTO SERVICE DOWN SOUTH, MAIDS AN' TH' LIKE.
SHE WROTE EVERY COUPLE O' DAYS, SENT MONEY WHEN SHE COULD. IT WAS ALL FINE FER A COUPLE O' WEEKS, THEN NOTHIN'. NOT A WORD.
DAVY, WHY DIDN'T Y'CONTACT ME?
HOW? WHAT WITH? EVEN WI' KATIE'S MONEY WE WAS JUST SCRAPIN' BY. I HADDA JUMP A FREIGHT TRAIN T'GET HERE M'SEL!

AN' Y'FOUND THE AGENCY? ARE Y'SURE IT WAS THE RIGHT ONE?

AH'M NO FOOL MAN. COURSE IT WAS. 'CEPT NAEBODY'D BEEN THERE IN MONTHS, MEBBE YEARS...

...THAT'S WHEN AH LOST MA RAG.

KNOCK KNOCK

EXCUSE THE INTRUSION GENTLEMEN, BUT I THINK I'VE FINALLY MANAGED TO SMOOTH THINGS OVER.

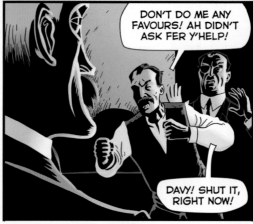

DON'T DO ME ANY FAVOURS! AH DIDN'T ASK FER Y'HELP!

DAVY! SHUT IT, RIGHT NOW!

IT'S ALL RIGHT SERGEANT. HE HAS EVERY RIGHT TO BE ANGRY.

SINCE THEY CAN'T LOCATE ANY OWNER OF THE BUILDING, THE CHARGES OF BREAKING AND ENTERING HAVE BEEN DROPPED.

YOUR ASSAULTING THE ARRESTING OFFICERS WAS MORE PROBLEMATIC, BUT THEY'VE AGREED TO RELEASE YOU, PROVIDED YOU RETURN HOME.

NO! NOT WHILE KATIE'S STILL MISSIN'!

YOU CAN DO HER MORE GOOD AS A FREE MAN THAN IN THIS DAMN CELL! BESIDES, THE SOONER WE RETURN TO GLASGOW, THE BETTER.

SIR?

YOUR FAMILY NEEDS YOU, SERGEANT. YOU'VE STOOD BY ME THROUGH THICK AND THIN. IT'S ONLY APPROPRIATE THAT I RETURN THE HONOUR.

IF WE'RE TO SOLVE THIS MYSTERY, THE BEST PLACE TO START IS AT THE BEGINNING, AND THERE IS NO TIME LIKE THE PRESENT.

SHALL WE?

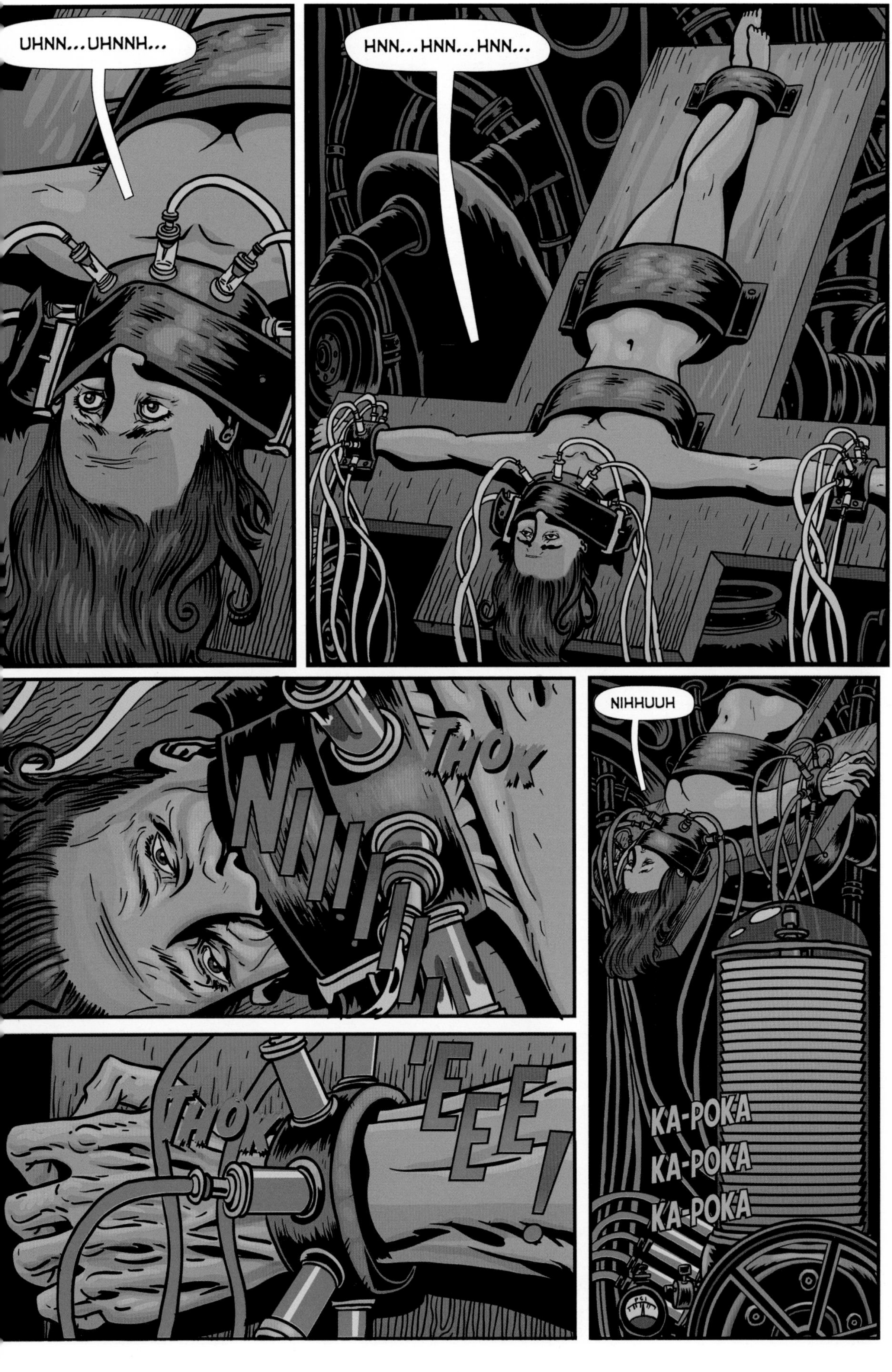
UHNN...UHNNH...
HNN...HNN...HNN...
NIIII
THOK
NIHHUUH
THOK
'EEE!
KA-POKA
KA-POKA
KA-POKA

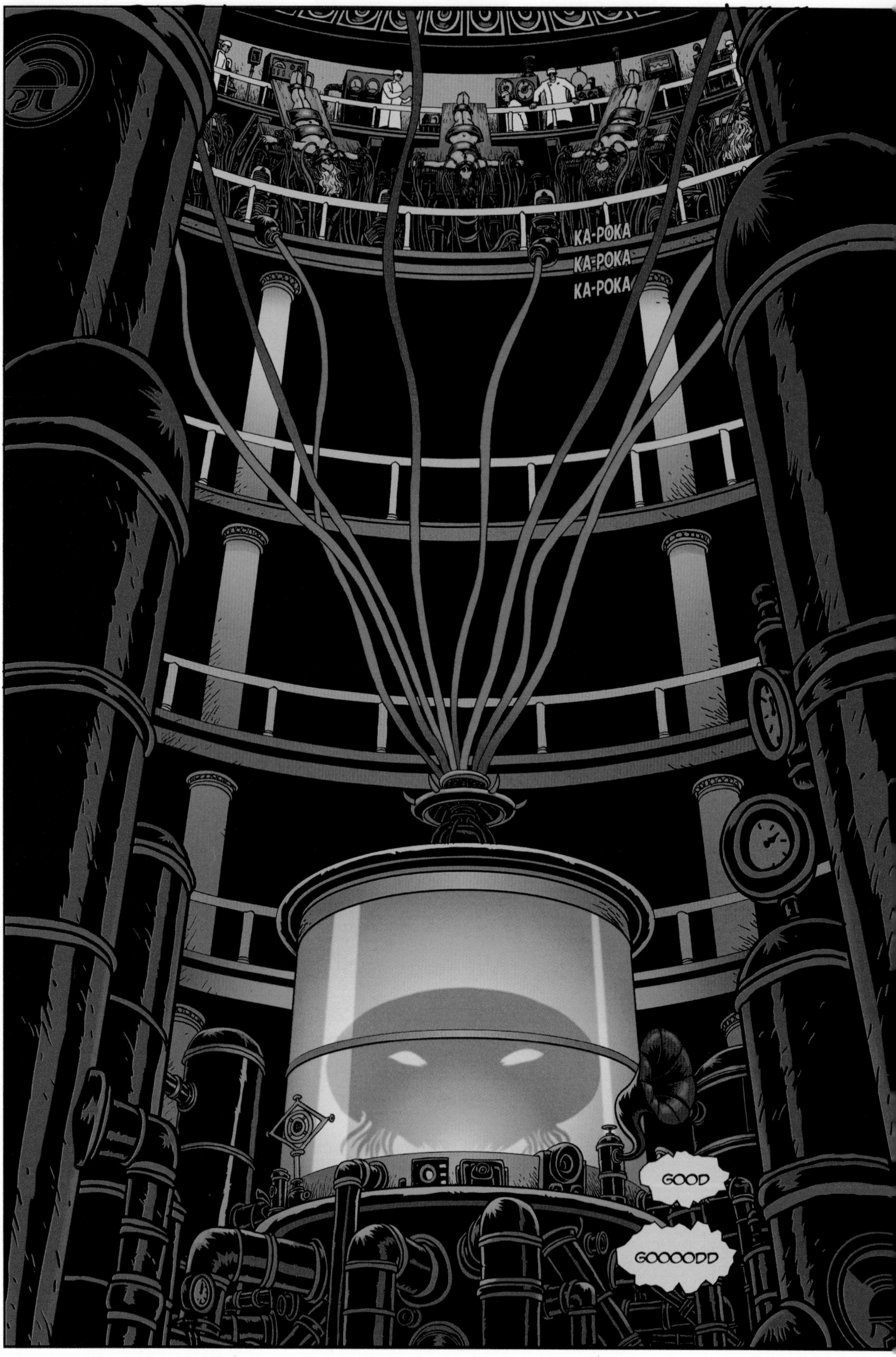
KA-POKA
KA-POKA
KA-POKA
GOOD
GOOOODD

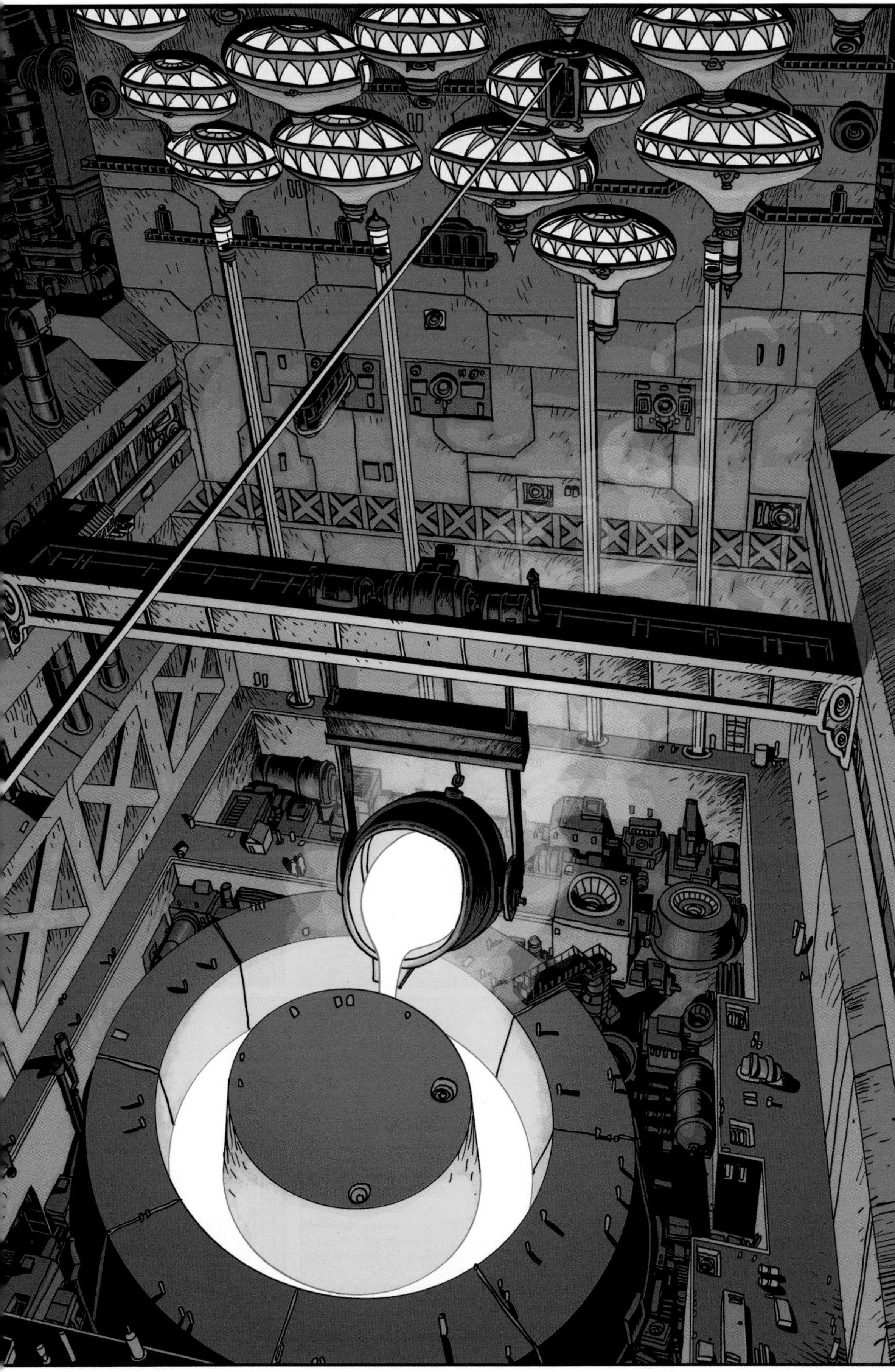

IS THIS THE LAST ONE? WILL IT BE COMPLETED IN TIME?

YES, SIR JOHN. EVERYTHING IS RUNNING TO SCHEDULE.

AND YESTERDAY'S LITTLE...INCIDENT?

IS IN HAND.

GOOD. GOOD.

HMM, I SHOULD LIKE TO SEE MORE, BUT I HAVE A SITTING IN THE HOUSE IN TWENTY MINUTES.

WALK WITH ME, DOCTOR.

DO YOU KNOW WHAT HAPPENED, REGARDING THE BODIES?

APPARENTLY, THE SITE MORTUARY FLOODED, IN THE RECENT RAINS. PERIL OF BUILDING ON THE THAMES FLOOD PLAIN, I'M AFRAID.

SEVERAL CRATES WASHED DOWN RIVER. NO ONE SAW THEM... NO ONE WHO MATTERS ANYWAY.

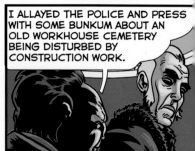

I ALLAYED THE POLICE AND PRESS WITH SOME BUNKUM ABOUT AN OLD WORKHOUSE CEMETERY BEING DISTURBED BY CONSTRUCTION WORK.

INGENIOUS...

(13) (12) (11) (10) (9) (8) (7) (6) (5) (4) (3) (2) (1) (G)

HOWEVER, I RECALL A SIMILAR OCCURRENCE AT THE OUTSET OF THE PROJECT, PROMPTING THE INSTALLATION OF THE INCINERATOR. WHY WASNT IT USED?

THERE'S A BACKLOG. THIS CLOSE TO COMPLETION MY MEN ARE WORKING AROUND THE CLOCK...

AND I AM ABOUT TO ADD A FURTHER LABOUR TO YOUR BURDENS.

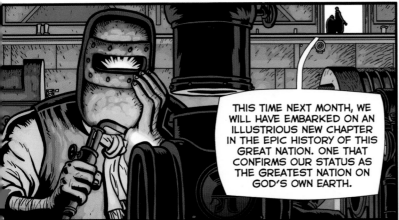

THIS TIME NEXT MONTH, WE WILL HAVE EMBARKED ON AN ILLUSTRIOUS NEW CHAPTER IN THE EPIC HISTORY OF THIS GREAT NATION. ONE THAT CONFIRMS OUR STATUS AS THE GREATEST NATION ON GOD'S OWN EARTH.

AND AS YOU KNOW, GOD IS AN ENGLISHMAN.

NOTHING MUST COMPROMISE THIS GOAL DOCTOR, NOTHING.

WE HAVE DONE MANY QUESTIONABLE THINGS TO REACH THIS POINT. NOW WE MUST GRIT OUR TEETH, GIRD OUR LOINS AND PUSH ON THAT EXTRA MILE. WE MUST WIPE THE SLATE CLEAN, DO YOU UNDERSTAND?

COMPLETELY.

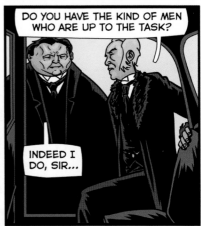

DO YOU HAVE THE KIND OF MEN WHO ARE UP TO THE TASK?

INDEED I DO, SIR...

"...IN FACT I HAVE JUST THE PAIR IN MIND."

HOW IS HE SERGEANT?

STILL SLEEPIN' LIKE A BAIRN. WAS THE SUPPER THAT DID FER HIM. HE'S NO HAD A DECENT MEAL IN MONTHS.

WHISKY?

AYE.

I CONFESS, I HAD HEARD THINGS WERE GRIM IN THE NORTH, BUT FROM WHAT DAVID DESCRIBED, THEY ARE NOTHING SHORT OF HELLISH.

AN' THERE'S ME SITTIN' ON MA ARSE IN LONDON, IN THE LAP O'BLOODY LUXURY WHILE MA KIN GO HUNGRY.

WHAT D'YE THINK TAE ALLA THIS SUR? KATE VANISHIN'. D'YE THINK SHE'S STILL ALIVE?

I PRAY SO, BUT LET'S NOT DWELL ON THE NEGATIVE. ABOVE ALL, OUR ENDEAVOURS REQUIRE HOPE.

I'VE STUDIED YOUR BROTHER'S POLICE STATEMENT AND WHILE JUSTIFIABLY EMOTIONAL, I'M ADAMANT HE'S TELLING THE TRUTH.

THE OFFICE HOUSING THE AGENCY THAT EMPLOYED YOUR MISSING NIECE THOUGH, IS ANOTHER MATTER ENTIRELY.

"YOU'LL RECALL THE POLICE COULD NOT TRACE THE OWNER OF THE BUILDING WHICH HAD ALLEGEDLY BEEN EMPTY FOR YEARS - A CURIOSITY IN ITSELF IN A CITY WHERE PROPERTY IS AT A PREMIUM."

"FURTHER INVESTIGATION REVEALED SEVERAL MORE ANOMALIES."

"THE ORIGINAL LOCK, WHICH ONE WOULD EXPECT TO BE RUSTED AND SEIZED, HAD BEEN OILED AND OPENED SMOOTHLY."

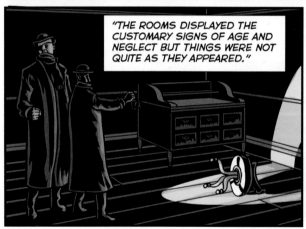

"THE ROOMS DISPLAYED THE CUSTOMARY SIGNS OF AGE AND NEGLECT BUT THINGS WERE NOT QUITE AS THEY APPEARED."

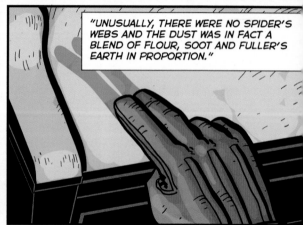

"UNUSUALLY, THERE WERE NO SPIDER'S WEBS AND THE DUST WAS IN FACT A BLEND OF FLOUR, SOOT AND FULLER'S EARTH IN PROPORTION."

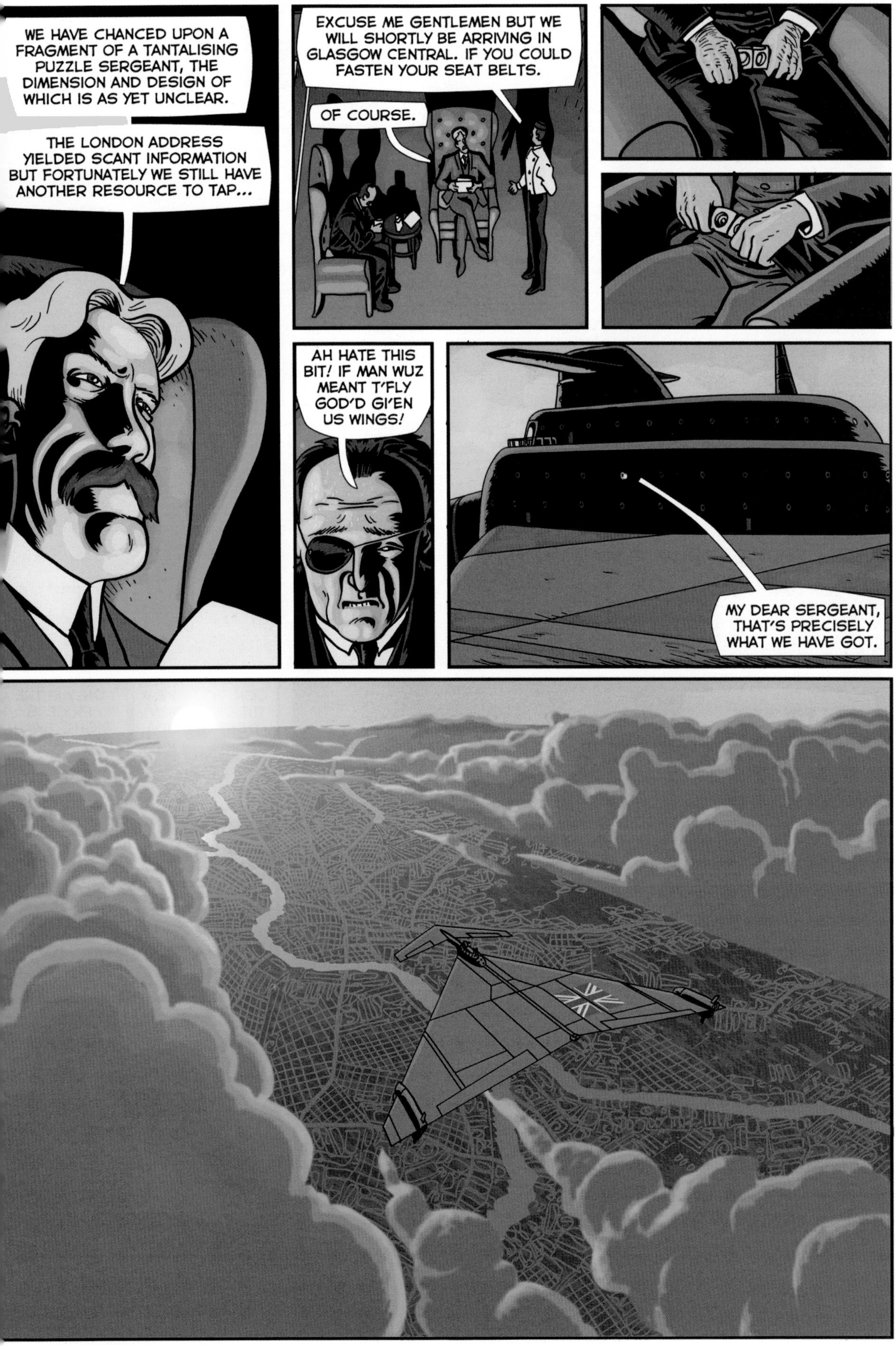
WE HAVE CHANCED UPON A FRAGMENT OF A TANTALISING PUZZLE SERGEANT, THE DIMENSION AND DESIGN OF WHICH IS AS YET UNCLEAR.
THE LONDON ADDRESS YIELDED SCANT INFORMATION BUT FORTUNATELY WE STILL HAVE ANOTHER RESOURCE TO TAP...
EXCUSE ME GENTLEMEN BUT WE WILL SHORTLY BE ARRIVING IN GLASGOW CENTRAL. IF YOU COULD FASTEN YOUR SEAT BELTS.
OF COURSE.
AH HATE THIS BIT! IF MAN WUZ MEANT T'FLY GOD'D GI'EN US WINGS!
MY DEAR SERGEANT, THAT'S PRECISELY WHAT WE HAVE GOT.

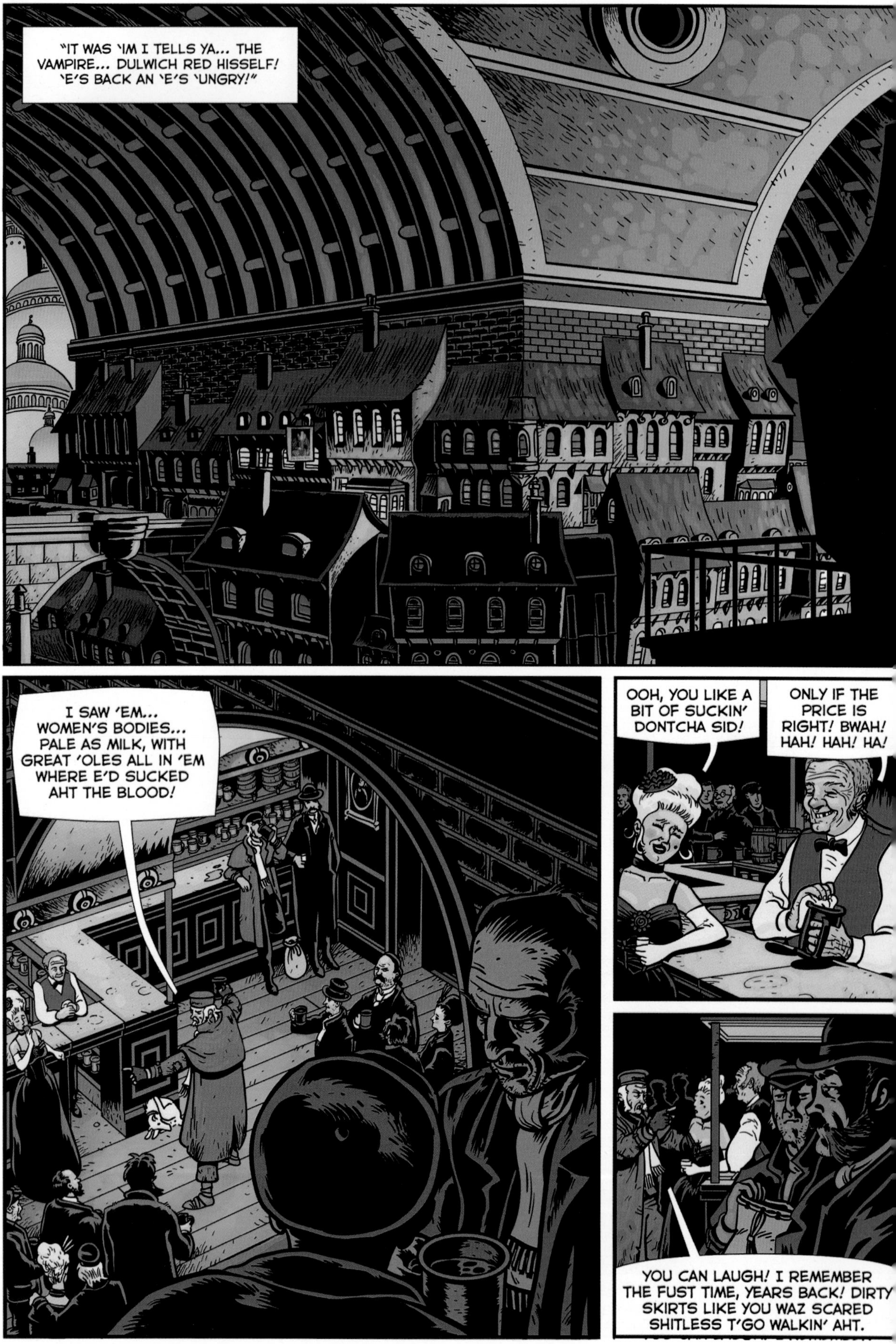
"IT WAS 'IM I TELLS YA... THE VAMPIRE... DULWICH RED HISSELF! 'E'S BACK AN 'E'S 'UNGRY!"
I SAW 'EM... WOMEN'S BODIES... PALE AS MILK, WITH GREAT 'OLES ALL IN 'EM WHERE E'D SUCKED AHT THE BLOOD!
OOH, YOU LIKE A BIT OF SUCKIN' DONTCHA SID!
ONLY IF THE PRICE IS RIGHT! BWAH! HAH! HAH! HA!
YOU CAN LAUGH! I REMEMBER THE FUST TIME, YEARS BACK! DIRTY SKIRTS LIKE YOU WAZ SCARED SHITLESS T'GO WALKIN' AHT.

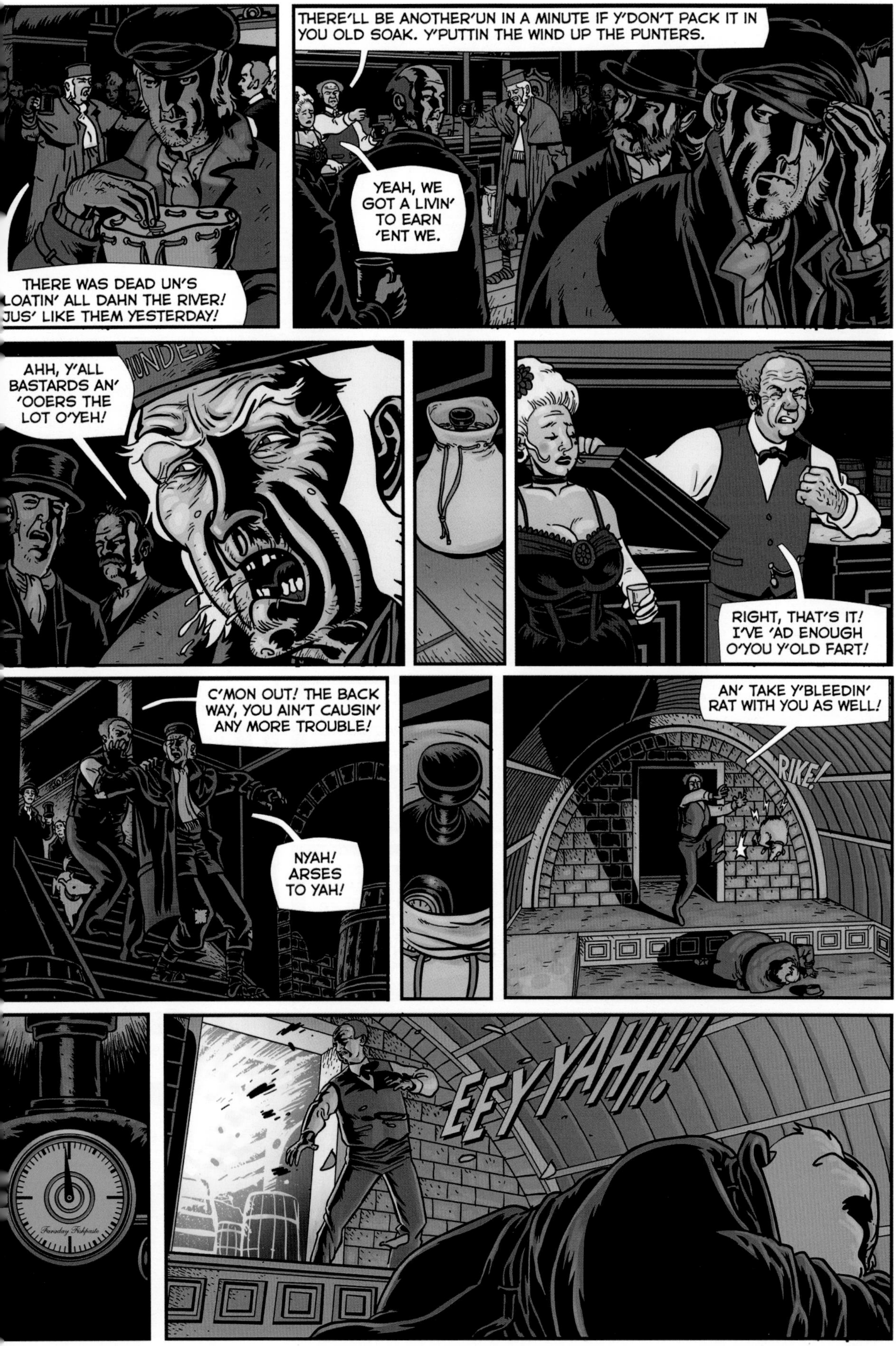
THERE WAS DEAD UN'S LOATIN' ALL DAHN THE RIVER! JUS' LIKE THEM YESTERDAY!
THERE'LL BE ANOTHER'UN IN A MINUTE IF Y'DON'T PACK IT IN YOU OLD SOAK. Y'PUTTIN THE WIND UP THE PUNTERS.
YEAH, WE GOT A LIVIN' TO EARN 'ENT WE.
AHH, Y'ALL BASTARDS AN' 'OOERS THE LOT O'YEH!
RIGHT, THAT'S IT! I'VE 'AD ENOUGH O'YOU Y'OLD FART!
C'MON OUT! THE BACK WAY, YOU AIN'T CAUSIN' ANY MORE TROUBLE!
NYAH! ARSES TO YAH!
AN' TAKE Y'BLEEDIN' RAT WITH YOU AS WELL!
RIKE!
Faraday Fishpaste
EEYYAHH!

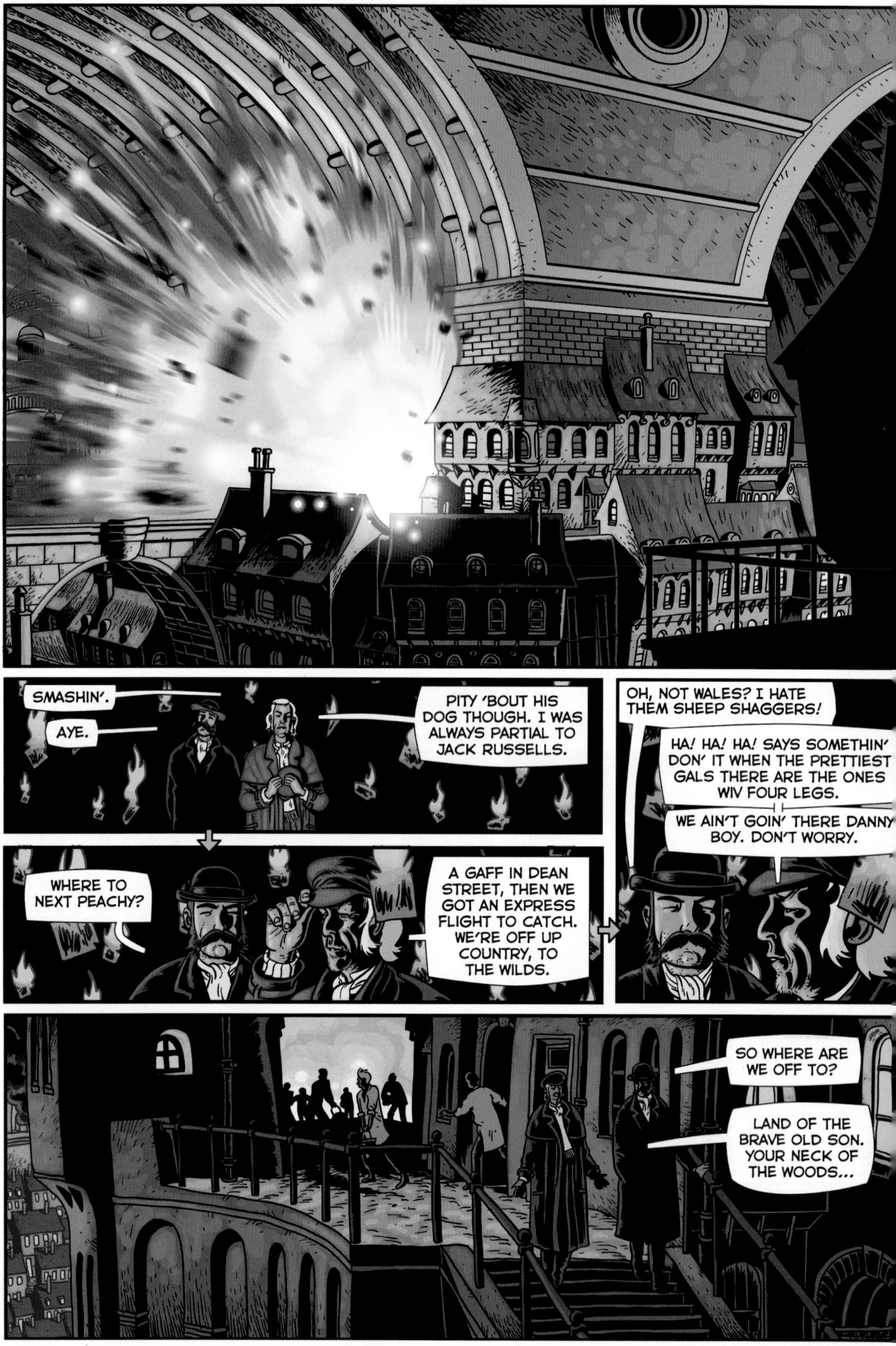
SMASHIN'.
AYE.
PITY 'BOUT HIS DOG THOUGH. I WAS ALWAYS PARTIAL TO JACK RUSSELLS.
WHERE TO NEXT PEACHY?
A GAFF IN DEAN STREET, THEN WE GOT AN EXPRESS FLIGHT TO CATCH. WE'RE OFF UP COUNTRY, TO THE WILDS.
OH, NOT WALES? I HATE THEM SHEEP SHAGGERS!
HA! HA! HA! SAYS SOMETHIN' DON' IT WHEN THE PRETTIEST GALS THERE ARE THE ONES WIV FOUR LEGS.
WE AIN'T GOIN' THERE DANNY BOY. DON'T WORRY.
SO WHERE ARE WE OFF TO?
LAND OF THE BRAVE OLD SON. YOUR NECK OF THE WOODS...

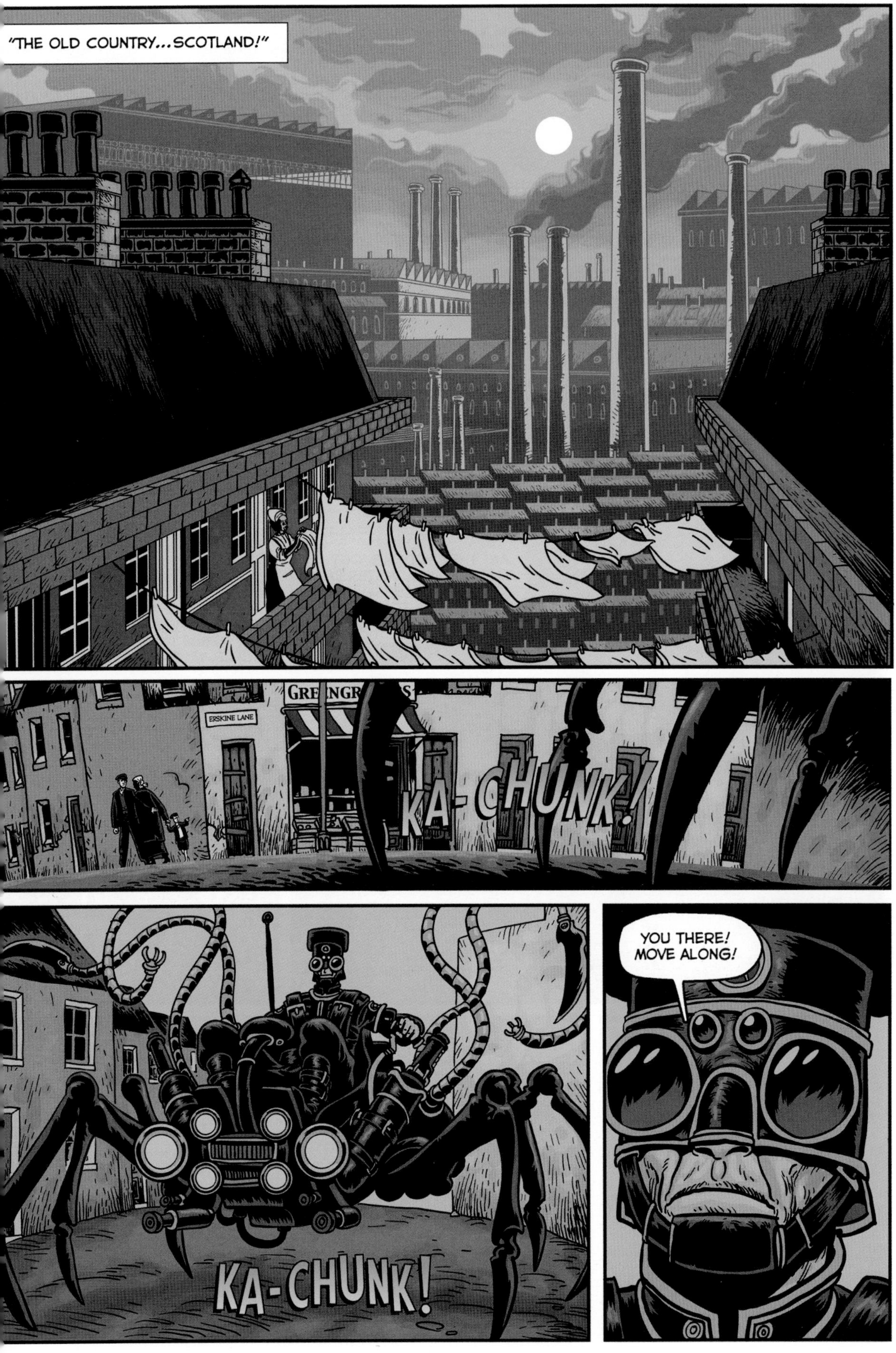
"THE OLD COUNTRY...SCOTLAND!"
ERSKINE LANE
KA-CHUNK!
KA-CHUNK!
YOU THERE! MOVE ALONG!

HE'S ROYAL ARTICULATED HUSSARS?

INDEED. THE GOVERNMENT ONLY DESPATCHES THEM TO EXTREME TROUBLE SPOTS IN THE EMPIRE. WHAT THE DEVIL ARE THEY DOING HERE?

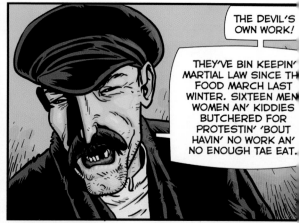

THE DEVIL'S OWN WORK!

THEY'VE BIN KEEPIN' MARTIAL LAW SINCE TH' FOOD MARCH LAST WINTER. SIXTEEN MEN WOMEN AN' KIDDIES BUTCHERED FOR PROTESTIN' 'BOUT HAVIN' NO WORK AN' NO ENOUGH TAE EAT.

AYE, THE PAPERS CALLED IT "BLOODY SUNDAY".

AN' THEY MADE US OUT TAE BE THE MONSTERS! SAID WE SMASHED UP FACTORIES, TORCHED TH'MILLS! ALL LIES!

Y'KNOW WE WORE OUR SUNDAY BEST TAE THE MARCH, TAE SHOW 'EM WE MEBBE POOR BUT WE'RE STILL PEOPLE, WI' PRIDE AN' SELF RESPEC'

AN' THEY CUT 'EM TAE PIECES WI' HEAT RAYS AN' SABRES!

EASY, DAVY.

BUT... THAT'S OBSCENE! THIS IS GREAT BRITAIN, THE HEART OF EMPIRE!

AYE SUR, AN' IT'S A COLD HEART TAE BE SURE.

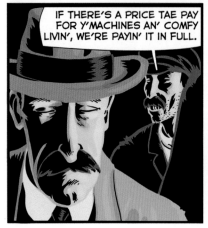

IF THERE'S A PRICE TAE PAY FOR Y'MACHINES AN' COMFY LIVIN', WE'RE PAYIN' IT IN FULL.

WE'RE HERE.

PRINTERS PR

KLEY & Co. Ltd
BER PRODUCTS

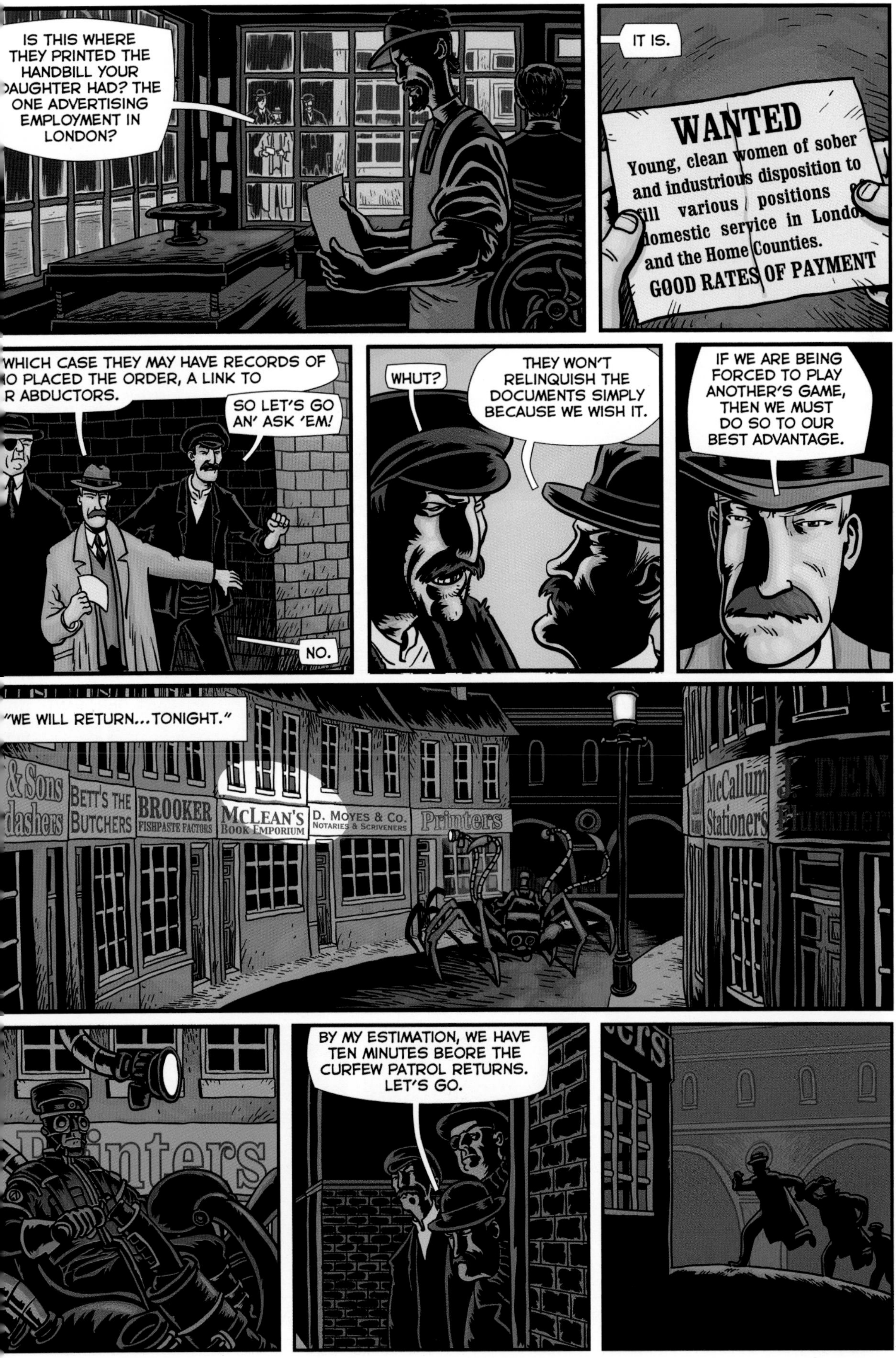
IS THIS WHERE THEY PRINTED THE HANDBILL YOUR DAUGHTER HAD? THE ONE ADVERTISING EMPLOYMENT IN LONDON?
IT IS.
WANTED
Young, clean women of sober and industrious disposition to fill various positions of domestic service in London and the Home Counties.
GOOD RATES OF PAYMENT
WHICH CASE THEY MAY HAVE RECORDS OF O PLACED THE ORDER, A LINK TO R ABDUCTORS.
SO LET'S GO AN' ASK 'EM!
NO.
WHUT?
THEY WON'T RELINQUISH THE DOCUMENTS SIMPLY BECAUSE WE WISH IT.
IF WE ARE BEING FORCED TO PLAY ANOTHER'S GAME, THEN WE MUST DO SO TO OUR BEST ADVANTAGE.
"WE WILL RETURN... TONIGHT."
& Sons
dashers
BETT'S THE BUTCHERS
BROOKER
FISHPASTE FACTORS
McLEAN'S
BOOK EMPORIUM
D. MOYES & CO.
NOTARIES & SCRIVENERS
Printers
McCallum
Stationers
Printers
BY MY ESTIMATION, WE HAVE TEN MINUTES BEORE THE CURFEW PATROL RETURNS. LET'S GO.

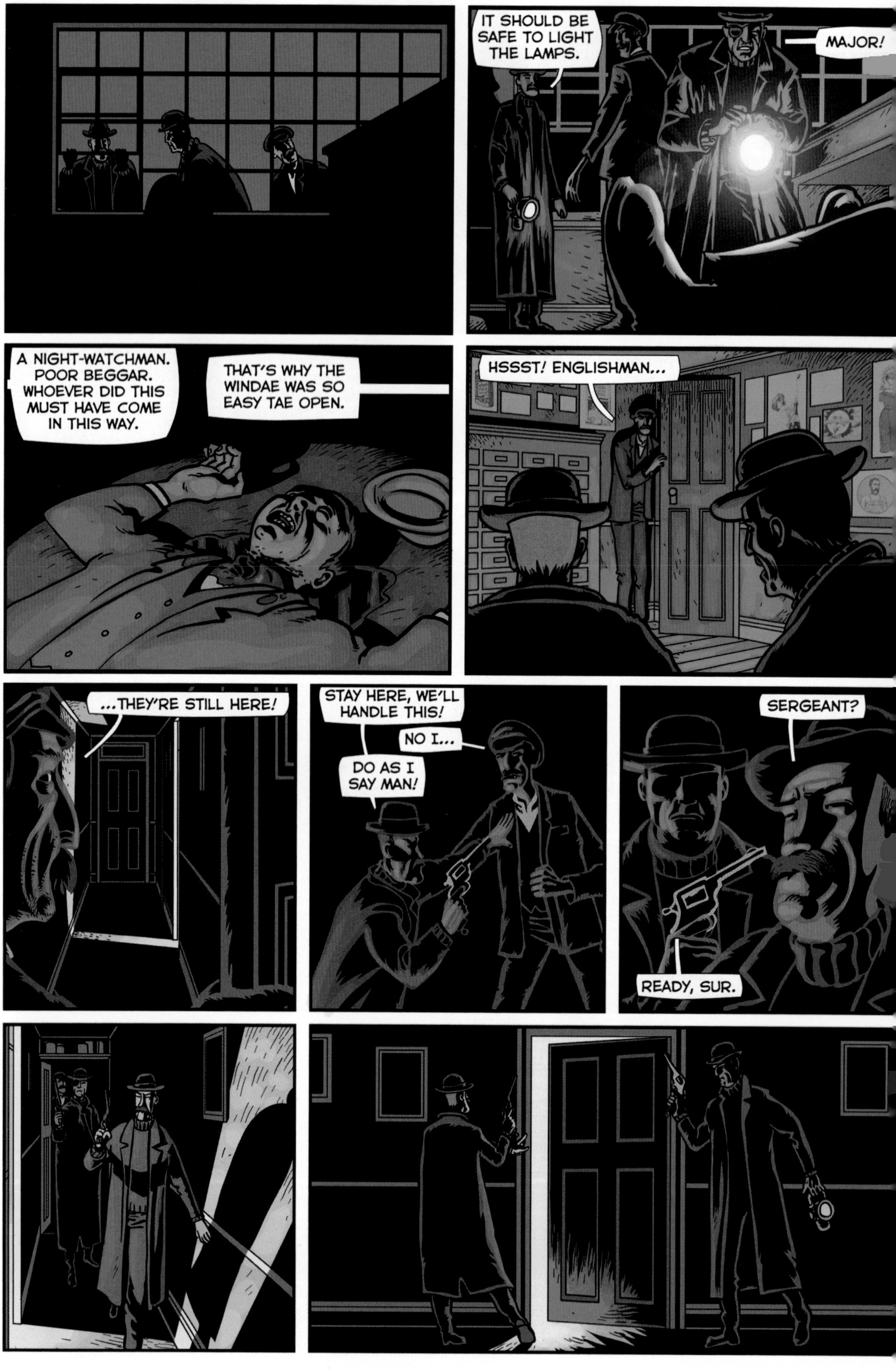
IT SHOULD BE SAFE TO LIGHT THE LAMPS.
MAJOR!
A NIGHT-WATCHMAN. POOR BEGGAR. WHOEVER DID THIS MUST HAVE COME IN THIS WAY.
THAT'S WHY THE WINDAE WAS SO EASY TAE OPEN.
HSSST! ENGLISHMAN...
...THEY'RE STILL HERE!
STAY HERE, WE'LL HANDLE THIS!
NO I...
DO AS I SAY MAN!
SERGEANT?
READY, SUR.

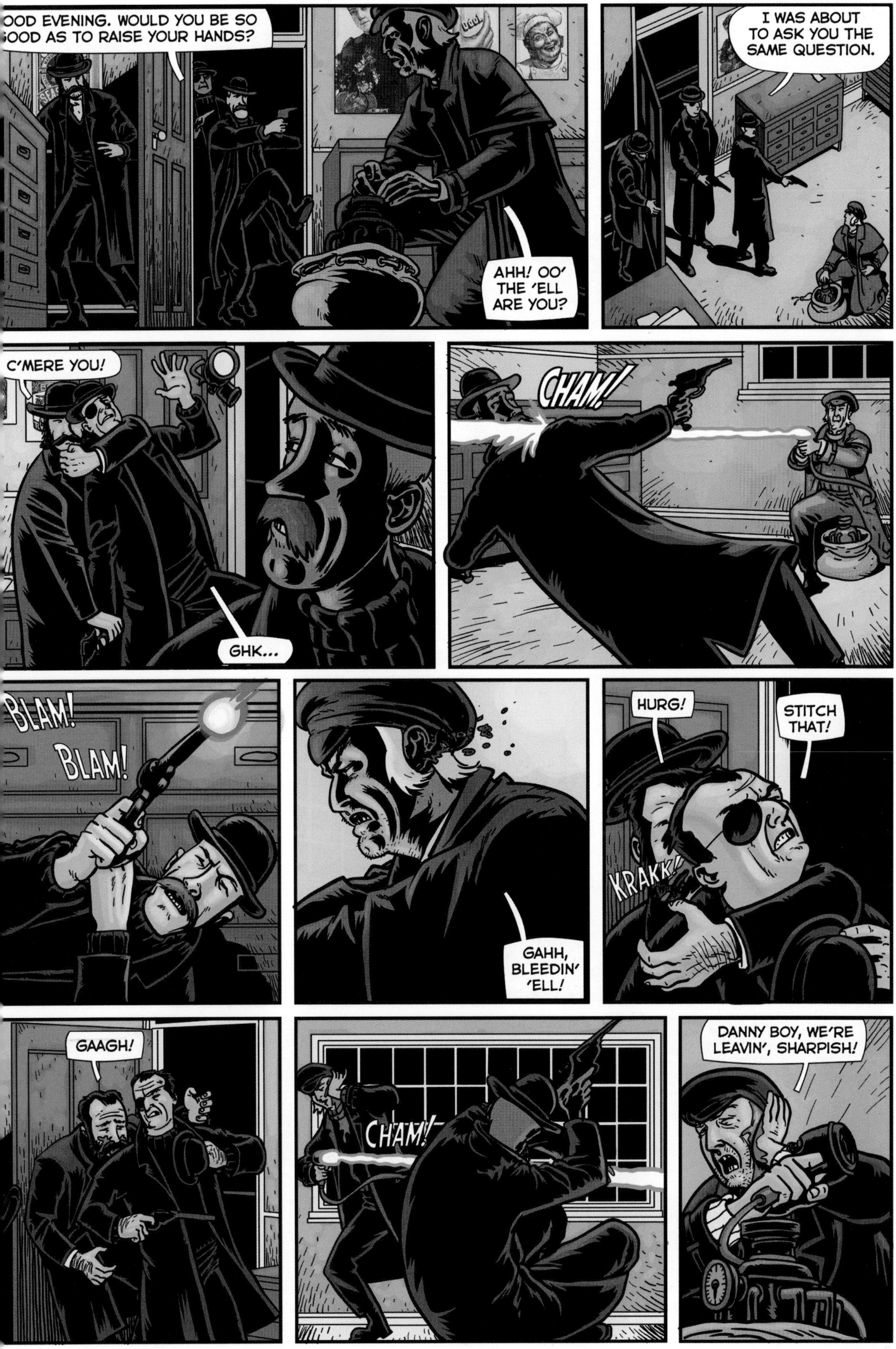
OOD EVENING. WOULD YOU BE SO GOOD AS TO RAISE YOUR HANDS?
AHH! OO' THE 'ELL ARE YOU?
I WAS ABOUT TO ASK YOU THE SAME QUESTION.
C'MERE YOU!
GHK...
CHAM!
BLAM!
BLAM!
GAHH, BLEEDIN' 'ELL!
HURG!
STITCH THAT!
KRAKK!
GAAGH!
CHAM!
DANNY BOY, WE'RE LEAVIN', SHARPISH!

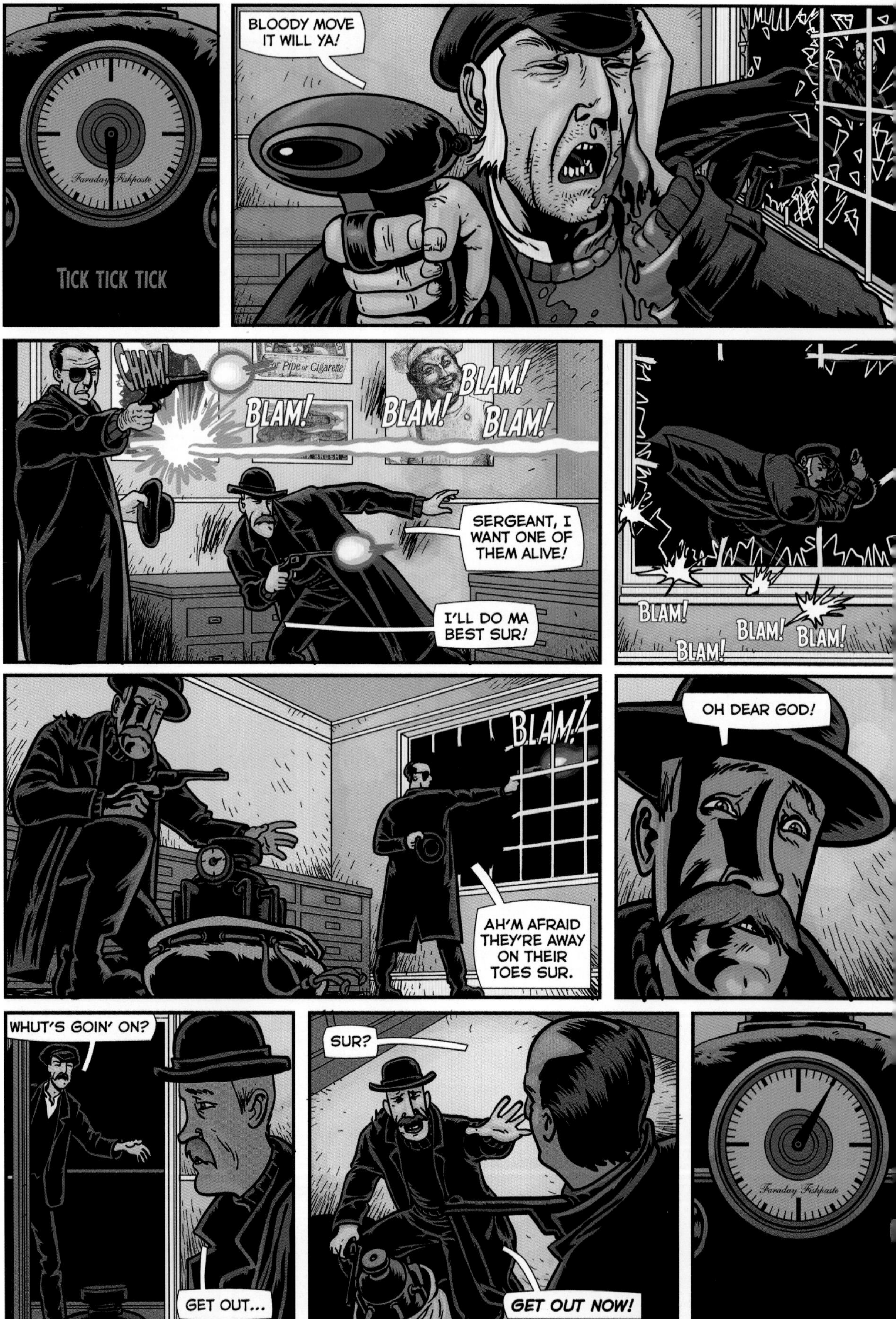
Faraday Fishpaste
TICK TICK TICK
BLOODY MOVE IT WILL YA!
BLAM!
BLAM!
BLAM!
BLAM!
SERGEANT, I WANT ONE OF THEM ALIVE!
I'LL DO MA BEST SUR!
BLAM!
BLAM!
BLAM!
BLAM!
BLAM!
AH'M AFRAID THEY'RE AWAY ON THEIR TOES SUR.
OH DEAR GOD!
WHUT'S GOIN' ON?
GET OUT...
SUR?
GET OUT NOW!
Faraday Fishpaste

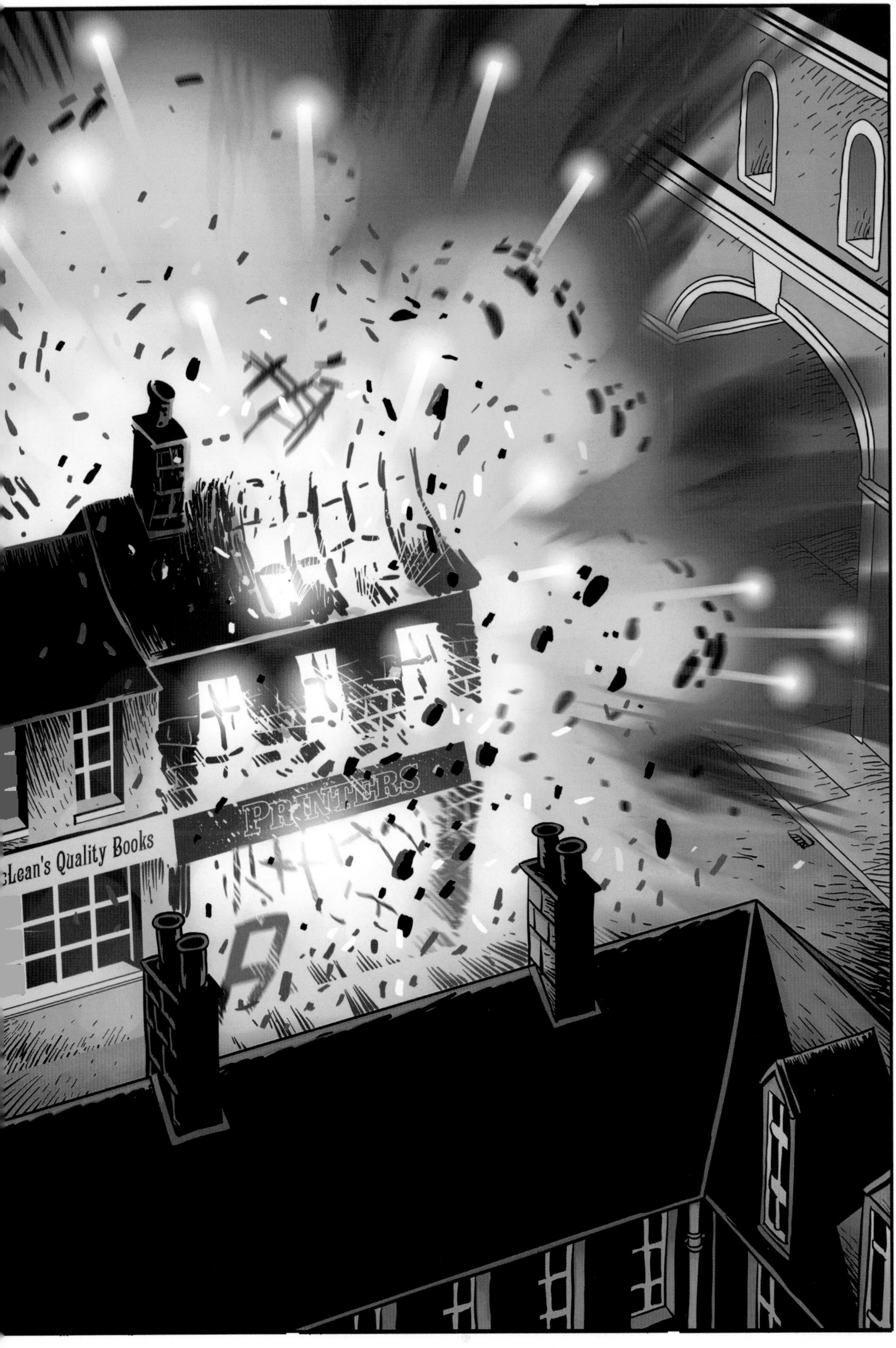
PRINTERS
cLean's Quality Books

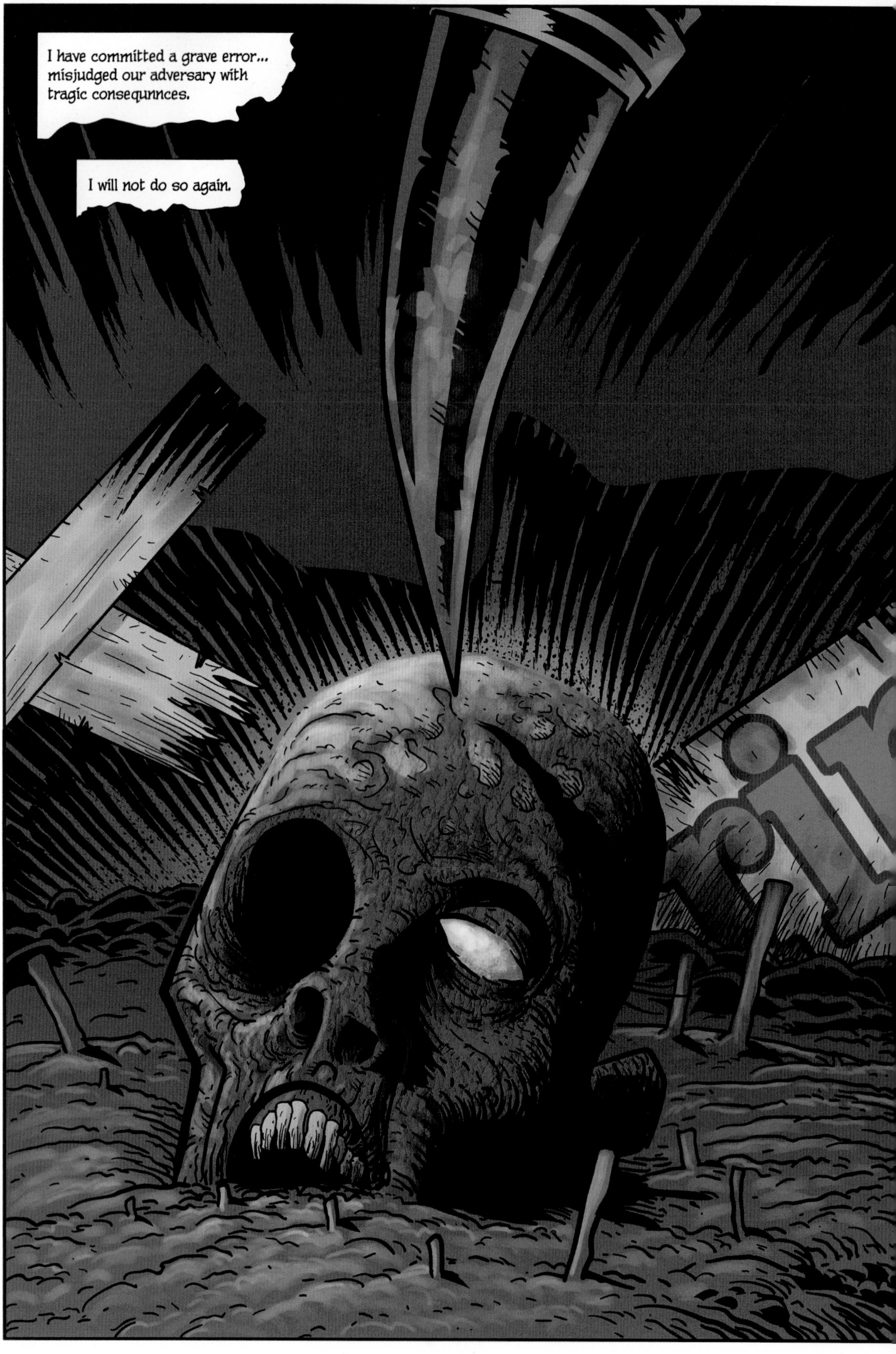
I have committed a grave error... misjudged our adversary with tragic consequnnces.
I will not do so again.

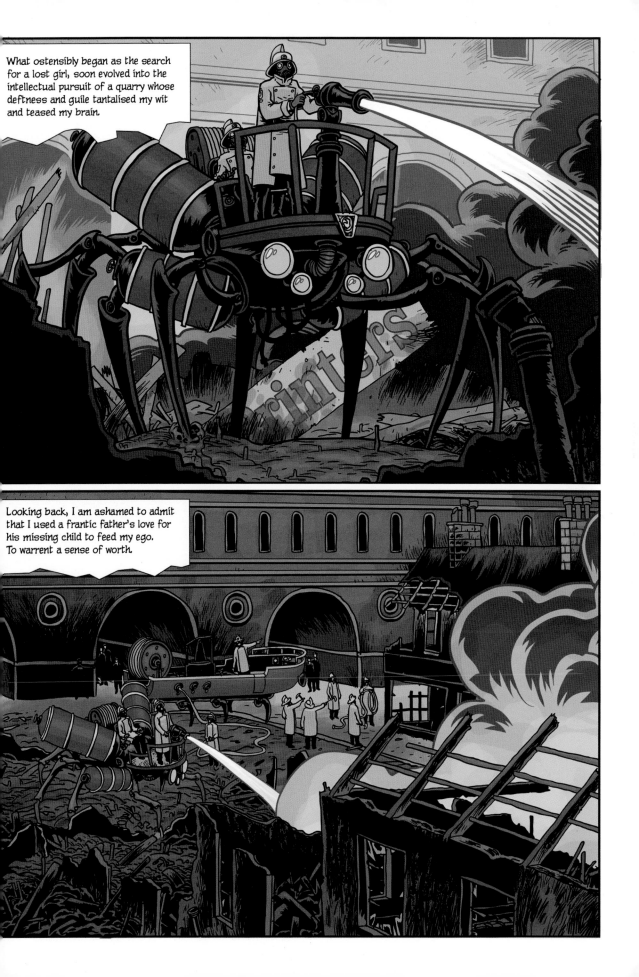

What ostensibly began as the search for a lost girl, soon evolved into the intellectual pursuit of a quarry whose deftness and guile tantalised my wit and teased my brain.

Looking back, I am ashamed to admit that I used a frantic father's love for his missing child to feed my ego. To warrent a sense of worth.

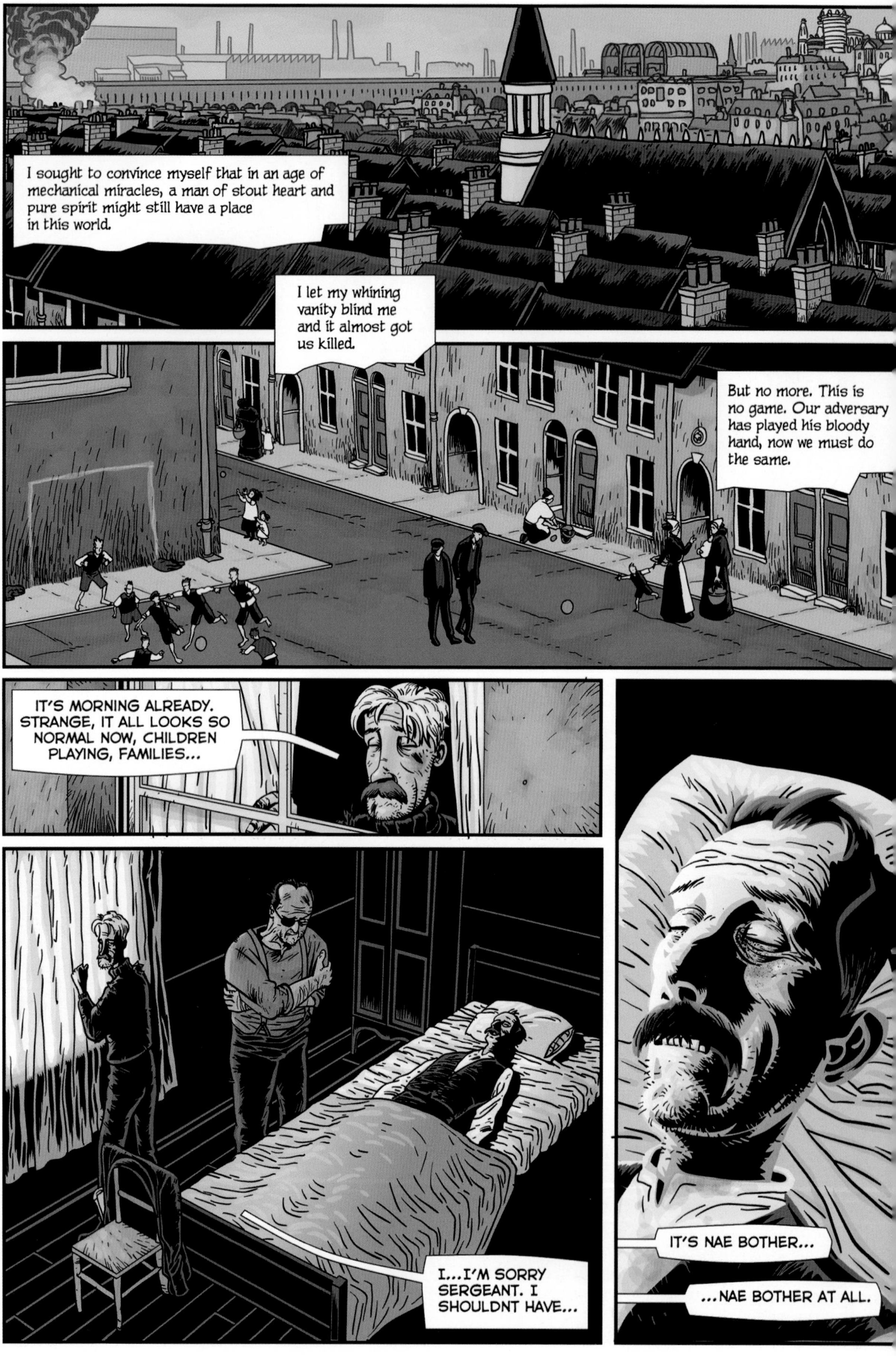
I sought to convince myself that in an age of mechanical miracles, a man of stout heart and pure spirit might still have a place in this world.
I let my whining vanity blind me and it almost got us killed.
But no more. This is no game. Our adversary has played his bloody hand, now we must do the same.
IT'S MORNING ALREADY. STRANGE, IT ALL LOOKS SO NORMAL NOW, CHILDREN PLAYING, FAMILIES...
I...I'M SORRY SERGEANT. I SHOULDNT HAVE...
IT'S NAE BOTHER...
...NAE BOTHER AT ALL.

I'M SORRY FOR YOUR LOSS, ERGEANT, HE WAS A FINE MAN.

AYE, HE WAS ALSO A CONTRARY BUGGER. TOO FOND O'THE BOTTLE AN TOO QUICK WI' HIS FISTS, BUT HE HAD A GOOD HEART.

WHAT WILL HAPPEN NOW?

ME AN MARIE... HIS MISSUS, WE'LL WASH AN' DRESS 'IM FER THE FUNERAL. PUT 'IM IN HIS SUNDAY BEST.

WON'T YOU REQUIRE A DEATH CERTIFICATE FIRST?

NAW. THE AMOUNT OF FOLKS DYIN' UP HERE, YON DOCTOR'LL GI' US A SCRIP JUST ON OUR SAY SO.

HE'LL NO BE FUSSED ABOUT SEEIN' ANOTHER CORPSE.

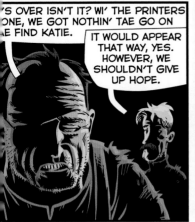

'S OVER ISN'T IT? WI' THE PRINTERS ONE, WE GOT NOTHIN' TAE GO ON E FIND KATIE.

IT WOULD APPEAR THAT WAY, YES. HOWEVER, WE SHOULDN'T GIVE UP HOPE.

HOPE...AYE.

WELL, I'D BEST SEE TAE ME AN MINE.

CAN I HELP IN ANY WAY?

AYE, THANK YOU SIR. COULD Y'GO LIGHT A FIRE IN THE GRATE DOWN-STAIRS, BOIL SOME WATER FER DAVY'S WASH?

CERTAINLY.

HERE'S A PAPER IN MA POCKET, TAKE IT. IT'LL DO F'KINDLIN.

GOOD GOD ALMIGHTY!!

June 20th, 1900 Price 3d

DOG-EA

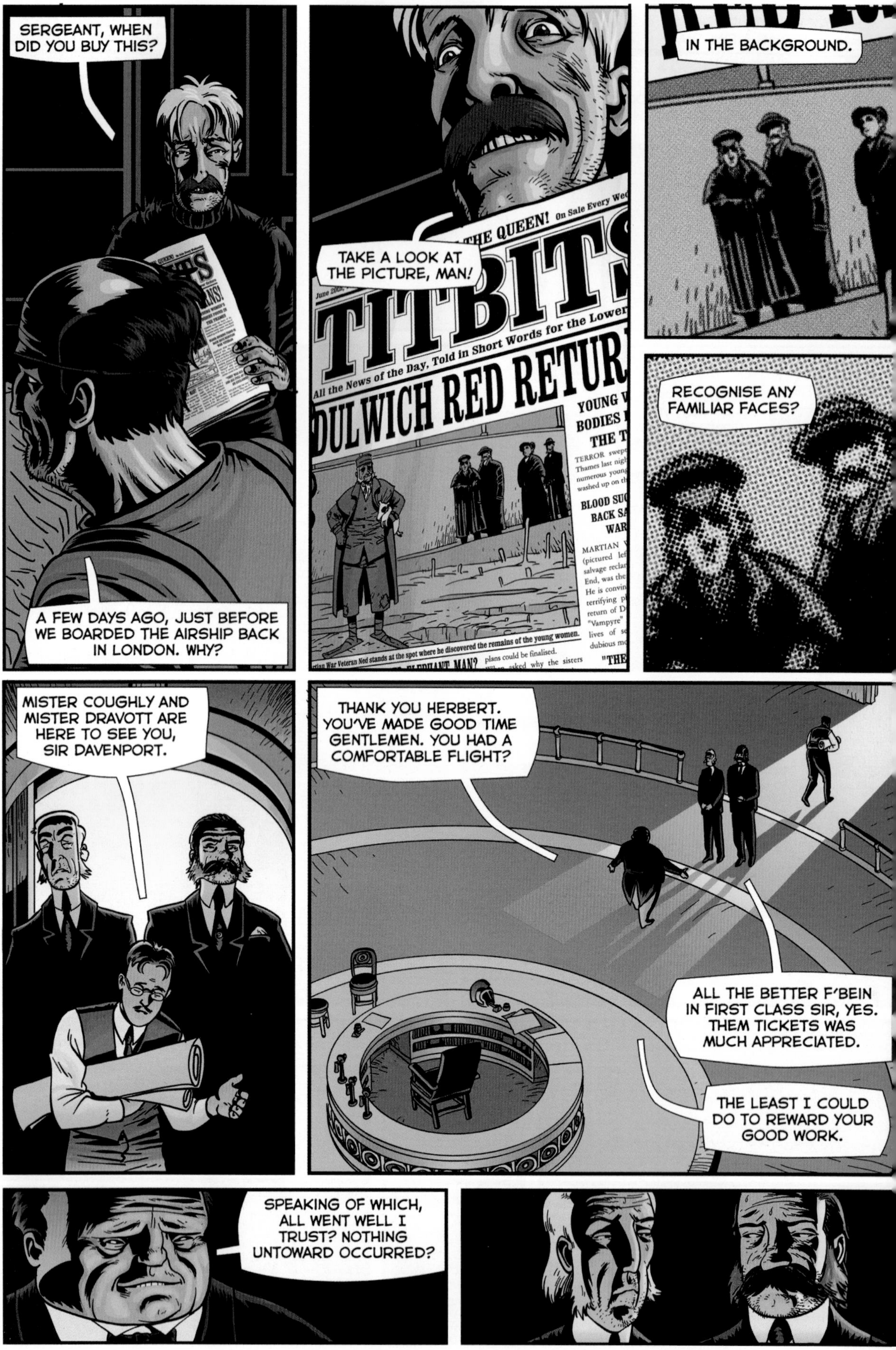
SERGEANT, WHEN DID YOU BUY THIS?
A FEW DAYS AGO, JUST BEFORE WE BOARDED THE AIRSHIP BACK IN LONDON. WHY?
TAKE A LOOK AT THE PICTURE, MAN!
TITBITS
All the News of the Day, Told in Short Words for the Lower
DULWICH RED RETUR
IN THE BACKGROUND.
RECOGNISE ANY FAMILIAR FACES?
MISTER COUGHLY AND MISTER DRAVOTT ARE HERE TO SEE YOU, SIR DAVENPORT.
THANK YOU HERBERT. YOU'VE MADE GOOD TIME GENTLEMEN. YOU HAD A COMFORTABLE FLIGHT?
ALL THE BETTER F'BEIN IN FIRST CLASS SIR, YES. THEM TICKETS WAS MUCH APPRECIATED.
THE LEAST I COULD DO TO REWARD YOUR GOOD WORK.
SPEAKING OF WHICH, ALL WENT WELL I TRUST? NOTHING UNTOWARD OCCURRED?

WHY DO I FIND YOUR HESITATION A CAUSE FOR CONCERN?

DON'T WORRY, WE DONE THE JOB SIR. RIGHT AND PROPER.

THAT PRINTERS SHOP WAS BLOWN TO KINGDOM COME... ALONG WITH A COUPLE OF BLOKES WE WASN'T EXPECTING.

WHAT MANNER OF MEN WERE THESE... BLOKES?

ONE WAS A BIG STRAPPING JOCK LIKE DANNY ERE.

AYE, AN' THE OTHER WAS A GENT LIKE YER SEL. HE WAS ONLY A STRIP O'WIND, BUT HE WAS A SCRAPPER AN' NO MISTAKE.

THEY WAS A TASTY PAIR. FULL O'PISS AN VINEGAR.

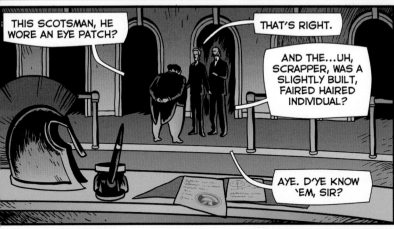

THIS SCOTSMAN, HE WORE AN EYE PATCH?

THAT'S RIGHT.

AND THE...UH, SCRAPPER, WAS A SLIGHTLY BUILT, FAIRED HAIRED INDIVIDUAL?

AYE. D'YE KNOW 'EM, SIR?

IN A MANNER OF SPEAKING.

SO, THEY ARE DEAD YOU SAY?

YES, SIR. THEY WAS STILL INSIDE WHEN THE SHOP WENT UP. NO WAY THEY COULDA GOT CLEAR IN TIME.

INDEED...

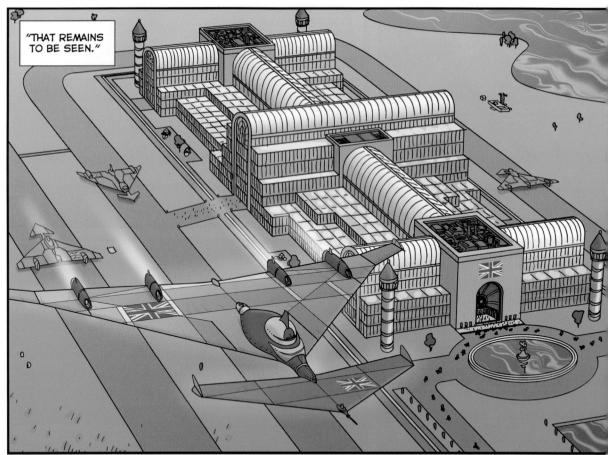

"THAT REMAINS TO BE SEEN."
CABBIE!
THE EAST END, MY GOOD MAN. WALFORD VIADUCT AND DON'T SPARE THE HORSEPOWER!
RIGHTCHOO ARE GUV'NOR.
IF THIS ITEM IS CORRECT, THIS OLD NED CHARACTER IS A REGULAR PATRON AT THE QUEEN BESS PUBLIC HOUSE.
EVEN IF HE ISN'T THERE PRESENTLY, I DARE SAY THE LOCALS MAY KNOW HIS WHEREABOUTS?
TITBITS
DULWICH RED RETURNS!
AYE...

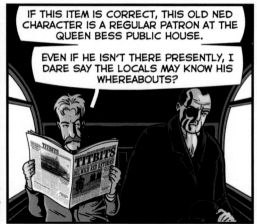

SERGEANT, I BITTERLY REGRET MY NOT STAYING FOR THE FUNERAL BUT THERE WAS NO NEED FOR YOU TO ACCOMPANY ME.

WHAT I MEAN TO SAY IS, YOUR PLACE IS WITH YOUR FAMILY...

NO SIR, IT IS NOT!!

...IT WAS MA CHOICE TAE COME. DAVY WOULDA WANTED ME TAE BE HERE.

NOW IF Y'DON'T MIND, THERE'S WORK TA BE DONE.

OF COURSE.

TITBITS

June 20th, 1900 Price 3d. GOD SAVE THE QUEE

WE CURRENTLY POSSESS SEVERAL PIECES TO THIS PUZZLE, BUT I FEEL THIS SEEMINGLY-INNOCUOUS NEWSPAPER ARTICLE IS THE KEY.

FIRST, I'LL HAZARD THAT KATE'S DISAPPEARANCE ISN'T A SINGULAR EVENT BUT ONE OF MANY. THAT DAMNED HANDBILL ENTICING YOUNG WOMEN FROM THE NORTH WITH PROMISES OF WORK, NEVER TO BE SEEN AGAIN.

I ALSO BELIEVE THIS HAS BEEN OCCURRING OVER MONTHS IF NOT YEARS. A SUPPOSITION COMPOUNDED BY THE GRISLY DISCOVERY OF THE WOMEN'S BODIES IN THE THAMES.

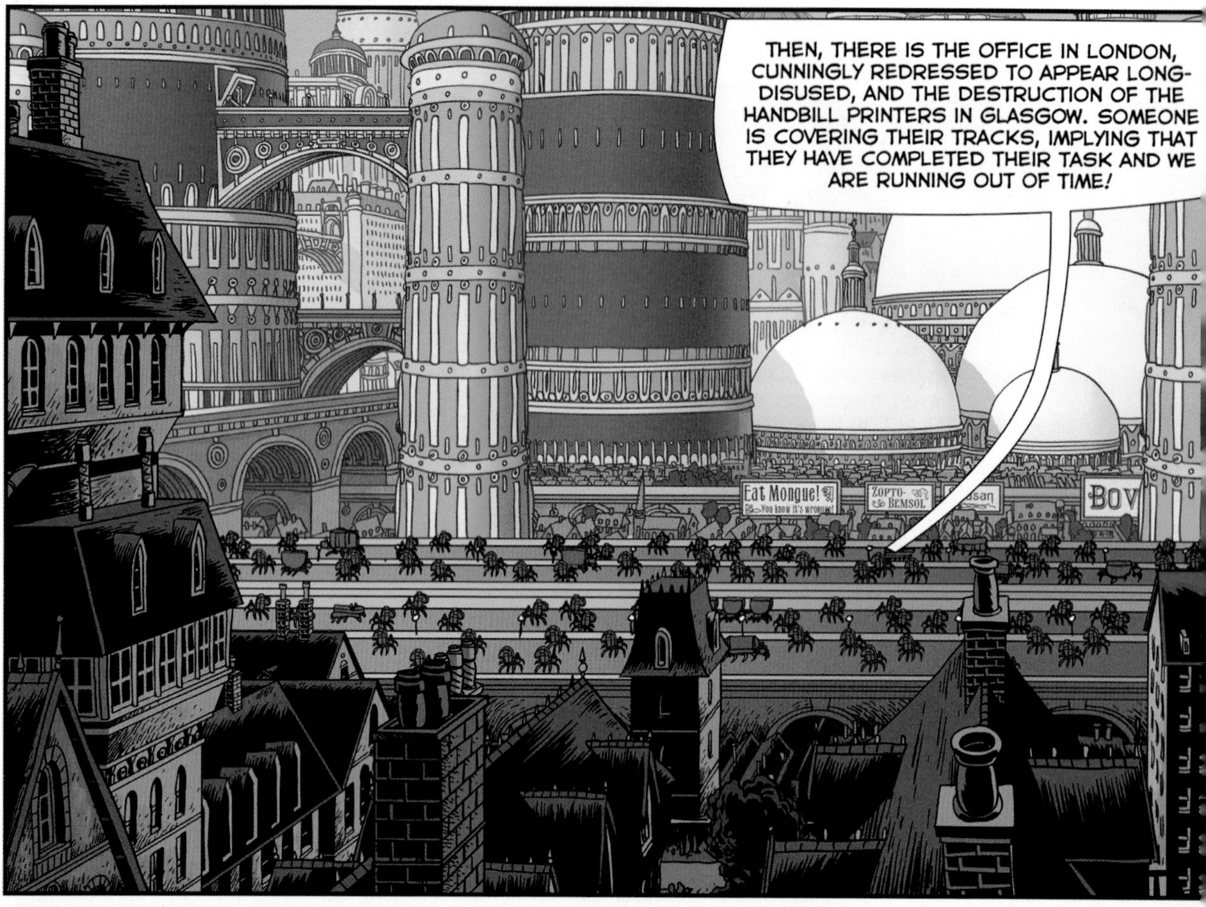
THEN, THERE IS THE OFFICE IN LONDON, CUNNINGLY REDRESSED TO APPEAR LONG-DISUSED, AND THE DESTRUCTION OF THE HANDBILL PRINTERS IN GLASGOW. SOMEONE IS COVERING THEIR TRACKS, IMPLYING THAT THEY HAVE COMPLETED THEIR TASK AND WE ARE RUNNING OUT OF TIME!
Eat Mongue!
ZOPTO-BEMSOL
BOV

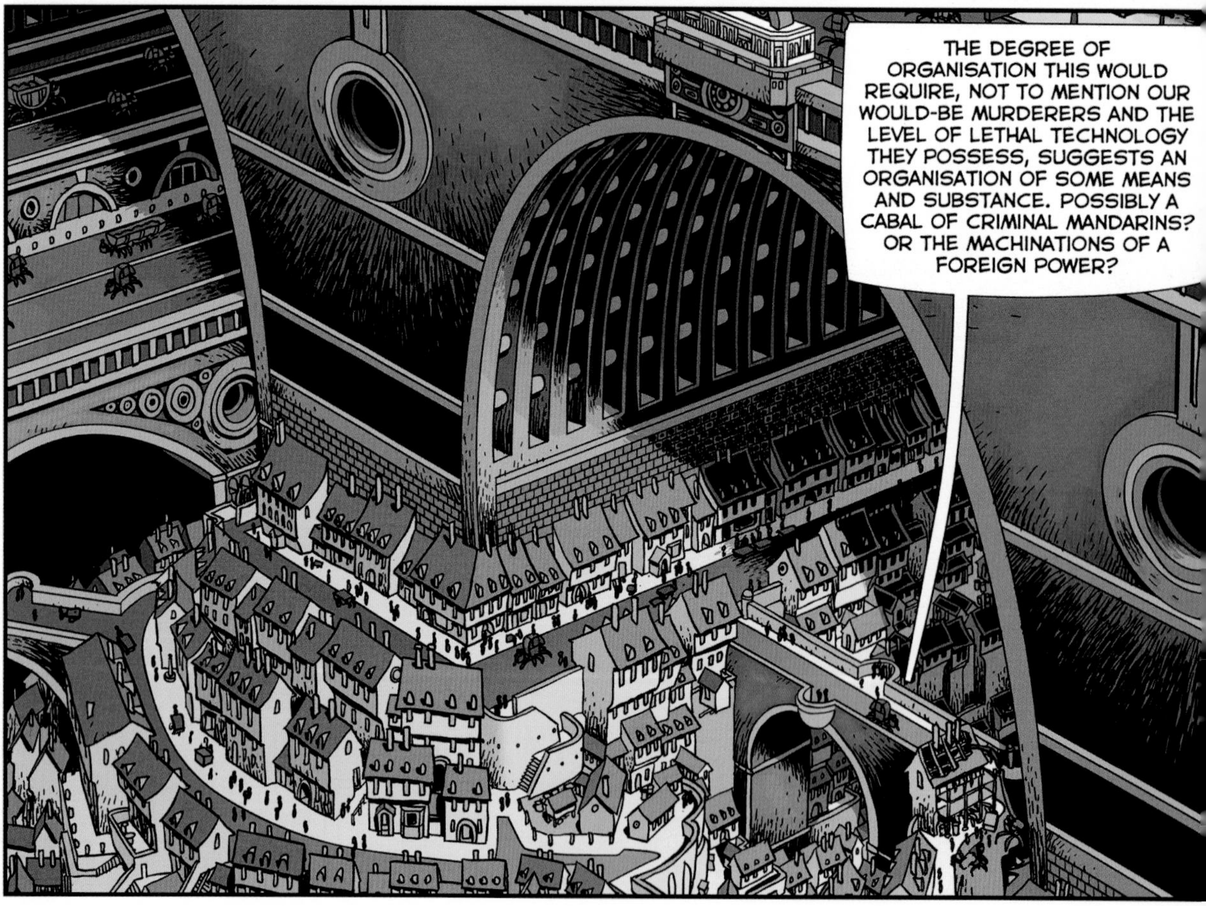
THE DEGREE OF ORGANISATION THIS WOULD REQUIRE, NOT TO MENTION OUR WOULD-BE MURDERERS AND THE LEVEL OF LETHAL TECHNOLOGY THEY POSSESS, SUGGESTS AN ORGANISATION OF SOME MEANS AND SUBSTANCE. POSSIBLY A CABAL OF CRIMINAL MANDARINS? OR THE MACHINATIONS OF A FOREIGN POWER?

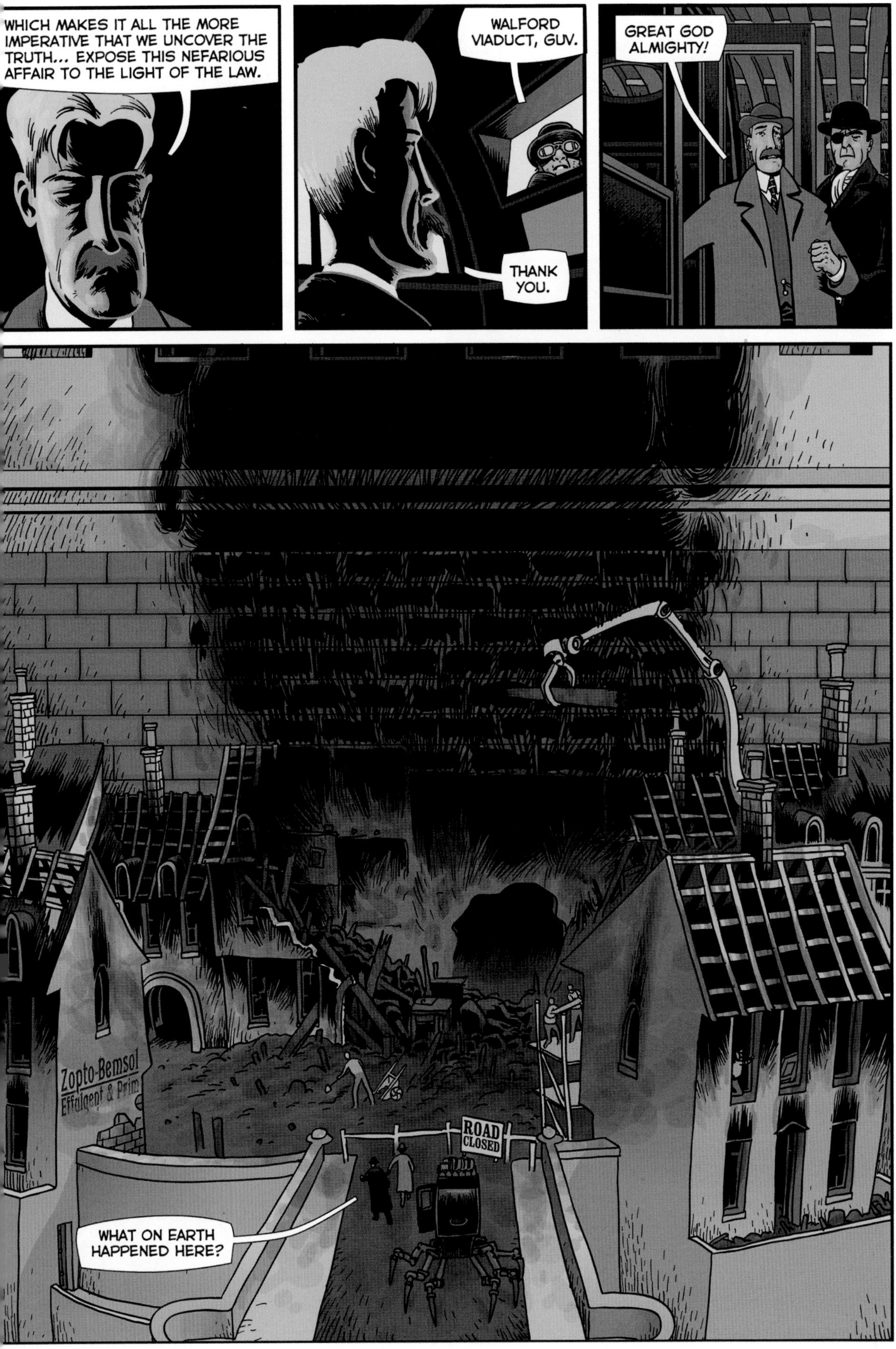

WHICH MAKES IT ALL THE MORE IMPERATIVE THAT WE UNCOVER THE TRUTH... EXPOSE THIS NEFARIOUS AFFAIR TO THE LIGHT OF THE LAW.
WALFORD VIADUCT, GUV.
THANK YOU.
GREAT GOD ALMIGHTY!
Zopto-Bemsol
Effulgent & Prim
ROAD CLOSED
WHAT ON EARTH HAPPENED HERE?

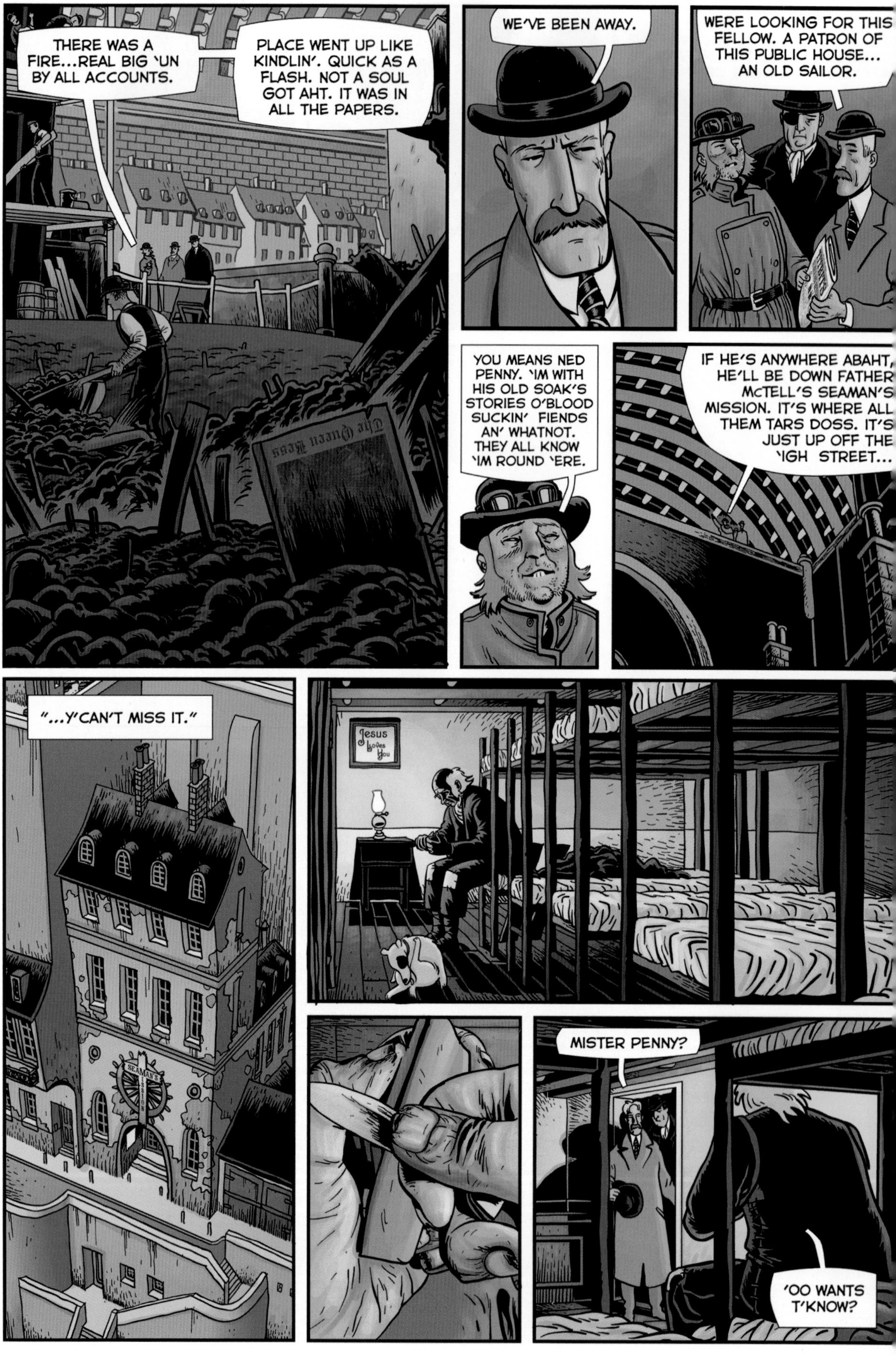
THERE WAS A FIRE...REAL BIG 'UN BY ALL ACCOUNTS.
PLACE WENT UP LIKE KINDLIN'. QUICK AS A FLASH. NOT A SOUL GOT AHT. IT WAS IN ALL THE PAPERS.
The Queen Bess
WE'VE BEEN AWAY.
WERE LOOKING FOR THIS FELLOW. A PATRON OF THIS PUBLIC HOUSE... AN OLD SAILOR.
YOU MEANS NED PENNY. 'IM WITH HIS OLD SOAK'S STORIES O'BLOOD SUCKIN' FIENDS AN' WHATNOT. THEY ALL KNOW 'IM ROUND 'ERE.
IF HE'S ANYWHERE ABAHT, HE'LL BE DOWN FATHER McTELL'S SEAMAN'S MISSION. IT'S WHERE ALL THEM TARS DOSS. IT'S JUST UP OFF THE 'IGH STREET...
"...Y'CAN'T MISS IT."
SEAMAN'S MISSION
Jesus Loves You
MISTER PENNY?
'OO WANTS T'KNOW?

MY NAME IS ROBERT AUTUMN, THIS IS MY MAN, MISTER CURRIE, WE'RE HERE TO...

Y'ERE ABOUT THE WOMEN, AINTCHA? WELL Y'CAN SOD OFF! I'M SICK O' YOU LOT TAKIN' THE MICKEY!

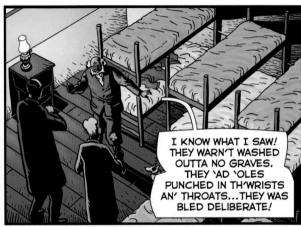

I KNOW WHAT I SAW! THEY WARN'T WASHED OUTTA NO GRAVES. THEY 'AD 'OLES PUNCHED IN TH'WRISTS AN' THROATS...THEY WAS BLED DELIBERATE!

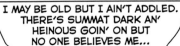

I MAY BE OLD BUT I AIN'T ADDLED. THERE'S SUMMAT DARK AN' HEINOUS GOIN' ON BUT NO ONE BELIEVES ME...

WE BELIEVE YOU. IN FACT, WE BELIEVE THE BODIES YOU FOUND ARE BUT THE TIP OF A GRISLY ICEBERG.

WE ARE INTENT ON EXPOSING THE TRUTH AND WE NEED YOUR HELP.

Jesus Loves You

YOU TALKS LIKE AN OFFICER. WHAT WAS YOU? ARMY?

THE COLDSTREAM GUARDS. BOTH OF US.

SERGEANT, RIGHT? YOU GOT THE LOOK.

COLOUR SERGEANT, AYE. YOU TOO?

THA'S RIGHT. I WAS GUNNERY SERGEANT... ON THE THUNDERCHILD.

THE IRONCLAD? I THOUGHT SHE WAS LOST WITH ALL HANDS DURING THE WAR?

NO...NOT ALL.

YOU SHOULDA SEEN 'ER THAT DAY BY GOD...

"...SPITTING FIRE AND ROARING LIKE A TIGER!"

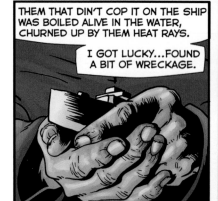

THEM THAT DIN'T COP IT ON THE SHIP WAS BOILED ALIVE IN THE WATER, CHURNED UP BY THEM HEAT RAYS.

I GOT LUCKY...FOUND A BIT OF WRECKAGE.

YOU WANTS T'FIND WHOEVER DID THEM GIRLS, THEN TAKE ME WITH YAH.

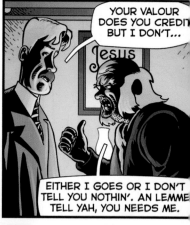

YOUR VALOUR DOES YOU CREDIT BUT I DON'T...

EITHER I GOES OR I DON'T TELL YOU NOTHIN'. AN LEMME TELL YAH, YOU NEEDS ME.

HOW'S THAT THEN?

ME OLD MAN WAS A RIVER CABBIE, HE KNEW THE TIDES AND CURRENTS LIKE THE BACK OF 'IS 'AND.

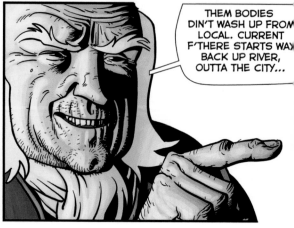

THEM BODIES DIN'T WASH UP FROM LOCAL. CURRENT F'THERE STARTS WAY BACK UP RIVER, OUTTA THE CITY...

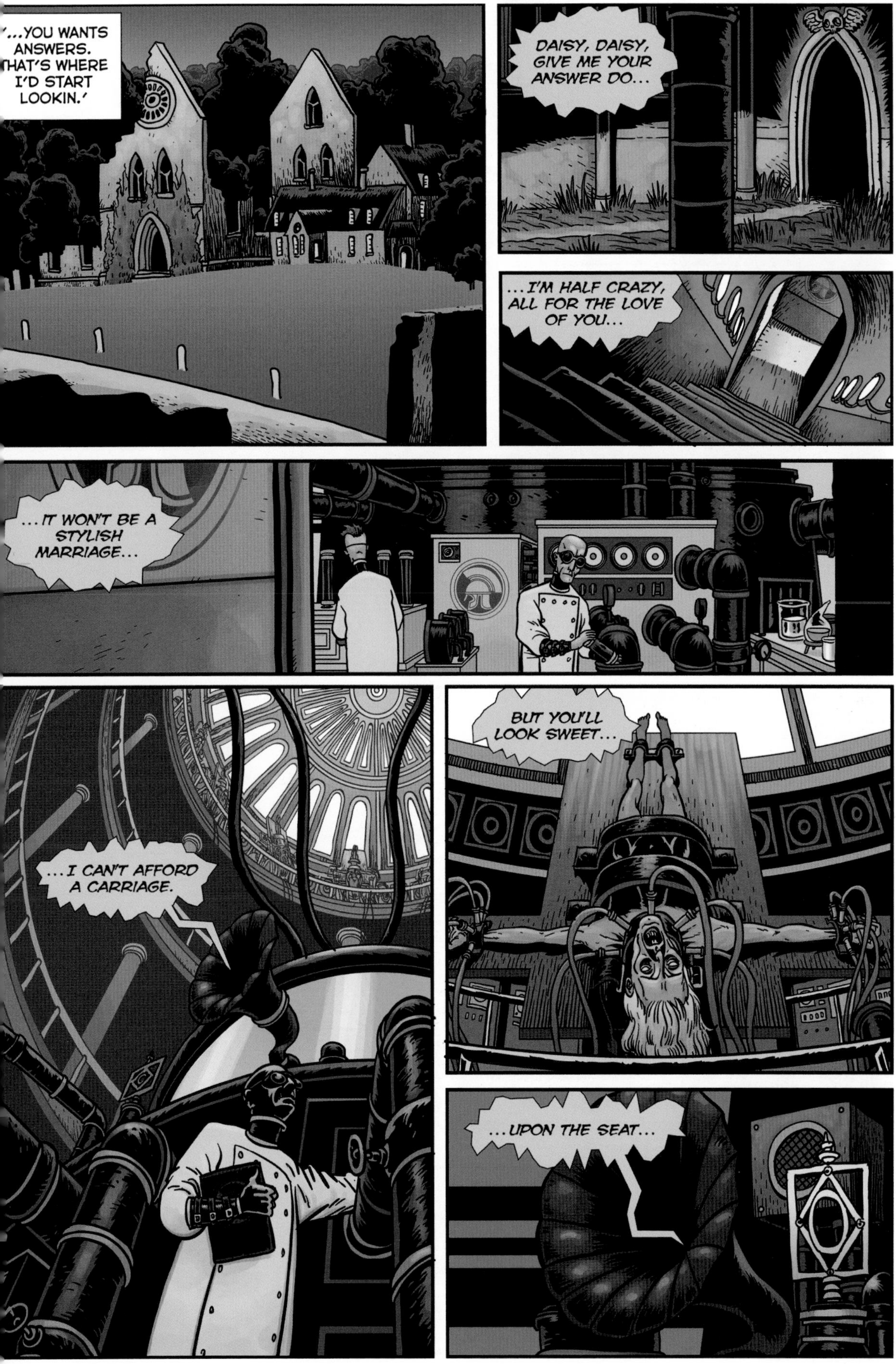
"...YOU WANTS ANSWERS. THAT'S WHERE I'D START LOOKIN.'
DAISY, DAISY, GIVE ME YOUR ANSWER DO...
...I'M HALF CRAZY, ALL FOR THE LOVE OF YOU...
...IT WON'T BE A STYLISH MARRIAGE...
...I CAN'T AFFORD A CARRIAGE.
BUT YOU'LL LOOK SWEET...
...UPON THE SEAT...

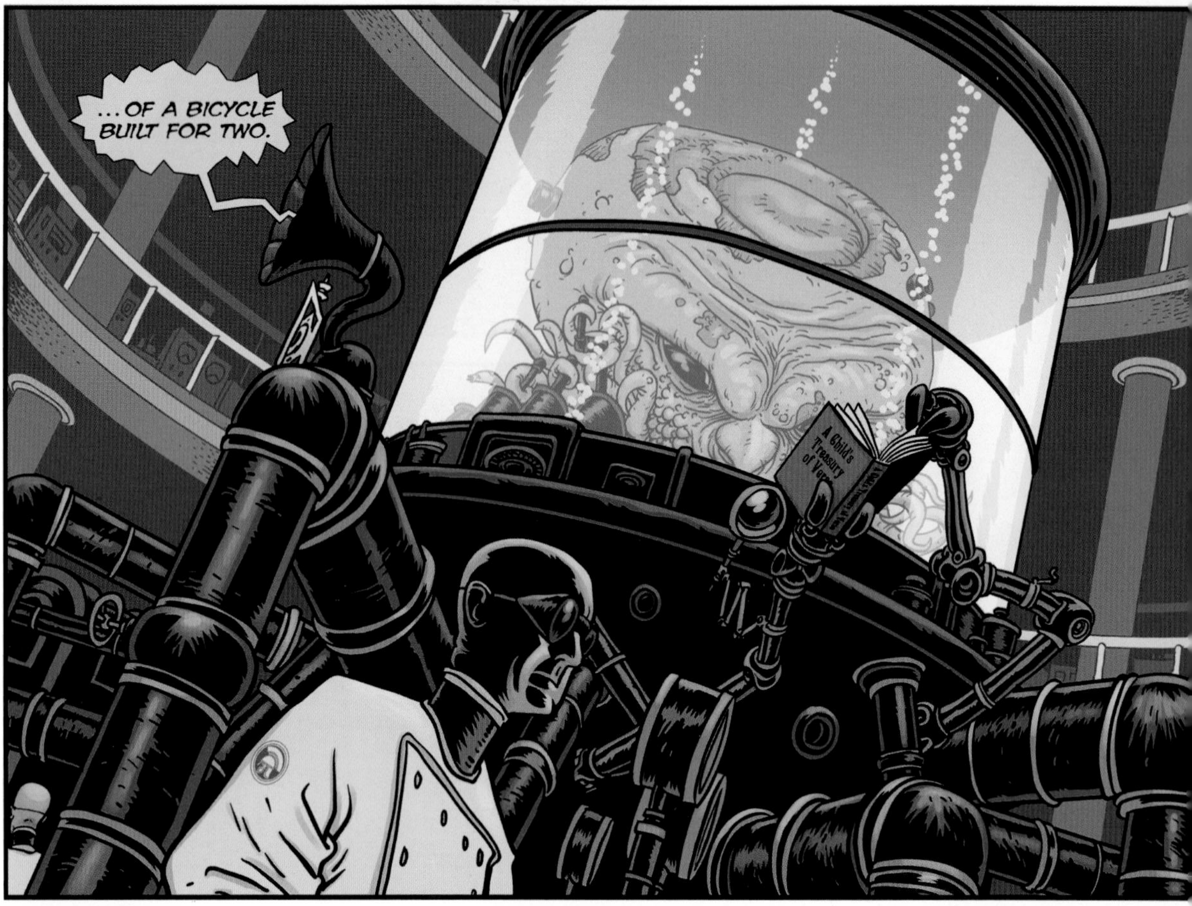
...OF A BICYCLE BUILT FOR TWO.
A Child's Treasury

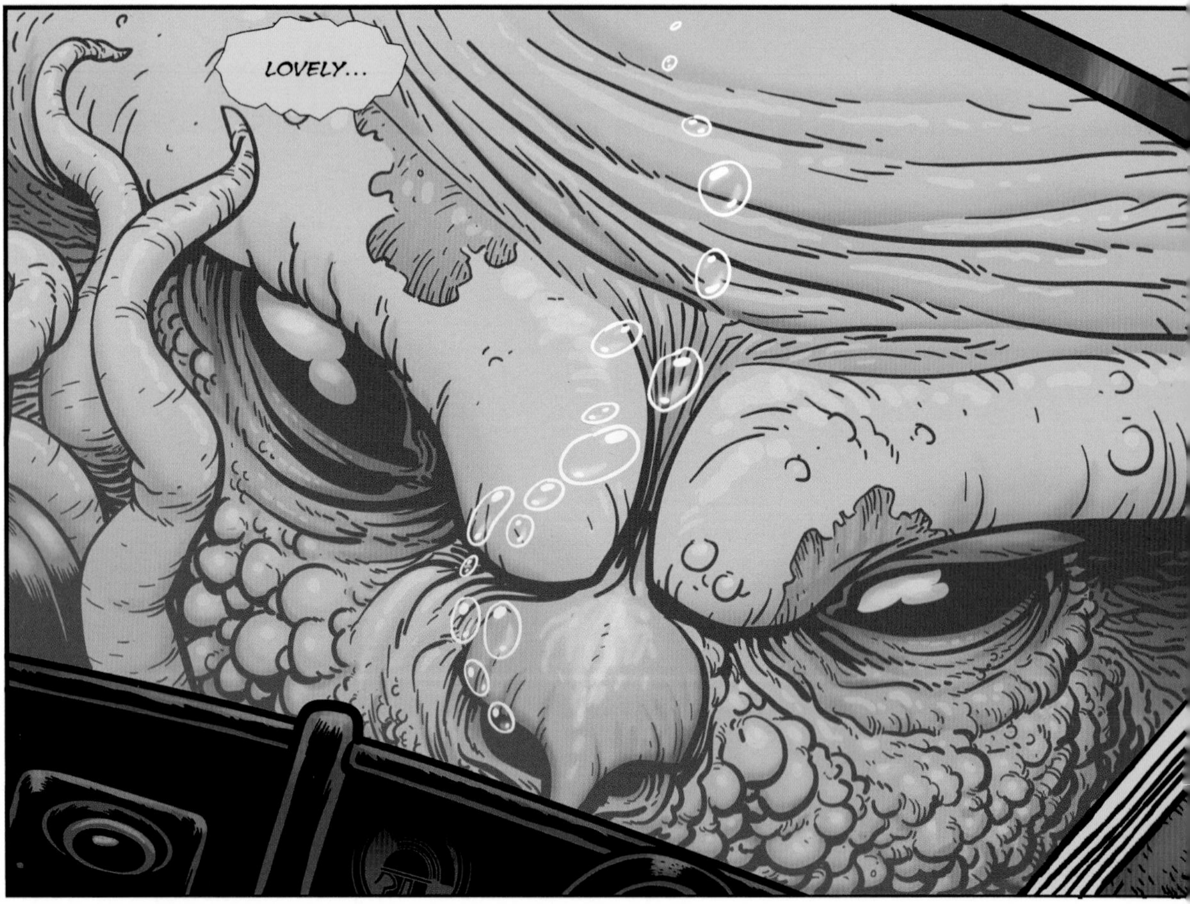
LOVELY...

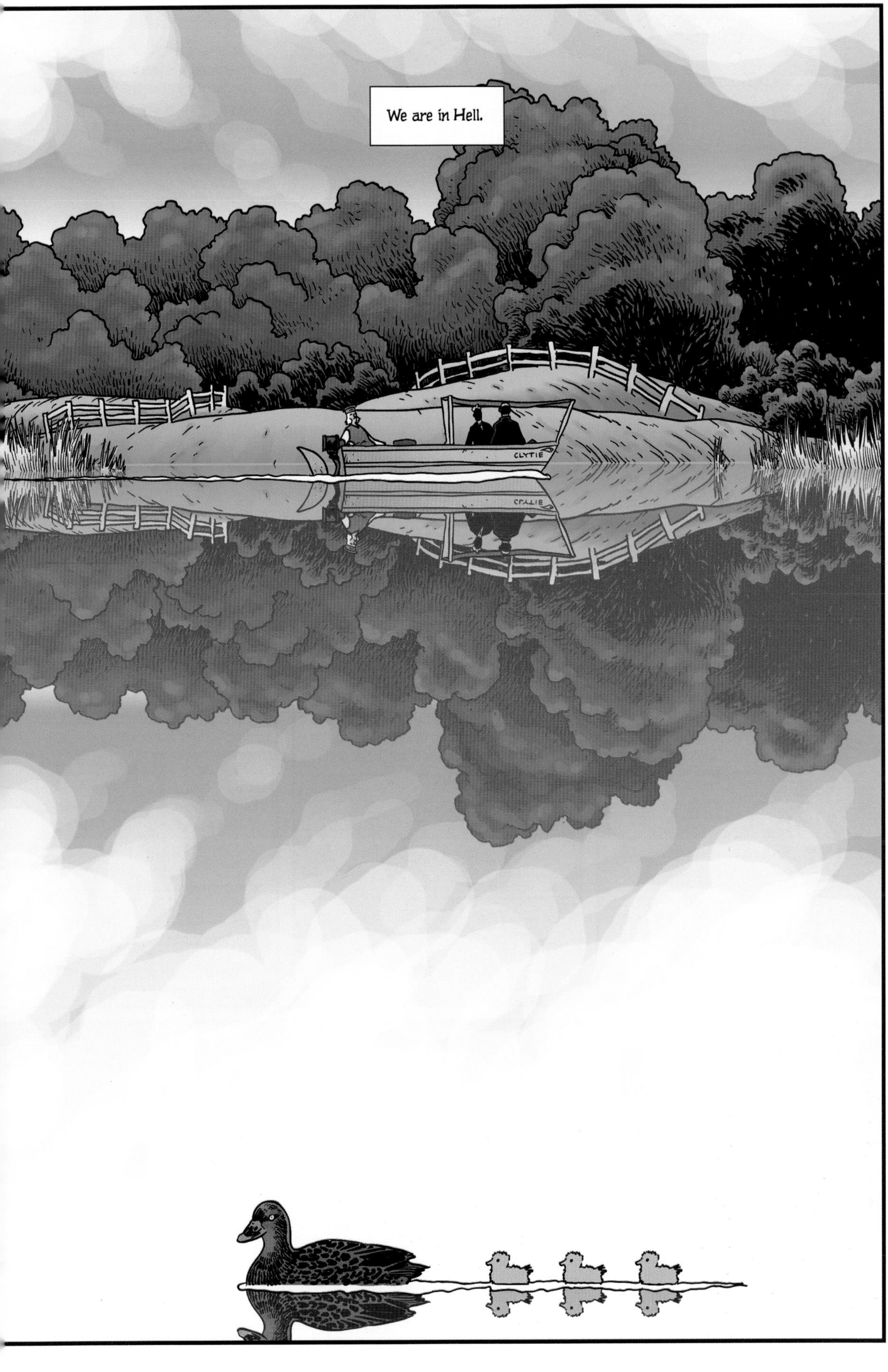
We are in Hell.
CLYTIE

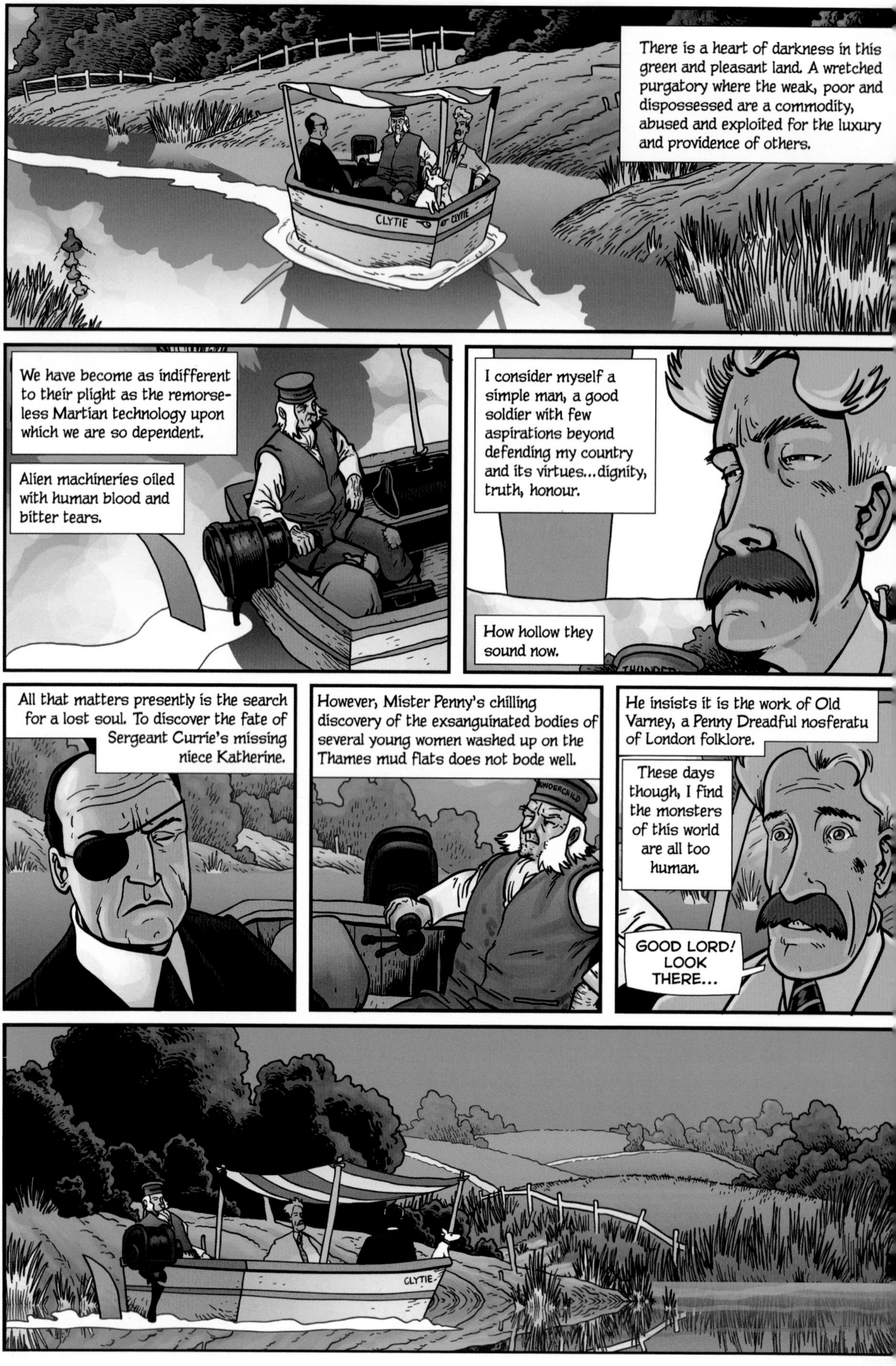
There is a heart of darkness in this green and pleasant land. A wretched purgatory where the weak, poor and dispossessed are a commodity, abused and exploited for the luxury and providence of others.
CLYTIE
CLYTIE
We have become as indifferent to their plight as the remorseless Martian technology upon which we are so dependent.
Alien machineries oiled with human blood and bitter tears.
I consider myself a simple man, a good soldier with few aspirations beyond defending my country and its virtues...dignity, truth, honour.
How hollow they sound now.
All that matters presently is the search for a lost soul. To discover the fate of Sergeant Currie's missing niece Katherine.
However, Mister Penny's chilling discovery of the exsanguinated bodies of several young women washed up on the Thames mud flats does not bode well.
He insists it is the work of Old Varney, a Penny Dreadful nosferatu of London folklore.
These days though, I find the monsters of this world are all too human.
GOOD LORD! LOOK THERE...
CLYTIE

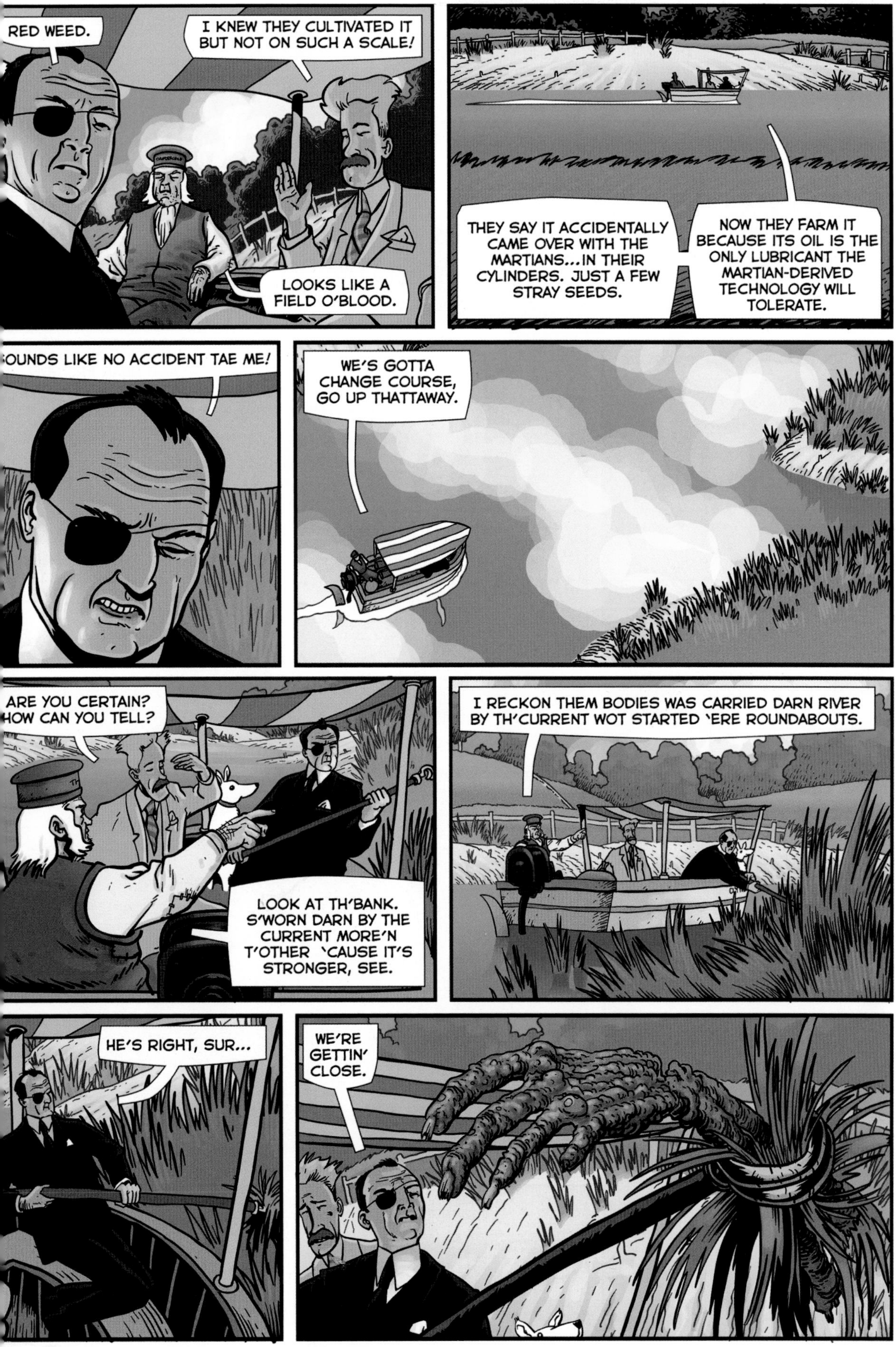
RED WEED.
I KNEW THEY CULTIVATED IT BUT NOT ON SUCH A SCALE!
LOOKS LIKE A FIELD O'BLOOD.
THEY SAY IT ACCIDENTALLY CAME OVER WITH THE MARTIANS...IN THEIR CYLINDERS. JUST A FEW STRAY SEEDS.
NOW THEY FARM IT BECAUSE ITS OIL IS THE ONLY LUBRICANT THE MARTIAN-DERIVED TECHNOLOGY WILL TOLERATE.
OUNDS LIKE NO ACCIDENT TAE ME!
WE'S GOTTA CHANGE COURSE, GO UP THATTAWAY.
ARE YOU CERTAIN? HOW CAN YOU TELL?
LOOK AT TH'BANK. S'WORN DARN BY THE CURRENT MORE'N T'OTHER 'CAUSE IT'S STRONGER, SEE.
I RECKON THEM BODIES WAS CARRIED DARN RIVER BY TH'CURRENT WOT STARTED 'ERE ROUNDABOUTS.
HE'S RIGHT, SUR...
WE'RE GETTIN' CLOSE.

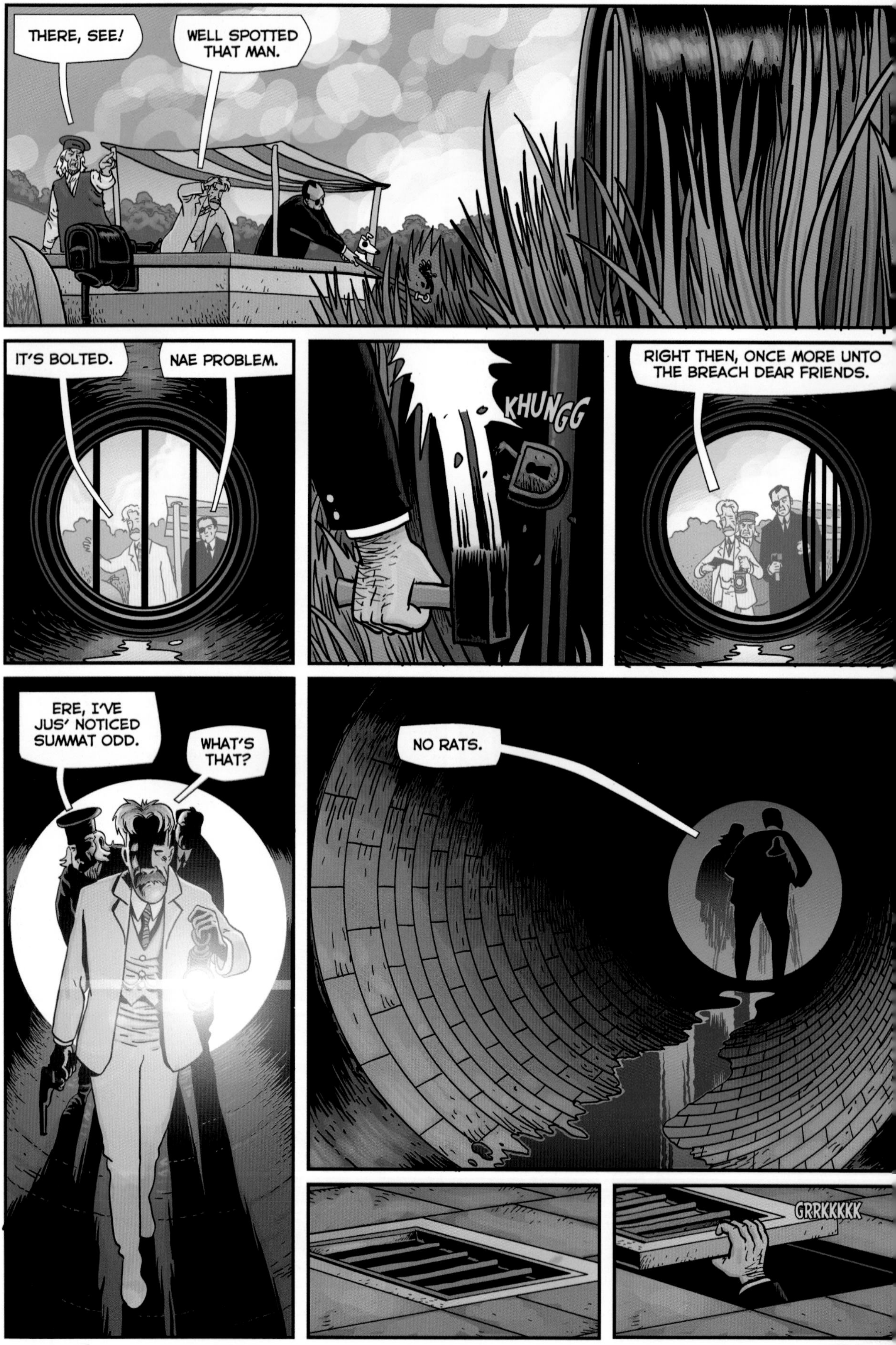
THERE, SEE!
WELL SPOTTED THAT MAN.
IT'S BOLTED.
NAE PROBLEM.
KHUNGG
RIGHT THEN, ONCE MORE UNTO THE BREACH DEAR FRIENDS.
ERE, I'VE JUS' NOTICED SUMMAT ODD.
WHAT'S THAT?
NO RATS.
GRRKKKKK

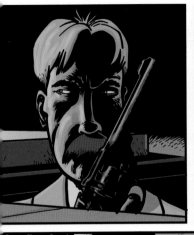

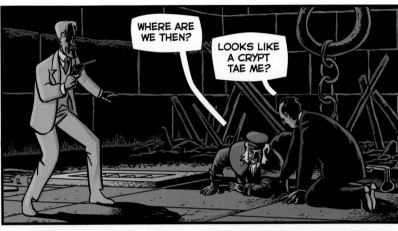

WHERE ARE WE THEN?
LOOKS LIKE A CRYPT TAE ME?
NO, ITS TOO LARGE. MORE LIKELY A CATACOMB. WE'RE BENEATH AN ABBEY OF SOME KIND, POSSIBLY A MONASTERY.
EXCEPT I FEAR THESE POOR SOULS ARE NOT THE ORIGINAL OCCUPANTS.
SEE 'OLES, THEY'S FULL OF 'OLES, JUS' LIKE I TOLD 'EM!
THUNDERCHILD
SUR, LOOK AT THIS.
A FURNACE?
AYE. ONE O'THEM NEW ONES. TH'KIND THAT USES A HEAT RAY 'STEAD O'COAL OR GAS.
AFTER PIRANESI

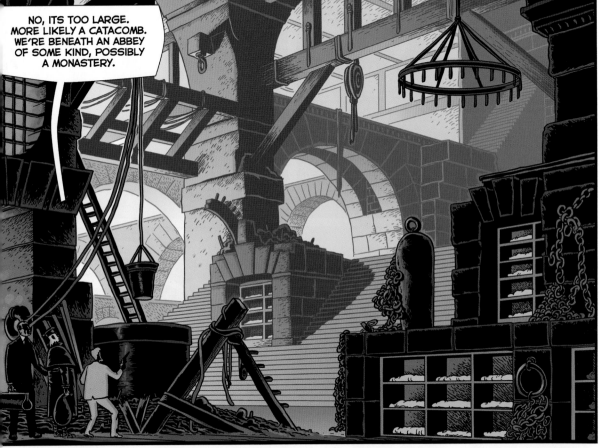

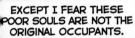

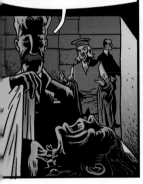

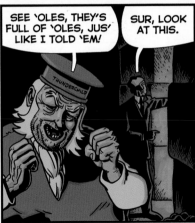

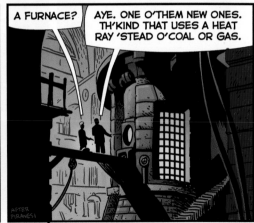

SEE HERE. THESE GOUGES ARE FRESH. THIS DEVICE HAS ONLY RECENTLY BEEN INSTALLED.

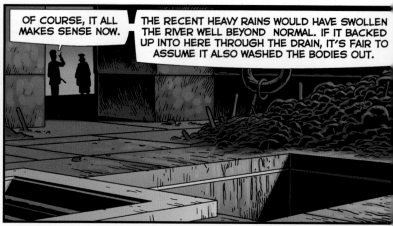

OF COURSE, IT ALL MAKES SENSE NOW.

THE RECENT HEAVY RAINS WOULD HAVE SWOLLEN THE RIVER WELL BEYOND NORMAL. IF IT BACKED UP INTO HERE THROUGH THE DRAIN, IT'S FAIR TO ASSUME IT ALSO WASHED THE BODIES OUT.

THEY WERE THEN CARRIED DOWN STREAM AND BEACHED ON THE MUD BANK WHEN THE TIDE RECEDED.

SO NOW THEY BURNS EM INSTEAD?

EXACTLY. SERGEANT, WE SHOULD - SERGEANT?

OH, DEAR LORD

THIS WHERE THEY KEPT 'EM. LIKE ANIMALS.

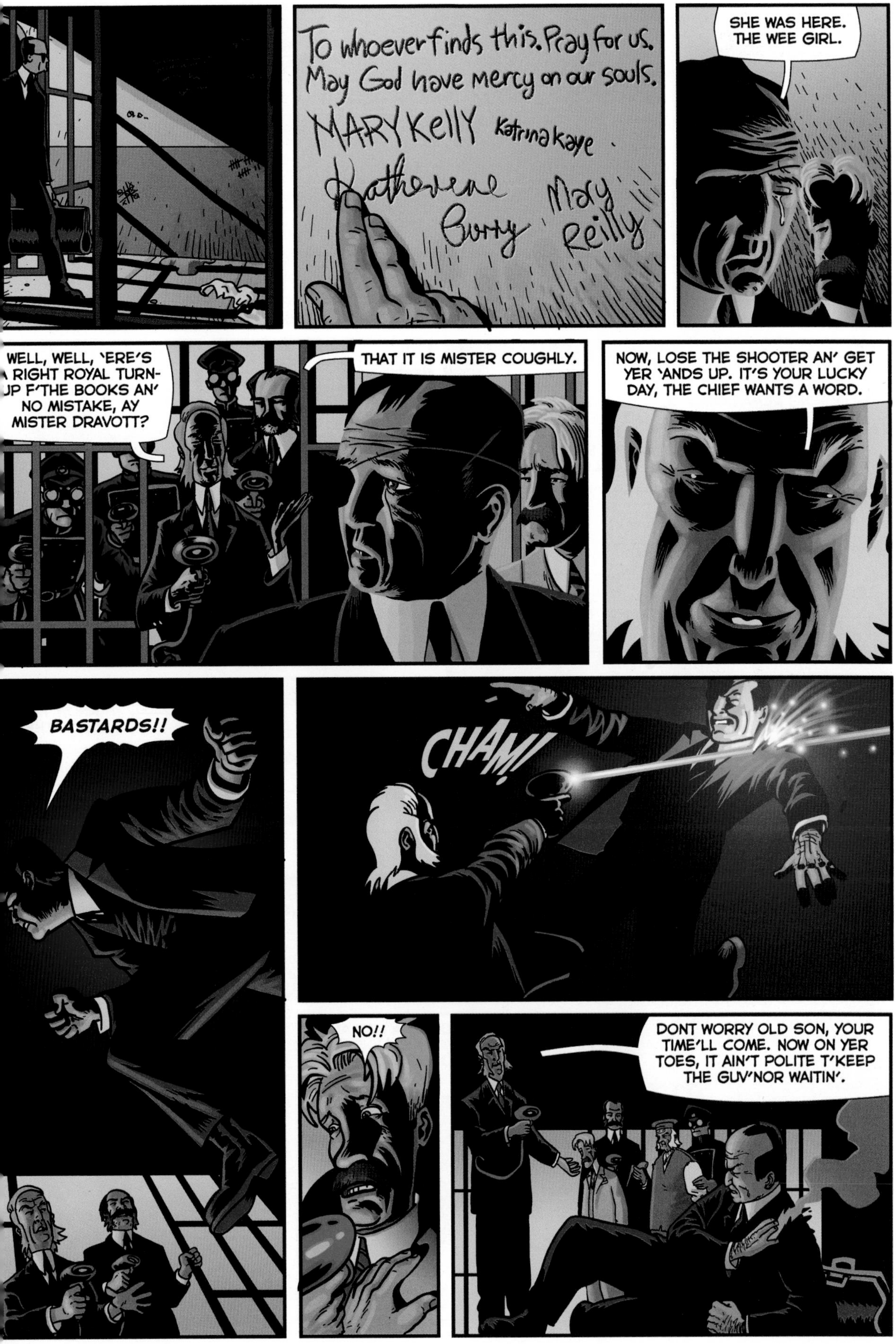
To whoever finds this. Pray for us.
May God have mercy on our souls.
MARY KELLY
Katrina kaye
Katherene Burry
Mary Reilly
SHE WAS HERE. THE WEE GIRL.
WELL, WELL, 'ERE'S RIGHT ROYAL TURN-UP F'THE BOOKS AN' NO MISTAKE, AY MISTER DRAVOTT?
THAT IT IS MISTER COUGHLY.
NOW, LOSE THE SHOOTER AN' GET YER 'ANDS UP. IT'S YOUR LUCKY DAY, THE CHIEF WANTS A WORD.
BASTARDS!!
CHAM!
NO!!
DONT WORRY OLD SON, YOUR TIME'LL COME. NOW ON YER TOES, IT AIN'T POLITE T'KEEP THE GUV'NOR WAITIN'.

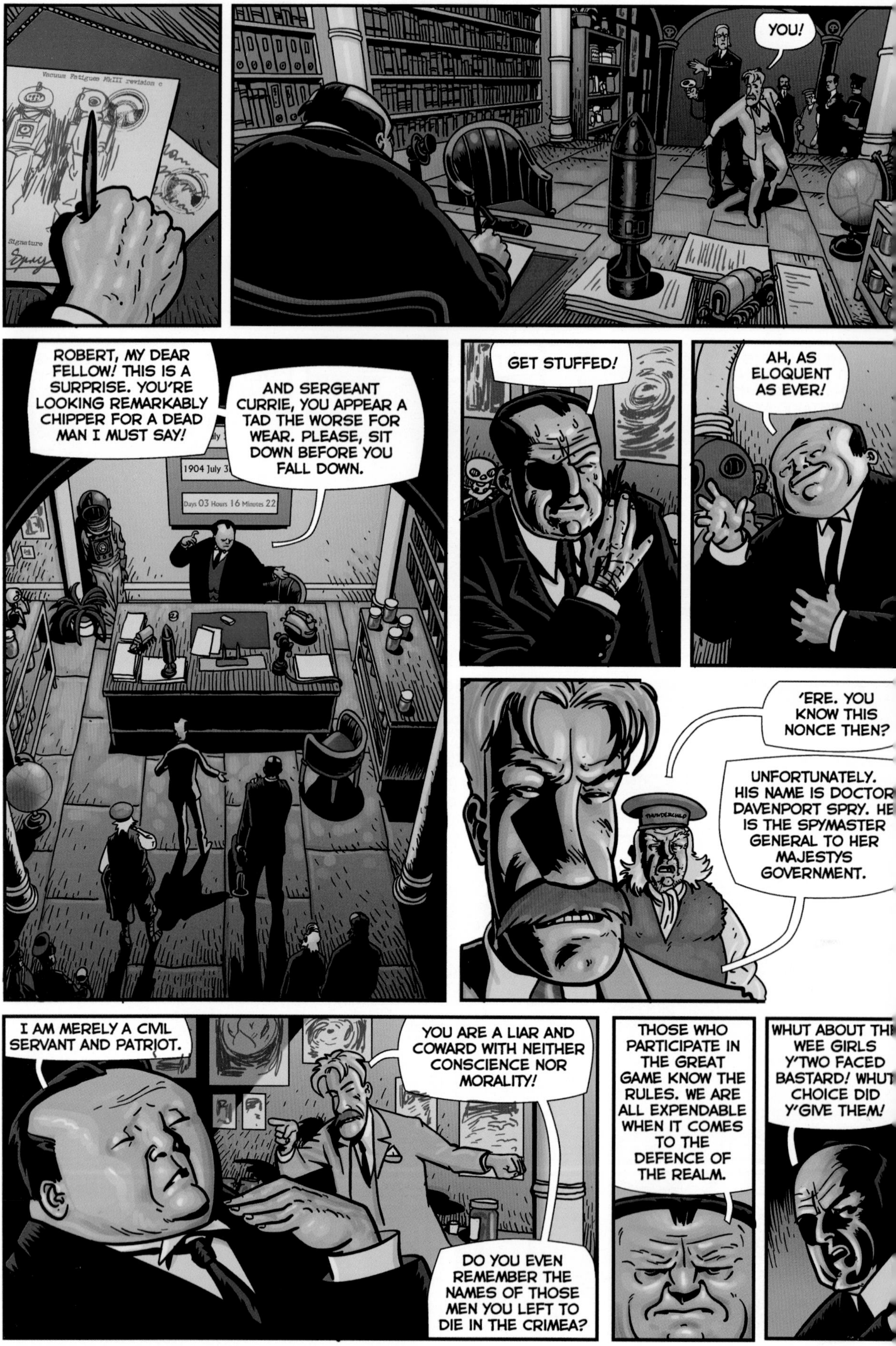

Vacuum Fatigues MkIII revision c
Signature
YOU!
ROBERT, MY DEAR FELLOW! THIS IS A SURPRISE. YOU'RE LOOKING REMARKABLY CHIPPER FOR A DEAD MAN I MUST SAY!
AND SERGEANT CURRIE, YOU APPEAR A TAD THE WORSE FOR WEAR. PLEASE, SIT DOWN BEFORE YOU FALL DOWN.
1904 July 3
Days 03 Hours 16 Minutes 22
GET STUFFED!
AH, AS ELOQUENT AS EVER!
'ERE. YOU KNOW THIS NONCE THEN?
THUNDERCHILD
UNFORTUNATELY. HIS NAME IS DOCTOR DAVENPORT SPRY. HE IS THE SPYMASTER GENERAL TO HER MAJESTYS GOVERNMENT.
I AM MERELY A CIVIL SERVANT AND PATRIOT.
YOU ARE A LIAR AND COWARD WITH NEITHER CONSCIENCE NOR MORALITY!
DO YOU EVEN REMEMBER THE NAMES OF THOSE MEN YOU LEFT TO DIE IN THE CRIMEA?
THOSE WHO PARTICIPATE IN THE GREAT GAME KNOW THE RULES. WE ARE ALL EXPENDABLE WHEN IT COMES TO THE DEFENCE OF THE REALM.
WHUT ABOUT TH WEE GIRLS Y'TWO FACED BASTARD! WHUT CHOICE DID Y'GIVE THEM!

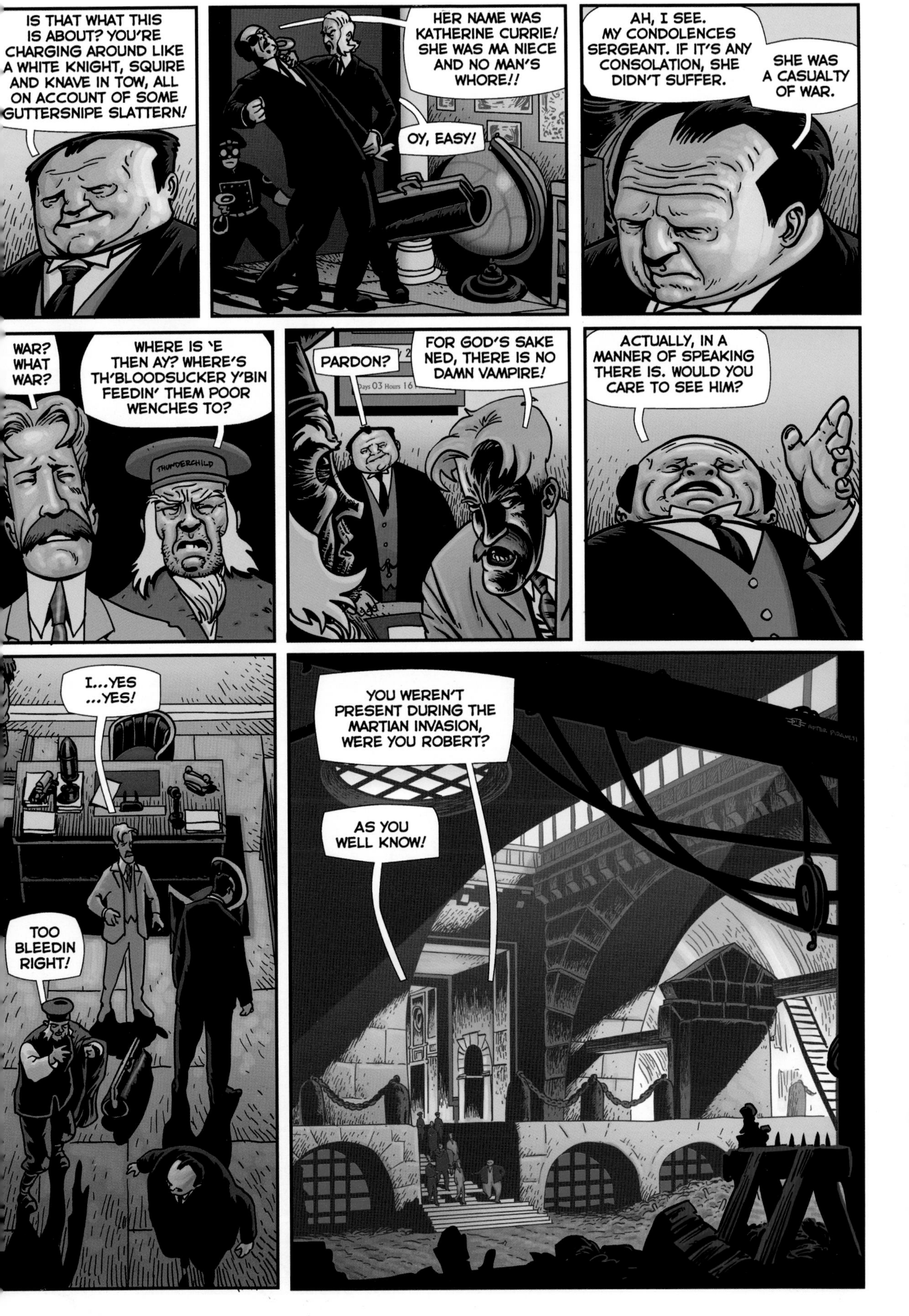
IS THAT WHAT THIS IS ABOUT? YOU'RE CHARGING AROUND LIKE A WHITE KNIGHT, SQUIRE AND KNAVE IN TOW, ALL ON ACCOUNT OF SOME GUTTERSNIPE SLATTERN!
HER NAME WAS KATHERINE CURRIE! SHE WAS MA NIECE AND NO MAN'S WHORE!!
OY, EASY!
AH, I SEE. MY CONDOLENCES SERGEANT. IF IT'S ANY CONSOLATION, SHE DIDN'T SUFFER.
SHE WAS A CASUALTY OF WAR.
WAR? WHAT WAR?
WHERE IS 'E THEN AY? WHERE'S TH'BLOODSUCKER Y'BIN FEEDIN' THEM POOR WENCHES TO?
THUNDERCHILD
PARDON?
FOR GOD'S SAKE NED, THERE IS NO DAMN VAMPIRE!
ACTUALLY, IN A MANNER OF SPEAKING THERE IS. WOULD YOU CARE TO SEE HIM?
I...YES ...YES!
TOO BLEEDIN RIGHT!
YOU WEREN'T PRESENT DURING THE MARTIAN INVASION, WERE YOU ROBERT?
AS YOU WELL KNOW!
AFTER PIRANESI

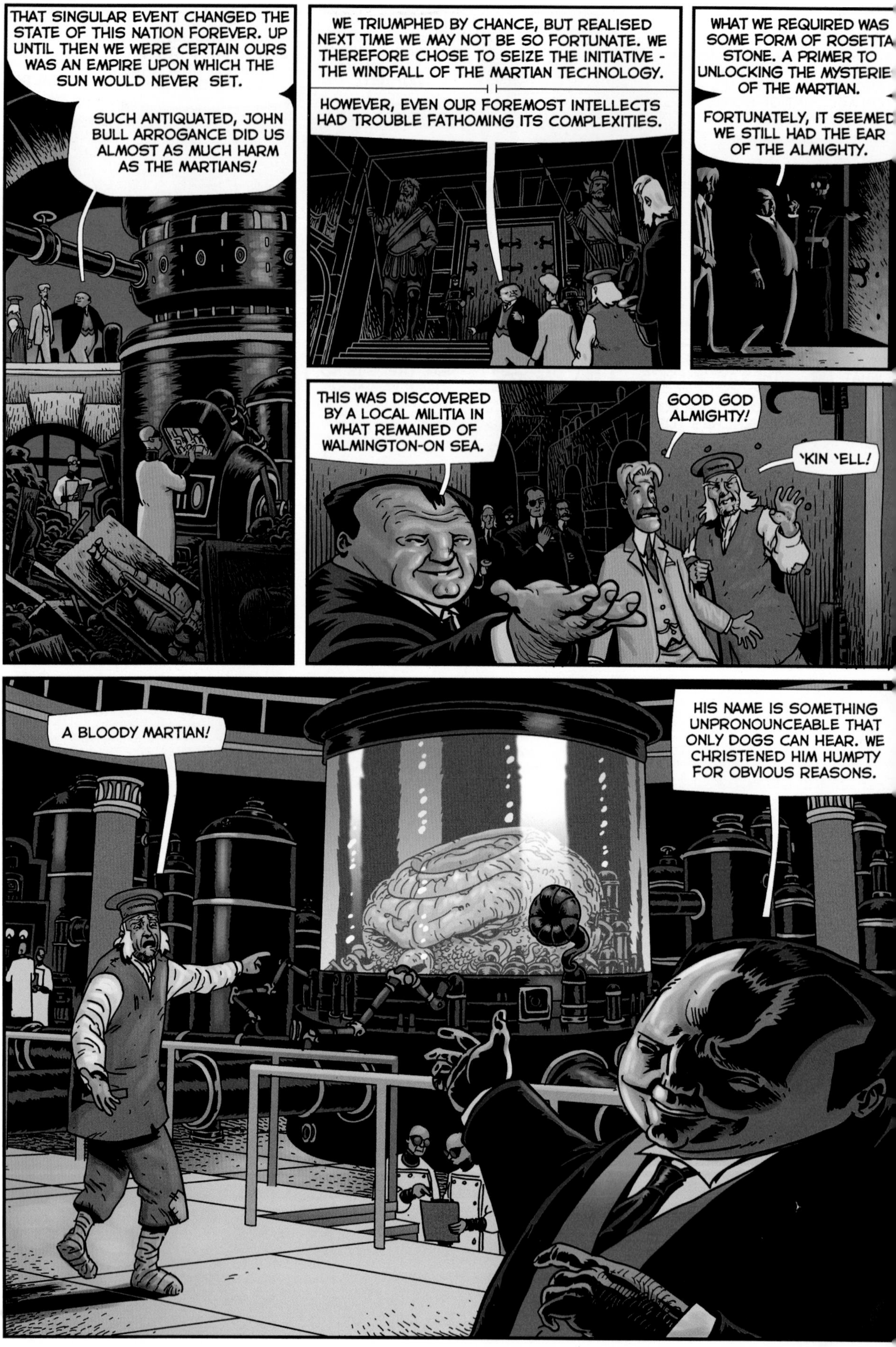
THAT SINGULAR EVENT CHANGED THE STATE OF THIS NATION FOREVER. UP UNTIL THEN WE WERE CERTAIN OURS WAS AN EMPIRE UPON WHICH THE SUN WOULD NEVER SET.
SUCH ANTIQUATED, JOHN BULL ARROGANCE DID US ALMOST AS MUCH HARM AS THE MARTIANS!
WE TRIUMPHED BY CHANCE, BUT REALISED NEXT TIME WE MAY NOT BE SO FORTUNATE. WE THEREFORE CHOSE TO SEIZE THE INITIATIVE - THE WINDFALL OF THE MARTIAN TECHNOLOGY.
HOWEVER, EVEN OUR FOREMOST INTELLECTS HAD TROUBLE FATHOMING ITS COMPLEXITIES.
WHAT WE REQUIRED WAS SOME FORM OF ROSETTA STONE. A PRIMER TO UNLOCKING THE MYSTERIE OF THE MARTIAN.
FORTUNATELY, IT SEEMED WE STILL HAD THE EAR OF THE ALMIGHTY.
THIS WAS DISCOVERED BY A LOCAL MILITIA IN WHAT REMAINED OF WALMINGTON-ON SEA.
GOOD GOD ALMIGHTY!
'KIN 'ELL!
A BLOODY MARTIAN!
HIS NAME IS SOMETHING UNPRONOUNCEABLE THAT ONLY DOGS CAN HEAR. WE CHRISTENED HIM HUMPTY FOR OBVIOUS REASONS.

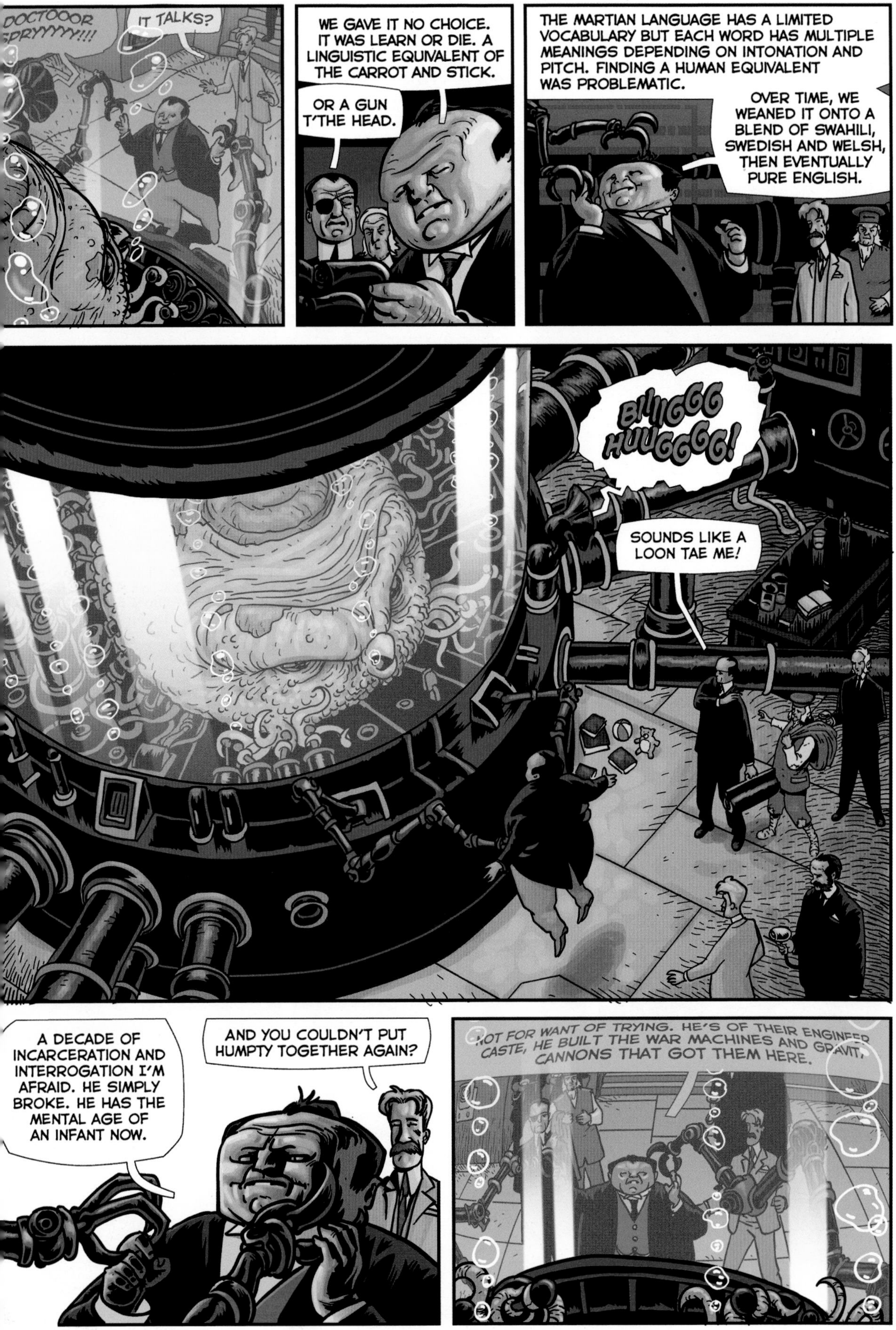
DOCTOOOR SPRYYYYY!!!
IT TALKS?
WE GAVE IT NO CHOICE. IT WAS LEARN OR DIE. A LINGUISTIC EQUIVALENT OF THE CARROT AND STICK.
OR A GUN T'THE HEAD.
THE MARTIAN LANGUAGE HAS A LIMITED VOCABULARY BUT EACH WORD HAS MULTIPLE MEANINGS DEPENDING ON INTONATION AND PITCH. FINDING A HUMAN EQUIVALENT WAS PROBLEMATIC.
OVER TIME, WE WEANED IT ONTO A BLEND OF SWAHILI, SWEDISH AND WELSH, THEN EVENTUALLY PURE ENGLISH.
BIIIGGG HUUGGGG!
SOUNDS LIKE A LOON TAE ME!
A DECADE OF INCARCERATION AND INTERROGATION I'M AFRAID. HE SIMPLY BROKE. HE HAS THE MENTAL AGE OF AN INFANT NOW.
AND YOU COULDN'T PUT HUMPTY TOGETHER AGAIN?
NOT FOR WANT OF TRYING. HE'S OF THEIR ENGINEER CASTE, HE BUILT THE WAR MACHINES AND GRAVIT CANNONS THAT GOT THEM HERE.

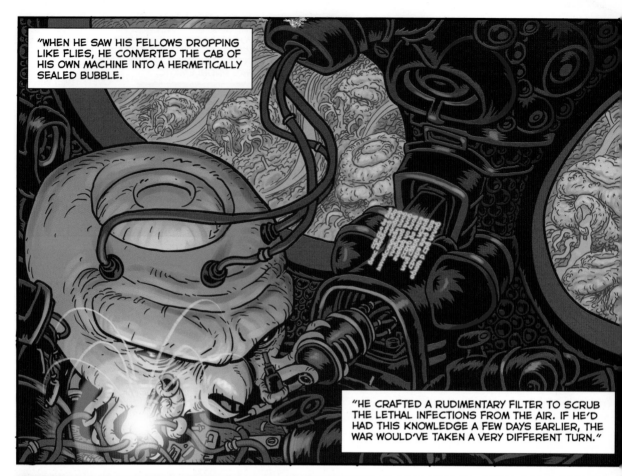

"WHEN HE SAW HIS FELLOWS DROPPING LIKE FLIES, HE CONVERTED THE CAB OF HIS OWN MACHINE INTO A HERMETICALLY SEALED BUBBLE."

"HE CRAFTED A RUDIMENTARY FILTER TO SCRUB THE LETHAL INFECTIONS FROM THE AIR. IF HE'D HAD THIS KNOWLEDGE A FEW DAYS EARLIER, THE WAR WOULD'VE TAKEN A VERY DIFFERENT TURN."

HIS EXPERTISE HAS PROVED INVALUABLE. THERE ISN'T A SINGLE MARTIAN DERIVED DEVICE IN USE, THAT DOESN'T OWE ITS ORIGIN TO THIS GHASTLY SQUAB.

OH, DEAR GOD. YOU FED THEM TO IT DIDN'T YOU? THE GIRLS.

I REMEMBER READING, DURING THE WAR, HOW THEY HERDED PEOPLE UP... LIKE CATTLE. BODIES WERE FOUND AFTERWARDS, DRAINED...BRITTLE...

...THEY DRANK THEIR BLOOD!

THEIR PHYSIOLOGY INDICATES THEY THRIVE ON A DIET OF PURE PROTEIN IN ITS SIMPLEST FORM...BLOOD. WE TRIED FEEDING HIM ANIMAL BLOOD, HE ALMOST DIED.

WE NEEDED ANOTHER ALTERNATIVE BEFORE HE STARVED TO DEATH. HE WAS TOO VITAL TO LOSE!

SO YOU LURED THEM HERE, THOSE POOR BLOODY GIRLS. YOU COAXED THEM FROM THEIR GODFORSAKEN GHETTOS WITH THE PROMISE OF A WAGE AND A WARM MEAL -

AND THEN YOU POURED THEM DOWN THAT THING'S GULLET, DIDN'T YOU, YOU BASTARD!

DAISY, DAISY, GIVE ME YOUR ANSWER DO I'M HALF CRAZY ALL FOR THE LOVE OF YOU

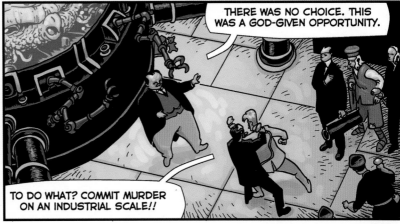

THERE WAS NO CHOICE. THIS WAS A GOD-GIVEN OPPORTUNITY.

TO DO WHAT? COMMIT MURDER ON AN INDUSTRIAL SCALE!!

T WON'T BE A STYLISH MARRIAGE

T CAN'T AFFORD A CARRIAGE

THEY WERE A MEANS TO AN END. IT WAS A NECESSARY EVIL. WE HAD TO LEARN EVERYTHING HE KNEW.

WHY? SO YOU COULD PUT A HEAT RAY COOKER IN EVERY KITCHEN! A DAMN ARACHNID HANSOM CAB ON EVERY STREET!

BUT YOU'LL LOOK SWEET UPON THE SEAT

OF A BICYCLE MADE FOR TWO

NO YOU FOOL, SO WE CAN INVADE MARS.

WE'RE GOING TO WAR!

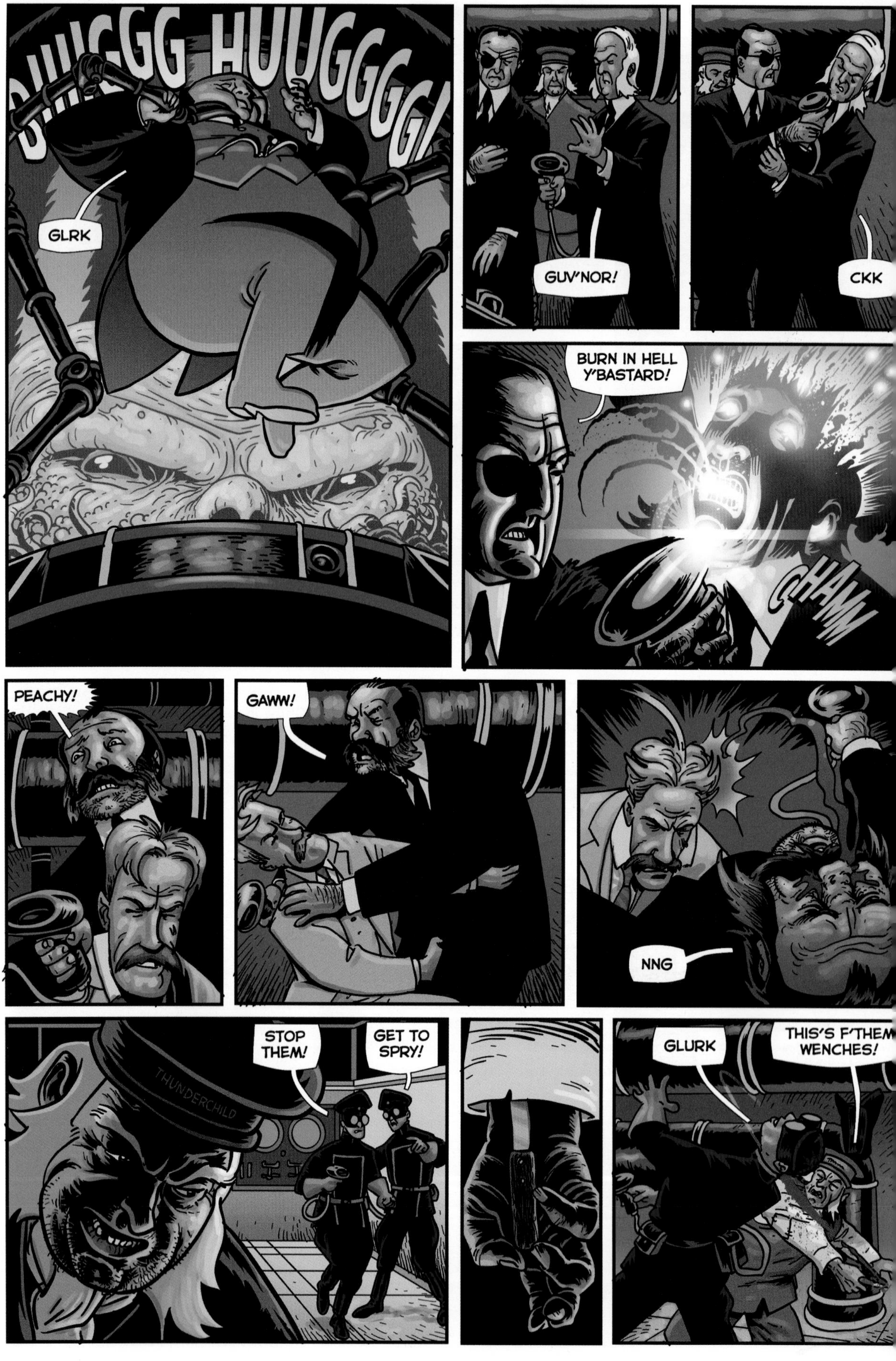
HUUGGG HUUGGGG!
GLRK
GUV'NOR!
CKK
BURN IN HELL Y'BASTARD!
CHAMM
PEACHY!
GAWW!
NNG
THUNDERCHILD
STOP THEM!
GET TO SPRY!
GLURK
THIS'S F'THEM WENCHES!

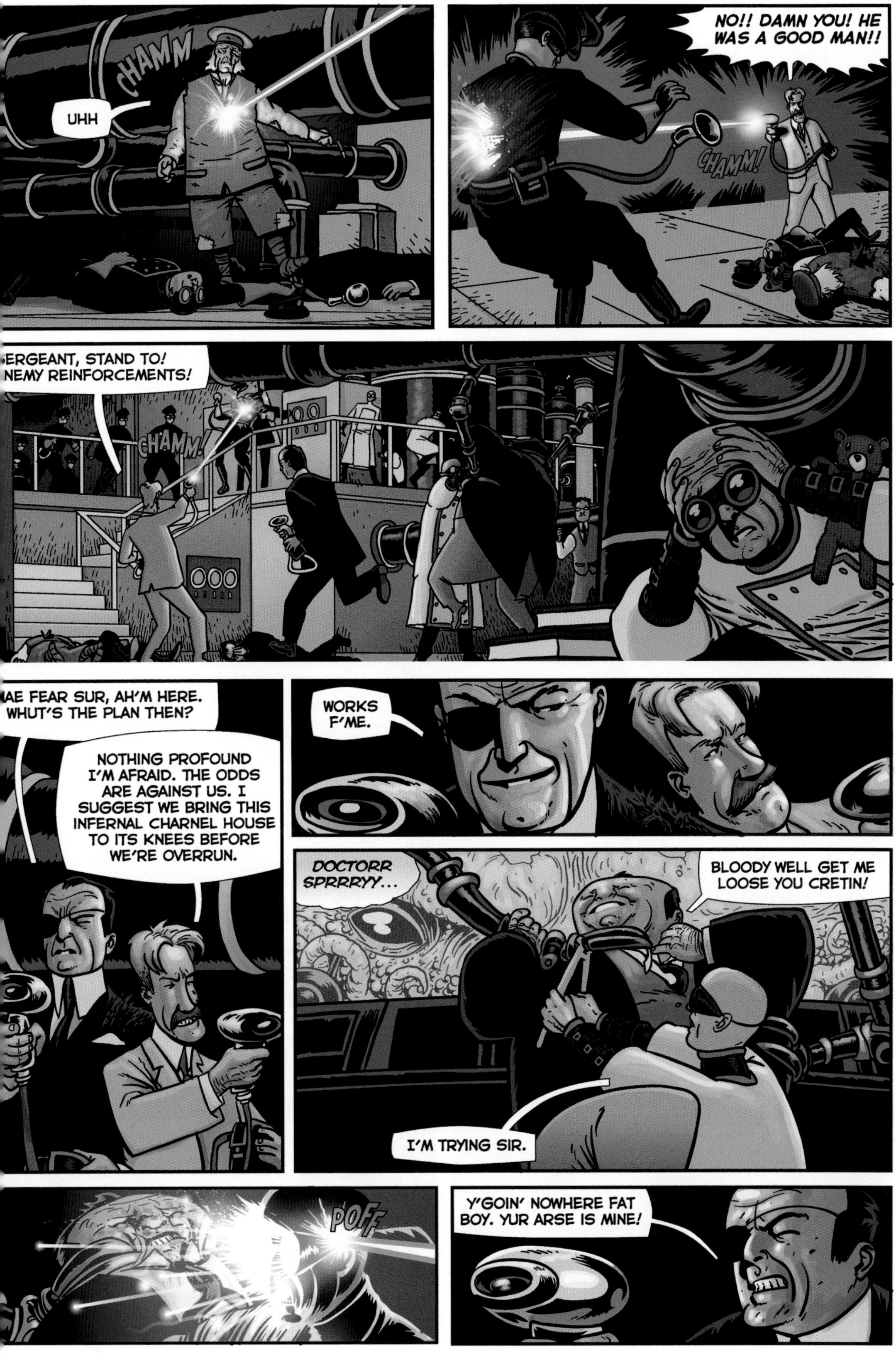
CHAMM
UHH
NO!! DAMN YOU! HE WAS A GOOD MAN!!
CHAMM!
ERGEANT, STAND TO! NEMY REINFORCEMENTS!
CHAMM!
AE FEAR SUR, AH'M HERE. WHUT'S THE PLAN THEN?
NOTHING PROFOUND I'M AFRAID. THE ODDS ARE AGAINST US. I SUGGEST WE BRING THIS INFERNAL CHARNEL HOUSE TO ITS KNEES BEFORE WE'RE OVERRUN.
WORKS F'ME.
DOCTORR SPRRRYY...
BLOODY WELL GET ME LOOSE YOU CRETIN!
I'M TRYING SIR.
POFF
Y'GOIN' NOWHERE FAT BOY. YUR ARSE IS MINE!

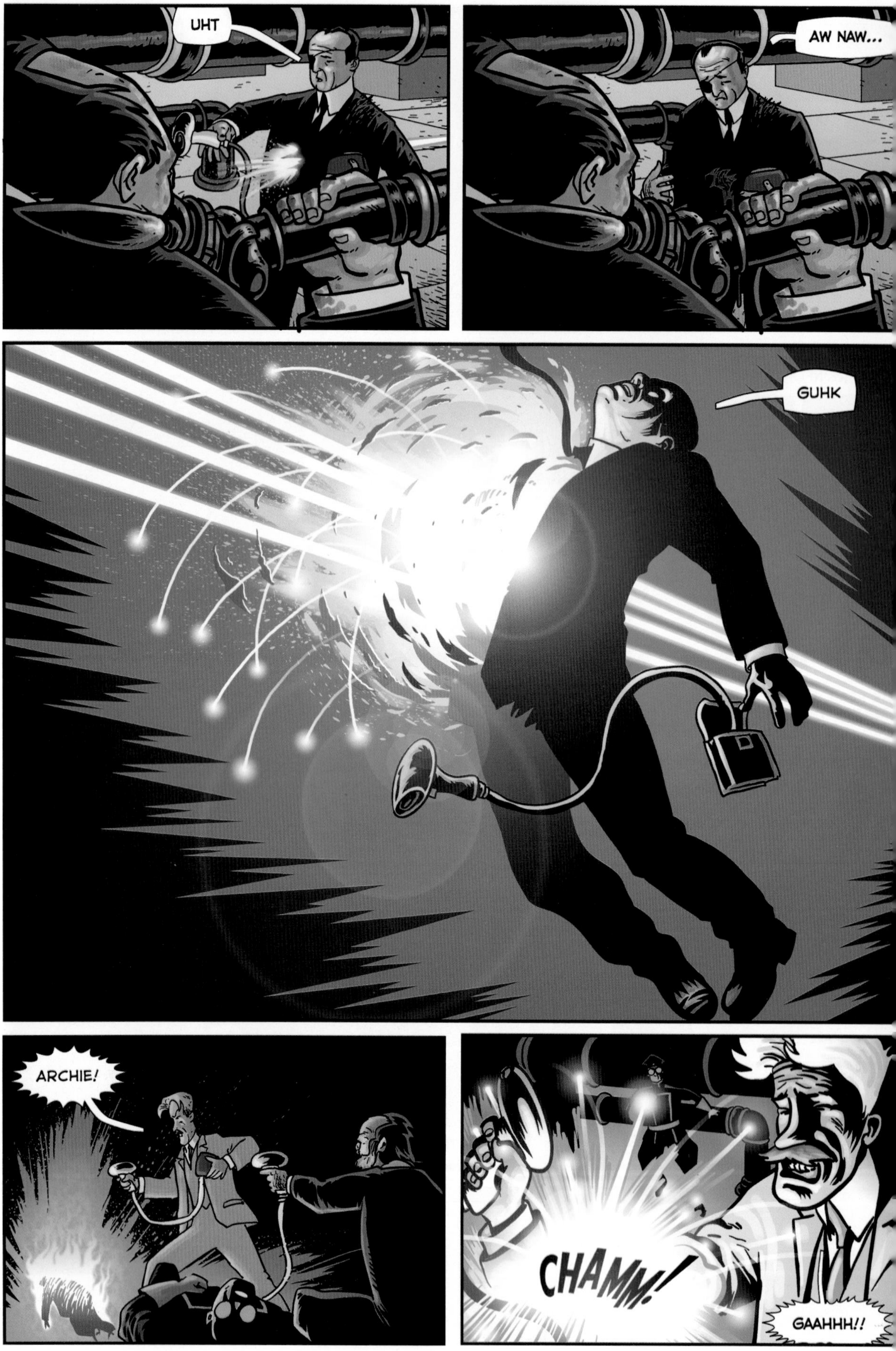
UHT
AW NAW...
GUHK
ARCHIE!
CHAMM!
GAAHHH!!

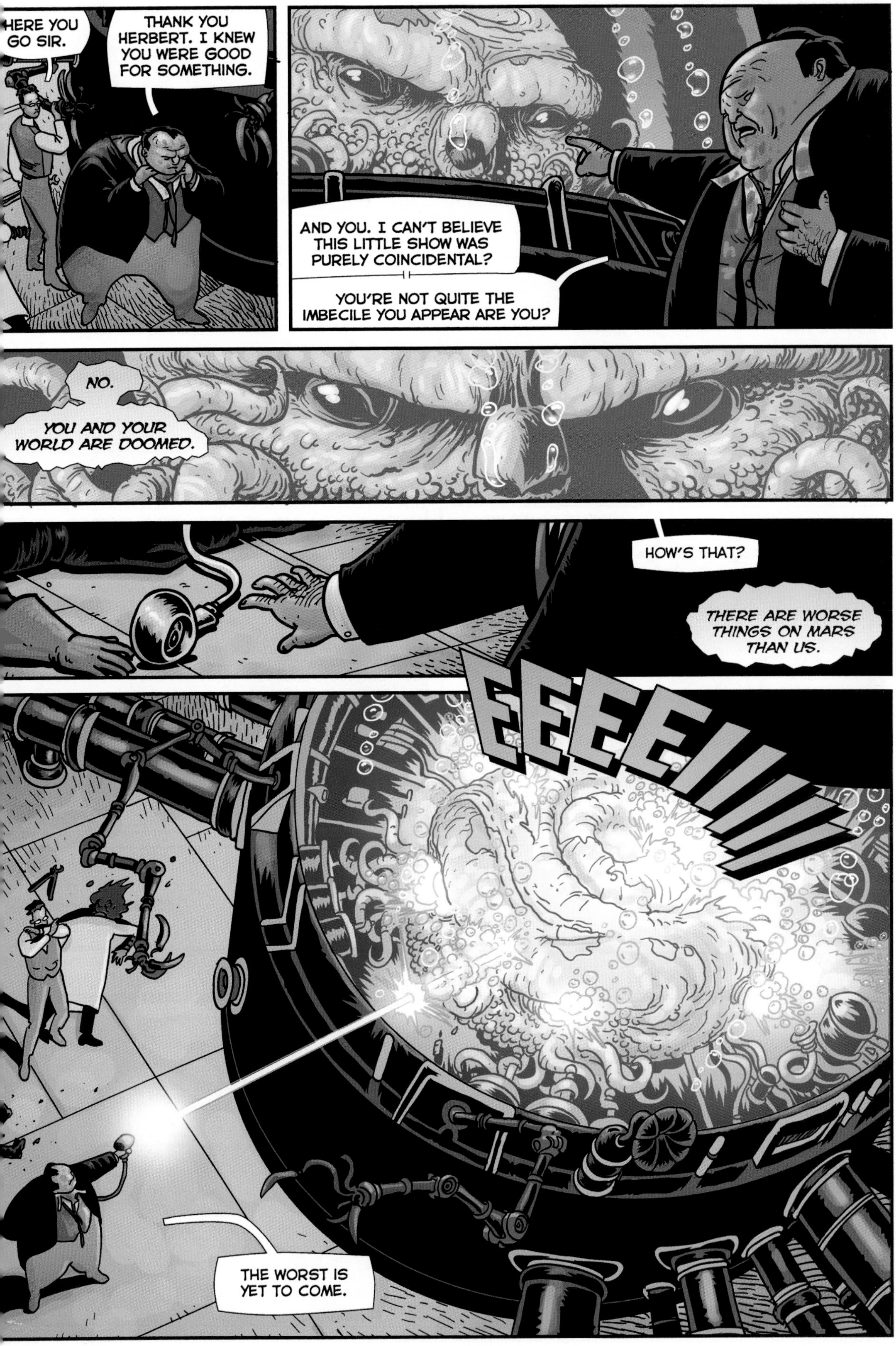
HERE YOU GO SIR.
THANK YOU HERBERT. I KNEW YOU WERE GOOD FOR SOMETHING.
AND YOU. I CAN'T BELIEVE THIS LITTLE SHOW WAS PURELY COINCIDENTAL?
YOU'RE NOT QUITE THE IMBECILE YOU APPEAR ARE YOU?
NO.
YOU AND YOUR WORLD ARE DOOMED.
HOW'S THAT?
THERE ARE WORSE THINGS ON MARS THAN US.
EEEEIIIII
THE WORST IS YET TO COME.

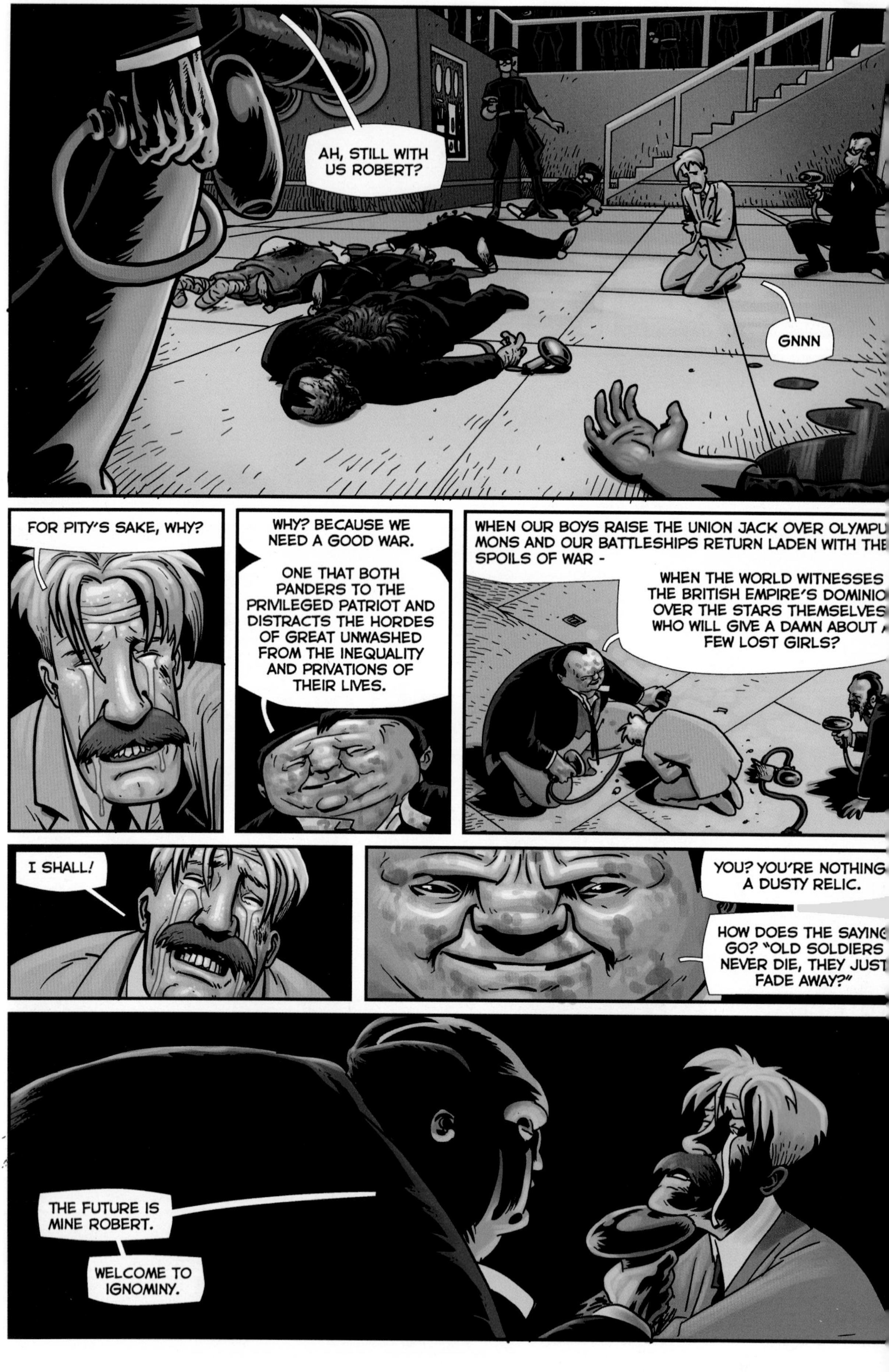
AH, STILL WITH US ROBERT?
GNNN
FOR PITY'S SAKE, WHY?
WHY? BECAUSE WE NEED A GOOD WAR.
ONE THAT BOTH PANDERS TO THE PRIVILEGED PATRIOT AND DISTRACTS THE HORDES OF GREAT UNWASHED FROM THE INEQUALITY AND PRIVATIONS OF THEIR LIVES.
WHEN OUR BOYS RAISE THE UNION JACK OVER OLYMPU MONS AND OUR BATTLESHIPS RETURN LADEN WITH THE SPOILS OF WAR -
WHEN THE WORLD WITNESSES THE BRITISH EMPIRE'S DOMINIO OVER THE STARS THEMSELVES WHO WILL GIVE A DAMN ABOUT A FEW LOST GIRLS?
I SHALL!
YOU? YOU'RE NOTHING A DUSTY RELIC.
HOW DOES THE SAYING GO? "OLD SOLDIERS NEVER DIE, THEY JUST FADE AWAY?"
THE FUTURE IS MINE ROBERT.
WELCOME TO IGNOMINY.

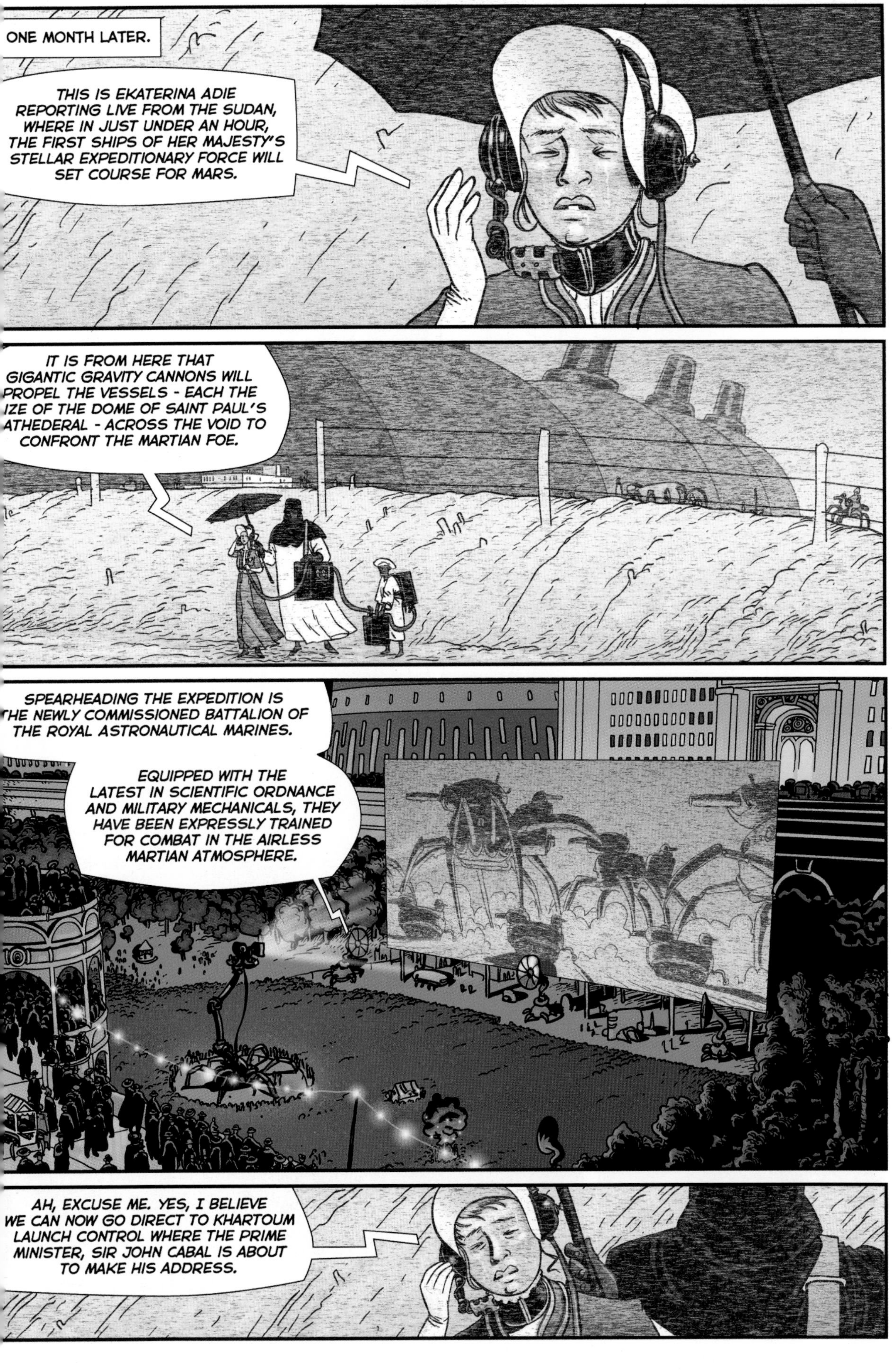
ONE MONTH LATER.
THIS IS EKATERINA ADIE REPORTING LIVE FROM THE SUDAN, WHERE IN JUST UNDER AN HOUR, THE FIRST SHIPS OF HER MAJESTY'S STELLAR EXPEDITIONARY FORCE WILL SET COURSE FOR MARS.
IT IS FROM HERE THAT GIGANTIC GRAVITY CANNONS WILL PROPEL THE VESSELS - EACH THE IZE OF THE DOME OF SAINT PAUL'S ATHEDERAL - ACROSS THE VOID TO CONFRONT THE MARTIAN FOE.
SPEARHEADING THE EXPEDITION IS HE NEWLY COMMISSIONED BATTALION OF THE ROYAL ASTRONAUTICAL MARINES.
EQUIPPED WITH THE LATEST IN SCIENTIFIC ORDNANCE AND MILITARY MECHANICALS, THEY HAVE BEEN EXPRESSLY TRAINED FOR COMBAT IN THE AIRLESS MARTIAN ATMOSPHERE.
AH, EXCUSE ME. YES, I BELIEVE WE CAN NOW GO DIRECT TO KHARTOUM LAUNCH CONTROL WHERE THE PRIME MINISTER, SIR JOHN CABAL IS ABOUT TO MAKE HIS ADDRESS.

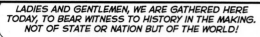

LADIES AND GENTLEMEN, WE ARE GATHERED HERE TODAY, TO BEAR WITNESS TO HISTORY IN THE MAKING. NOT OF STATE OR NATION BUT OF THE WORLD!

TEN YEARS AGO TO THIS DAY, THE MARTIAN RACE SET FOOT ON GOD'S OWN EARTH WITH THE OBJECTIVE OF SUBJUGATING HUMANITY BENEATH THE YOKE OF THEIR ALIEN TYRANNY.

THE BRIDGEHEAD OF THEIR VILE INTENT WAS THE VERY HEART OF THE CIVILISED WORLD, GREAT BRITAIN HERSELF. HOWEVER, WE HAVE REPULSED INVASIONS BEFORE, AS THE FRENCH AND SPANISH WILL ATTEST.

Live from Khartoum

AS ONE NATION WE RESISTED, SHOULDER-TO-SHOULDER. FROM OUR NOBLE MEN IN UNIFORM TO THE COMMON MAN IN THE STREET. WE STOOD FAST AND WITH THE AID OF THE ALMIGHTY WE PREVAILED.

NOW USING THE MARTIANS' OWN MACHINERIES AGAINST THEM, WE SHALL TAKE THE BATTLE BACK TO THEIR HOMES AND HEARTHS, WHERE WE WILL DELIVER SUCH A CRUSHING BLOW AS TO PREVENT THEM FROM EVER THREATENING OUR WORLD AGAIN!

BRITAIN ALONE BORE THE BRUNT OF THE CONFLICT WITHOUT THE SUPPORT OR SUCCOUR OF OUR NEIGHBOURS AND WE ASK NO ONE TO FIGHT OUR BATTLES FOR US NOW.

ON BEHALF OF MANKIND, WE WILL TAKE UP OUR SWORD ONCE MORE AND FORCE OUR FOE TO YIELD HIS WORLD TO US!

THIS ENTERPRISE HAS MADE DEMANDS OF US ALL, CALLED FOR A DEGREE OF SKILL AND SACRIFICE NOT SEEN SINCE THE WAR.

BUT AS THE GREAT LORD NELSON HIMSELF SAID TO HIS FLEET BEFORE THE BATTLE OF TRAFALGAR...

"ENGLAND EXPECTS EVERY MAN TO DO HIS DUTY." AND SO HE SHALL!

LYING BASTARD!!!

LIES! LIES! ALL LIES! THEY KILLED 'EM ALL, THOSE POOR BLOODY GIRLS! AND ARCHIE... DEAR ARCHIE... OH GOD!

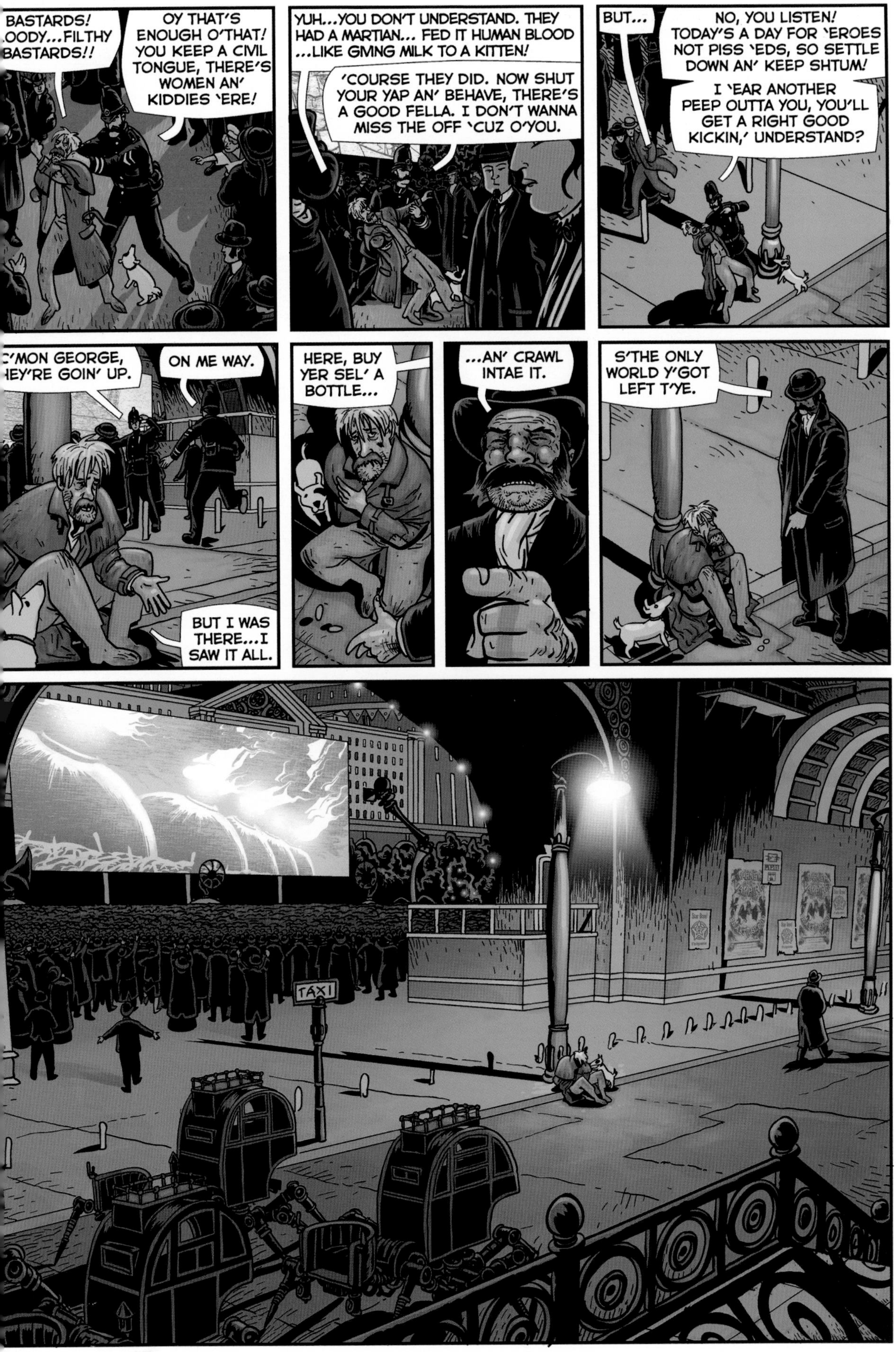

BASTARDS! LOODY...FILTHY BASTARDS!!
OY THAT'S ENOUGH O'THAT! YOU KEEP A CIVIL TONGUE, THERE'S WOMEN AN' KIDDIES 'ERE!
YUH...YOU DON'T UNDERSTAND. THEY HAD A MARTIAN... FED IT HUMAN BLOOD ...LIKE GIVING MILK TO A KITTEN!
'COURSE THEY DID. NOW SHUT YOUR YAP AN' BEHAVE, THERE'S A GOOD FELLA. I DON'T WANNA MISS THE OFF 'CUZ O'YOU.
BUT...
NO, YOU LISTEN! TODAY'S A DAY FOR 'EROES NOT PISS 'EDS, SO SETTLE DOWN AN' KEEP SHTUM!
I 'EAR ANOTHER PEEP OUTTA YOU, YOU'LL GET A RIGHT GOOD KICKIN,' UNDERSTAND?
C'MON GEORGE, HEY'RE GOIN' UP.
ON ME WAY.
BUT I WAS THERE...I SAW IT ALL.
HERE, BUY YER SEL' A BOTTLE...
...AN' CRAWL INTAE IT.
S'THE ONLY WORLD Y'GOT LEFT T'YE.
TAXI

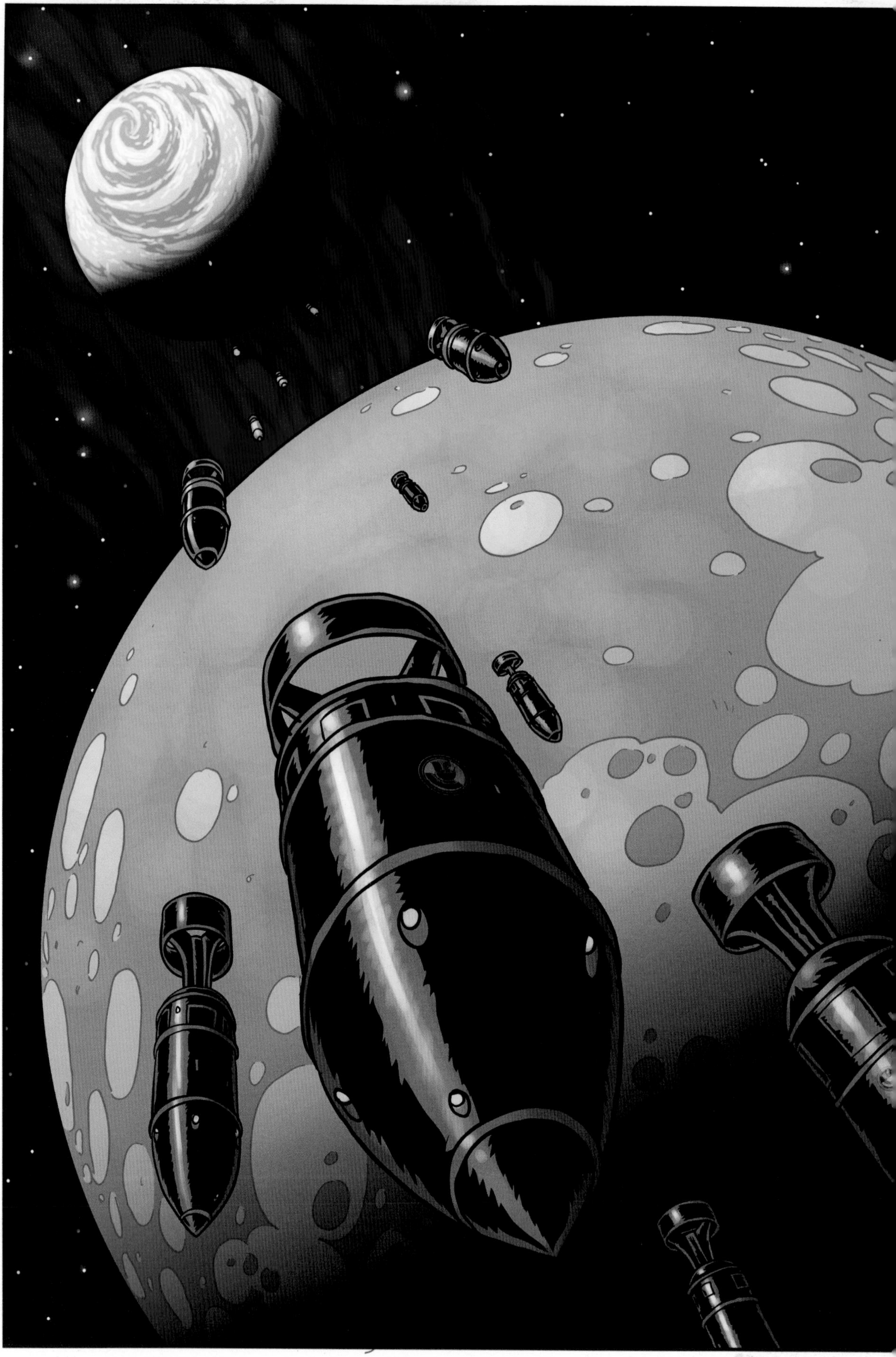

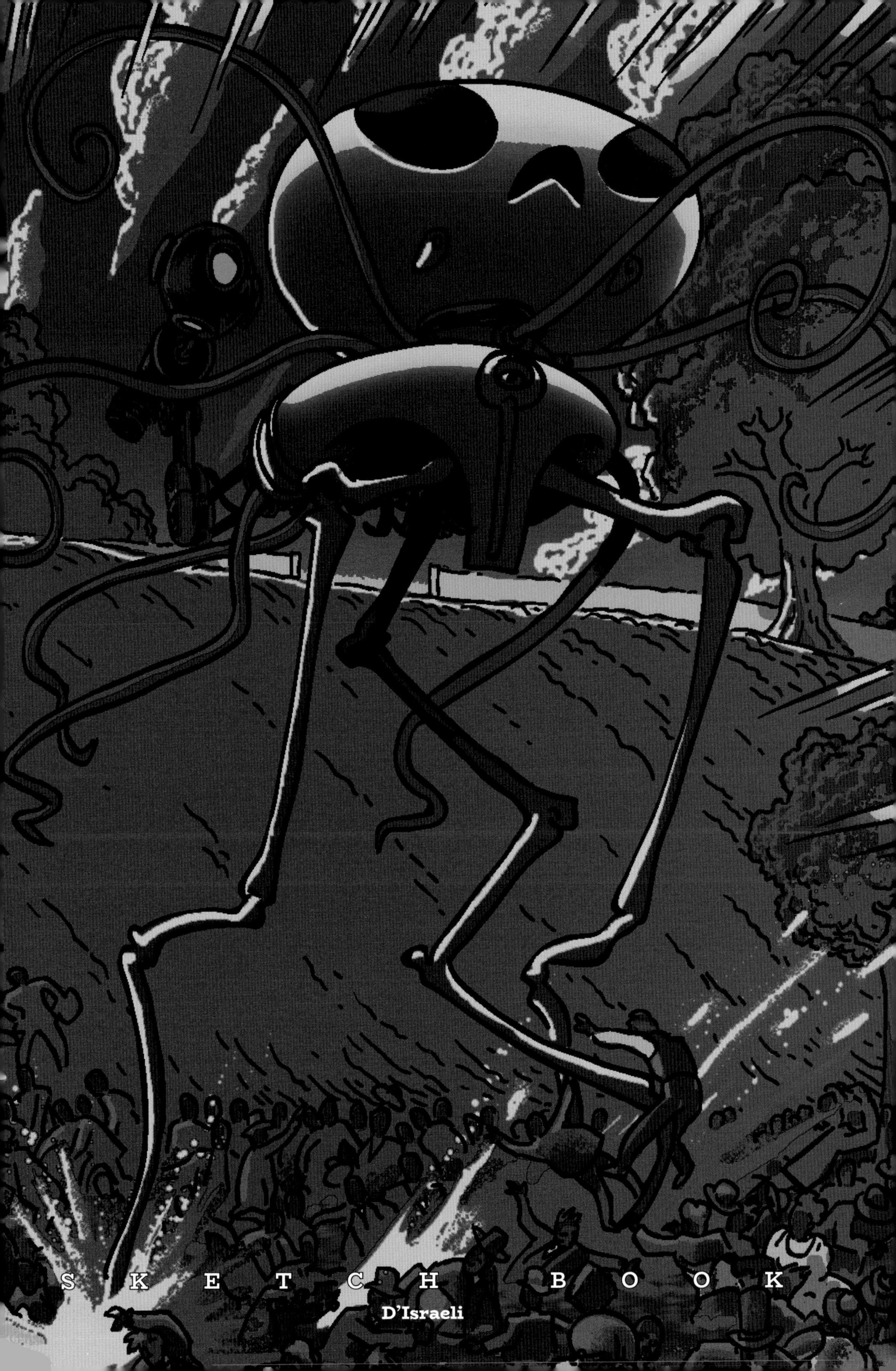

S K E T C H B O O K

D'Israeli

It's more than ten years since Ian Edginton and I first discussed the proposal which was to become *Scarlet Traces*. This first pen sketch is dated April 2nd, 1993.

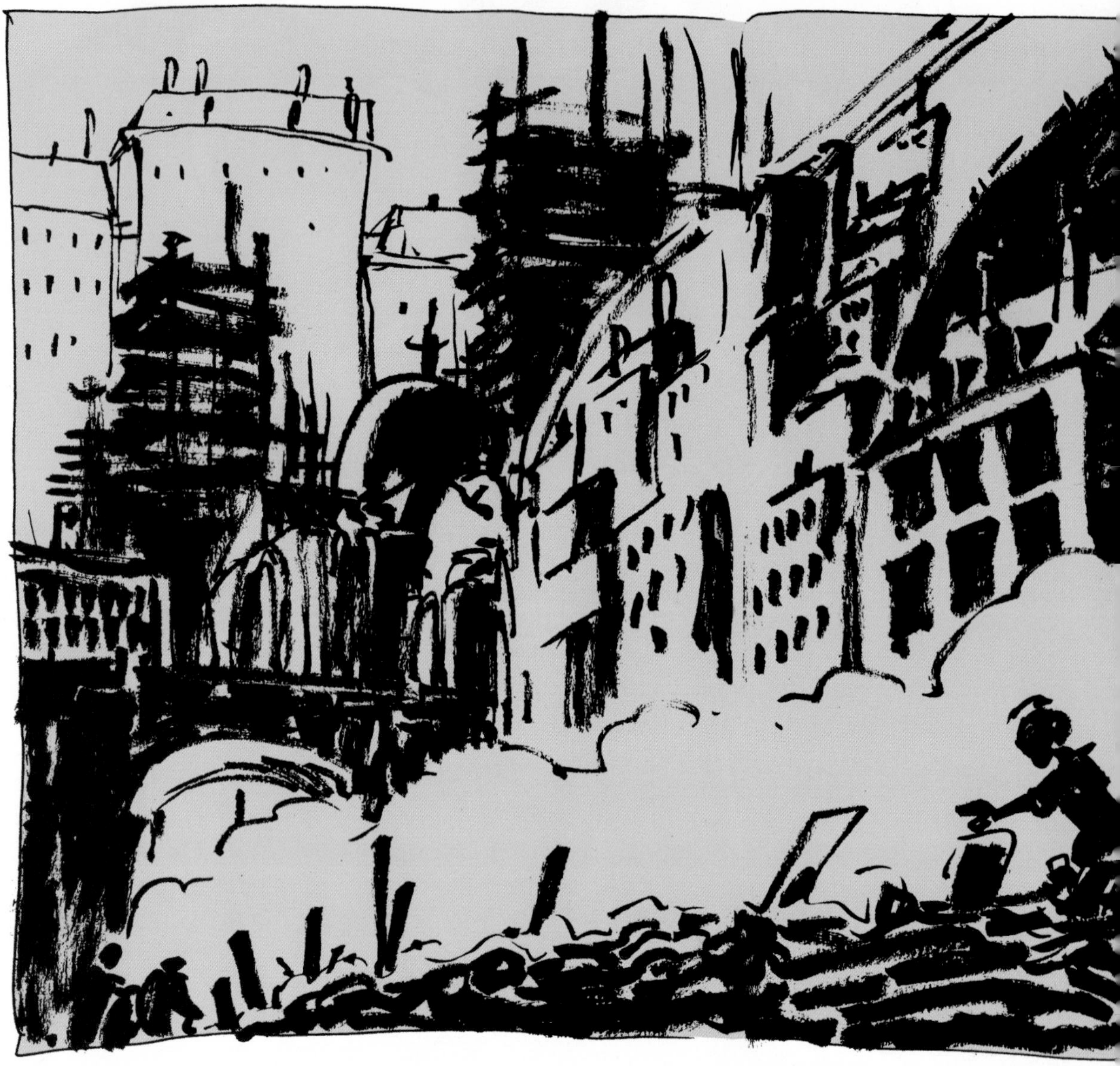

Although the Martians were long-defeated by the start of *Scarlet Traces*, we still needed a design for their Fighting Machines (far right).

Scarlet Traces was originally commissioned by Coolbeans Productions Ltd. for use on the web, which meant we could include limited amounts of animation.

Coolbeans animators actually built a CGI tripod (right) for a proposed animated intro, which sadly was never made. They did get as far as making it walk, no mean feat for a three-legged device.

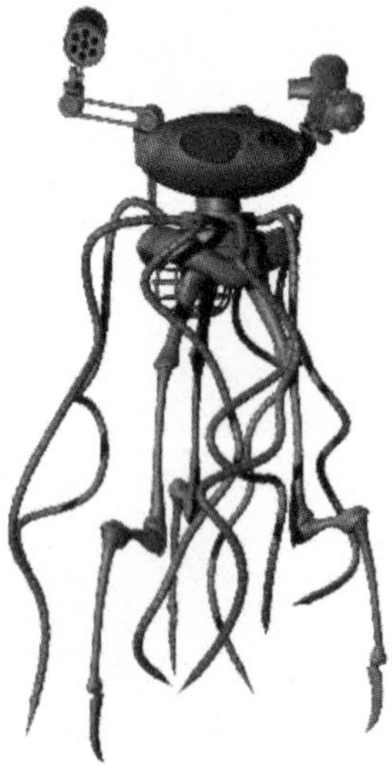

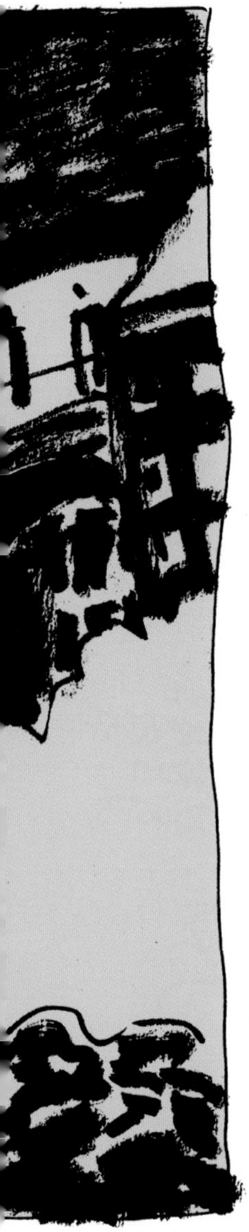

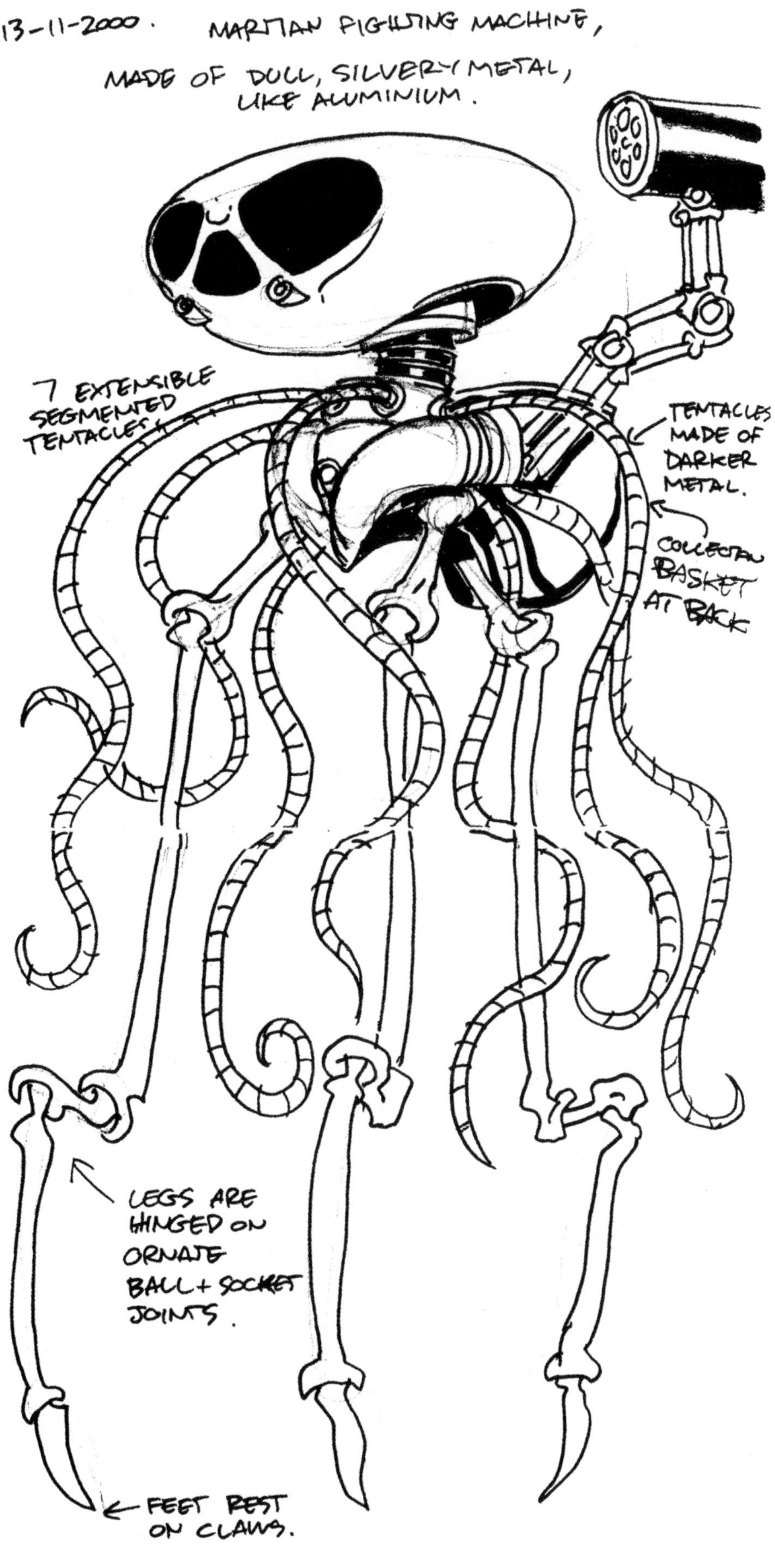
13-11-2000. MARTIAN FIGHTING MACHINE,
MADE OF DULL, SILVERY METAL, LIKE ALUMINIUM.
7 EXTENSIBLE SEGMENTED TENTACLES,
TENTACLES MADE OF DARKER METAL.
COLLECTION BASKET AT BACK
LEGS ARE HINGED ON ORNATE BALL + SOCKET JOINTS.
FEET REST ON CLAWS.

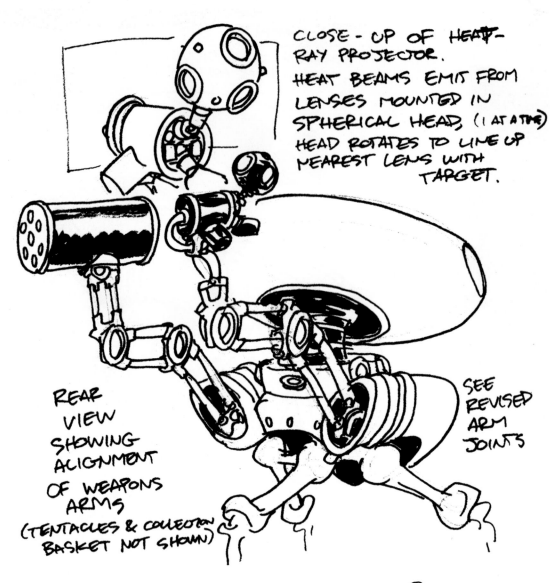

CLOSE-UP OF HEAT-RAY PROJECTOR.
HEAT BEAMS EMIT FROM LENSES MOUNTED IN SPHERICAL HEAD, (1 AT A TIME) HEAD ROTATES TO LINE UP NEAREST LENS WITH TARGET.

REAR VIEW SHOWING ALIGNMENT OF WEAPONS ARMS (TENTACLES & COLLECTION BASKET NOT SHOWN)

SEE REVISED ARM JOINTS

Because the Fighting Machine was to be built and animated, I had to draw it in detail from all angles, something I wouldn't need to do for a design appearing in an ordinary comic.

I also gave some thought to how the leg joints would work, and sketched out the rudiments of a walk cycle.

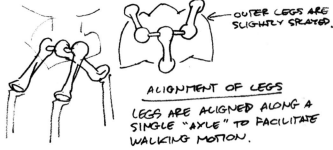

OUTER LEGS ARE SLIGHTLY SPLAYED.

ALIGNMENT OF LEGS
LEGS ARE ALIGNED ALONG A SINGLE "AXLE" TO FACILITATE WALKING MOTION.

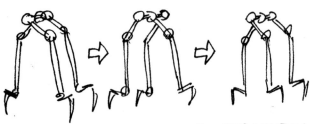

WALKING MOTION - TWO OUTER LEGS MOVE IN OPPOSITION TO INNER LEG. "ANKLE" JOINTS REVERSE

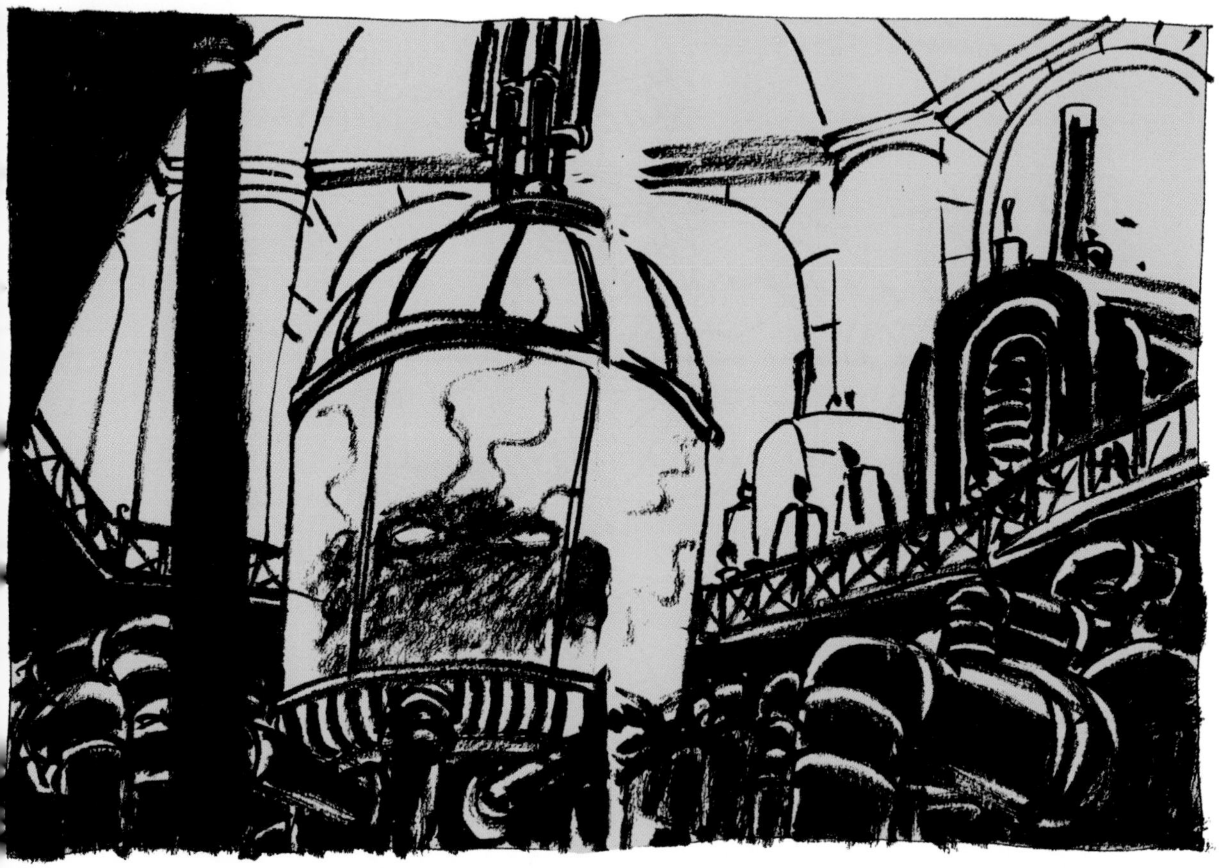

Above: the original sketch for the Martian tank room at Carfax Abbey.
The basic layout was there from the start, though the room became a lot taller.

Below: the Martians, based closely on Wells' description.

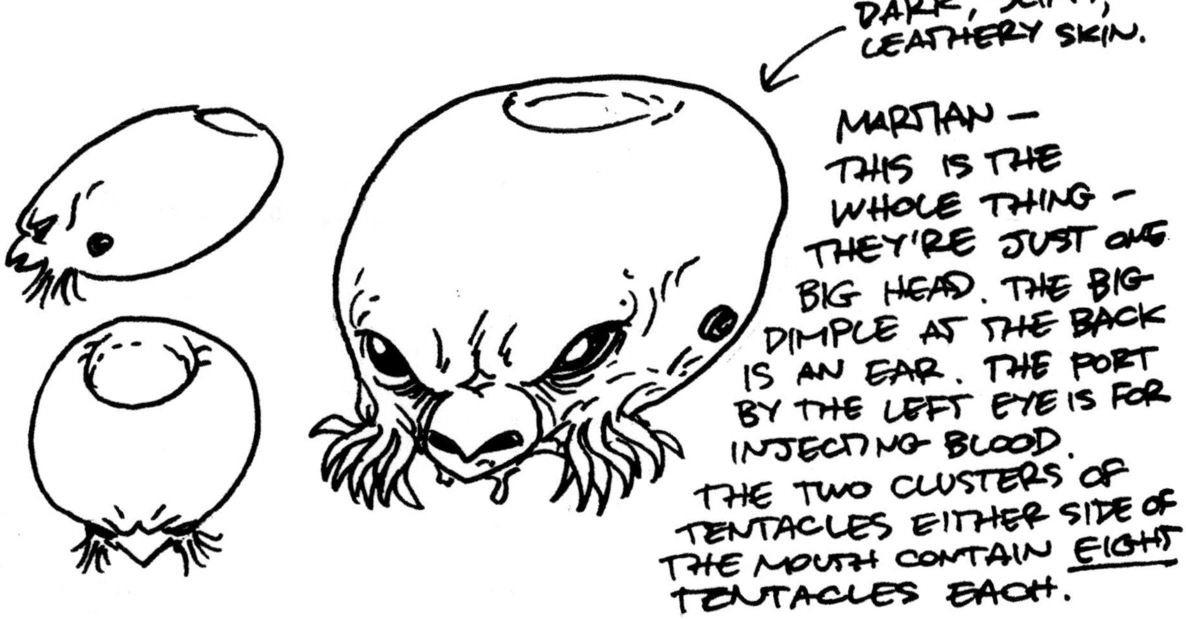
DARK, SLIMY, LEATHERY SKIN.
MARTIAN – THIS IS THE WHOLE THING – THEY'RE JUST ONE BIG HEAD. THE BIG DIMPLE AT THE BACK IS AN EAR. THE PORT BY THE LEFT EYE IS FOR INJECTING BLOOD.
THE TWO CLUSTERS OF TENTACLES EITHER SIDE OF THE MOUTH CONTAIN EIGHT TENTACLES EACH.

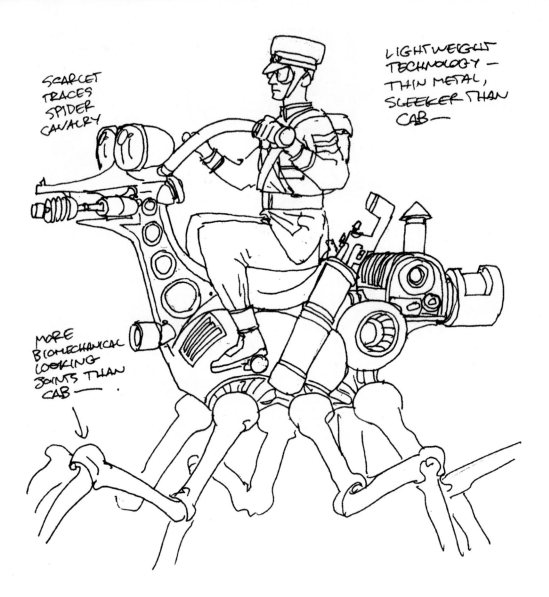

SCARLET TRACES SPIDER CAVALRY

LIGHTWEIGHT TECHNOLOGY — THIN METAL, SLEEKER THAN CAB —

MORE BIOMECHANICAL LOOKING JOINTS THAN CAB —

Above and right: whenever I collaborate with Ian Edginton, he always comes up with the best visual ideas. He was the one who suggested a Victorian world full of legged vehicles made with re-engineered Martian technology.

These are the first and final sketches for the "Spider Cavalry," the replacement for the Horse Guards.

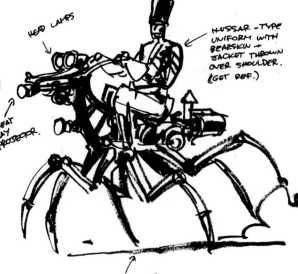

'IL-1-2000.
SCARLET TRACES — "SPIDER CAVALRY"

HEAD LAMPS

HUSSAR-TYPE UNIFORM WITH BEARSKIN + JACKET THROWN OVER SHOULDER. (GET REF.)

HEAT RAY PROJECTOR.

6 LEGS.

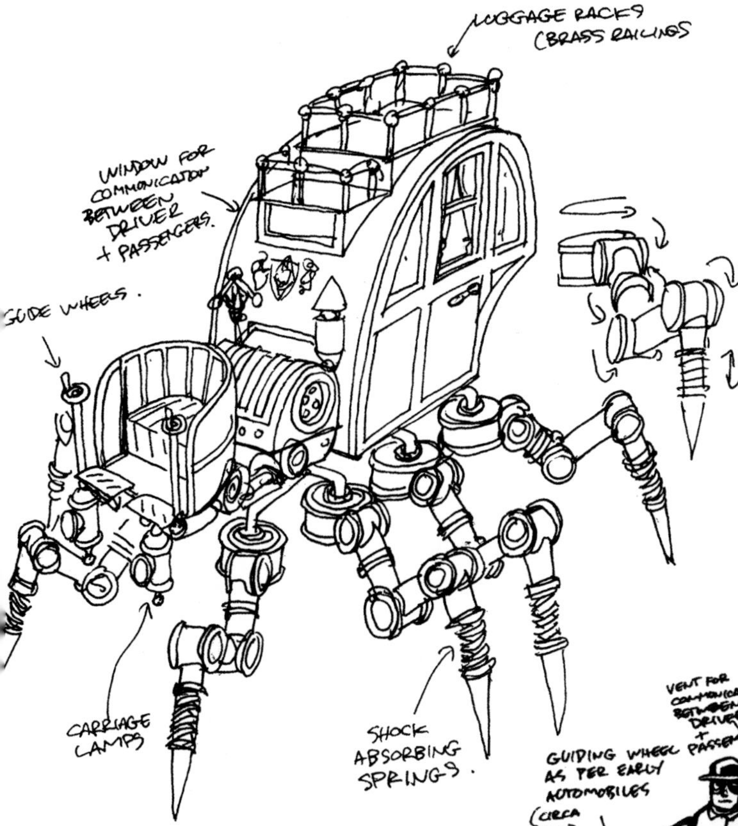
LUGGAGE RACKS
(BRASS RAILINGS
WINDOW FOR COMMUNICATION BETWEEN DRIVER + PASSENGERS.
SIDE WHEELS.
CARRIAGE LAMPS
SHOCK ABSORBING SPRINGS.

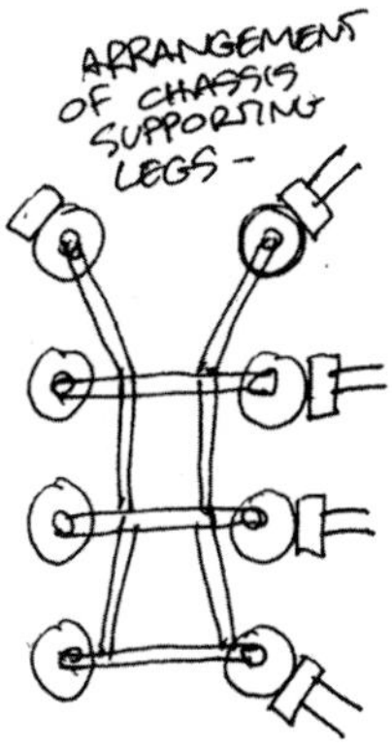
ARRANGEMENT OF CHASSIS SUPPORTING LEGS -

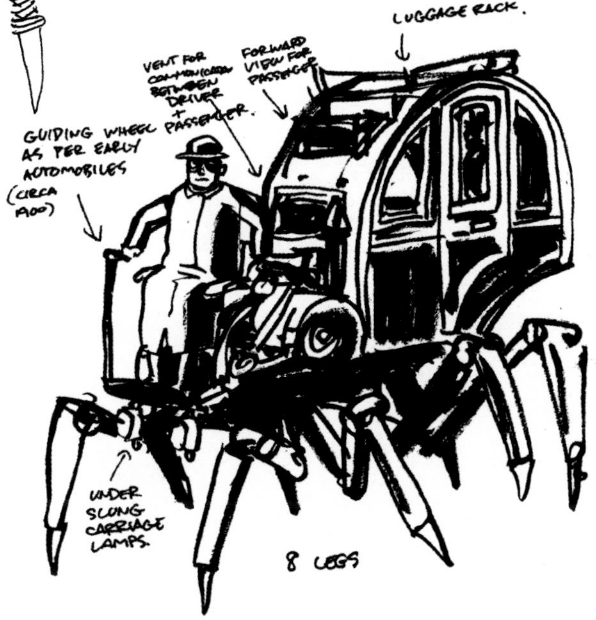
LUGGAGE RACK.
VENT FOR COMMUNICATION BETWEEN DRIVER + PASSENGER.
FORWARD VIEW FOR PASSENGER
GUIDING WHEEL AS PER EARLY AUTOMOBILES (CIRCA 1900)
UNDER SLUNG CARRIAGE LAMPS.
8 LEGS

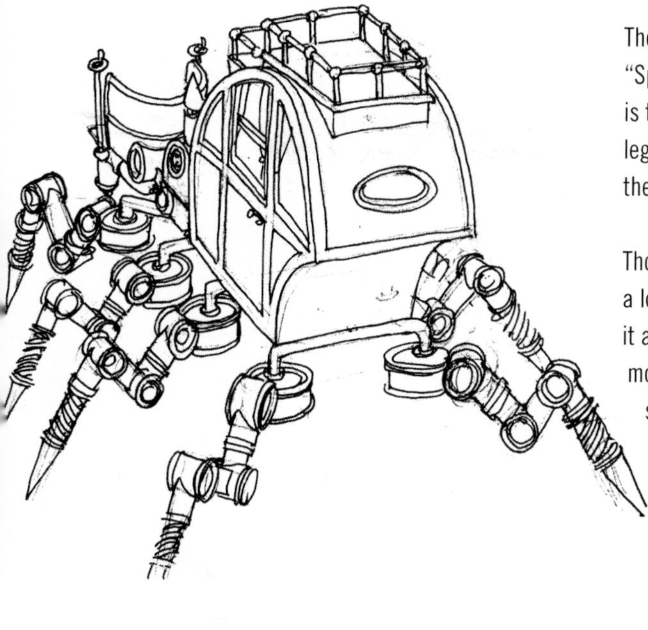

The piece de resistance of *Scarlet Traces* has to be the "Spider Cabs," again thought up by Ian. The basic idea is to have a Hansom cab mounted on eight mechanical legs. The driver's position and controls are based on the very earliest automobiles.

Though the Spider Cabs are a favourite of mine, they're a lot of work – if you're drawing a street full of traffic it adds up to an awful lot of legs. You'll notice that most of the busy street views in Scarlet Traces are seen from a distance, so I don't have to draw too many cabs in detail. I will also confess to cloning a single tiny cab lots of times in some shots!

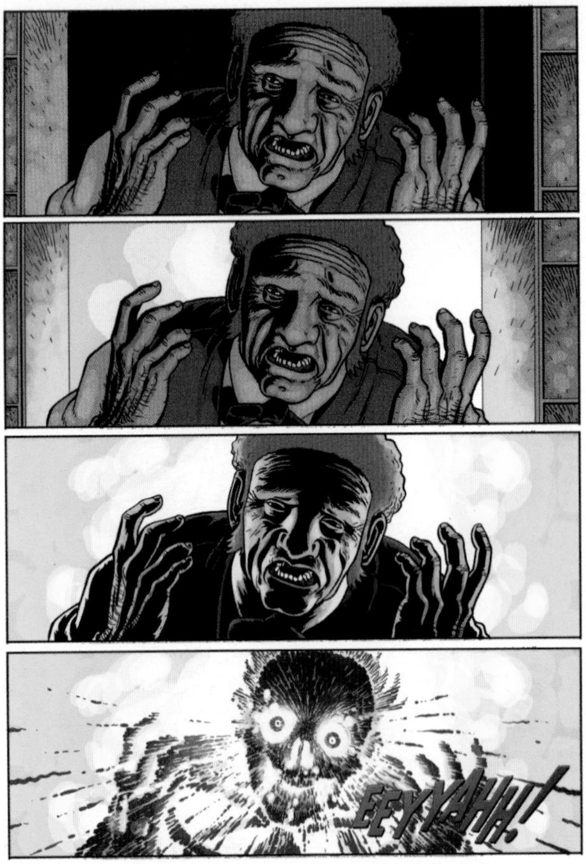
EEYYAHH!

In *Scarlet Traces*' original web incarnation, most of the pages included limited animation effects. Many of these panels had to be altered or dropped, as we'd have had to include all the animated frames as separate comic panels to really make sense of them, and from a storytelling point of view they didn't warrant taking up that much space.

Left: the original, animated last panel showing Sid the Landlord being blown up in gruesome detail. We substituted this with a wider shot showing Sid being blown off his feet as a fireball surges down the stairs from the pub.

Below: on the next page, we kept the basic shot, but I re-painted the explosion to make it more dynamic. The original fireball had to be kept simple for animation purposes, the movement supplying the dynamism. And yes, I did re-use the wide shot of the pub, but by the time I'd worked out how to overlay all the explosions and areas where the background is lit by the fireball, it didn't feel as if I'd saved much time!

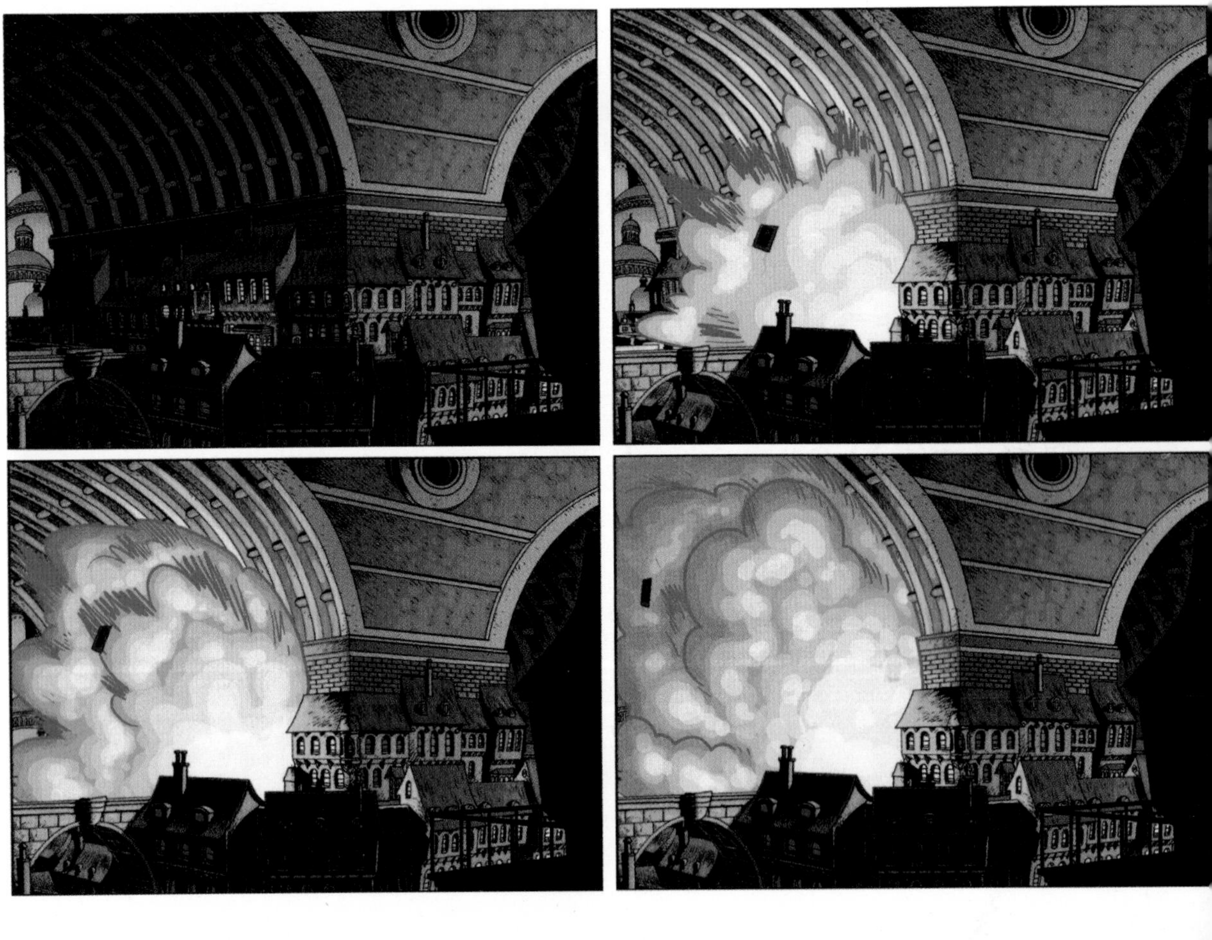

Above: We regretted having to drop this page as it showed Ned's motivation for going into danger. The shot of Pikey straining at the lead is one of my favourites from the whole story. I think Pikey's fab, and that he should get his own series.

Left: A bizarre twist on Archie Currie's death scene, done as an April Fool's joke, though it only reached the pencil state. Note the blue pencil I use to rough out my drawing, and the perspective grids, which I use obsessively, even when it's only for a couple of lines on the floor, as here.

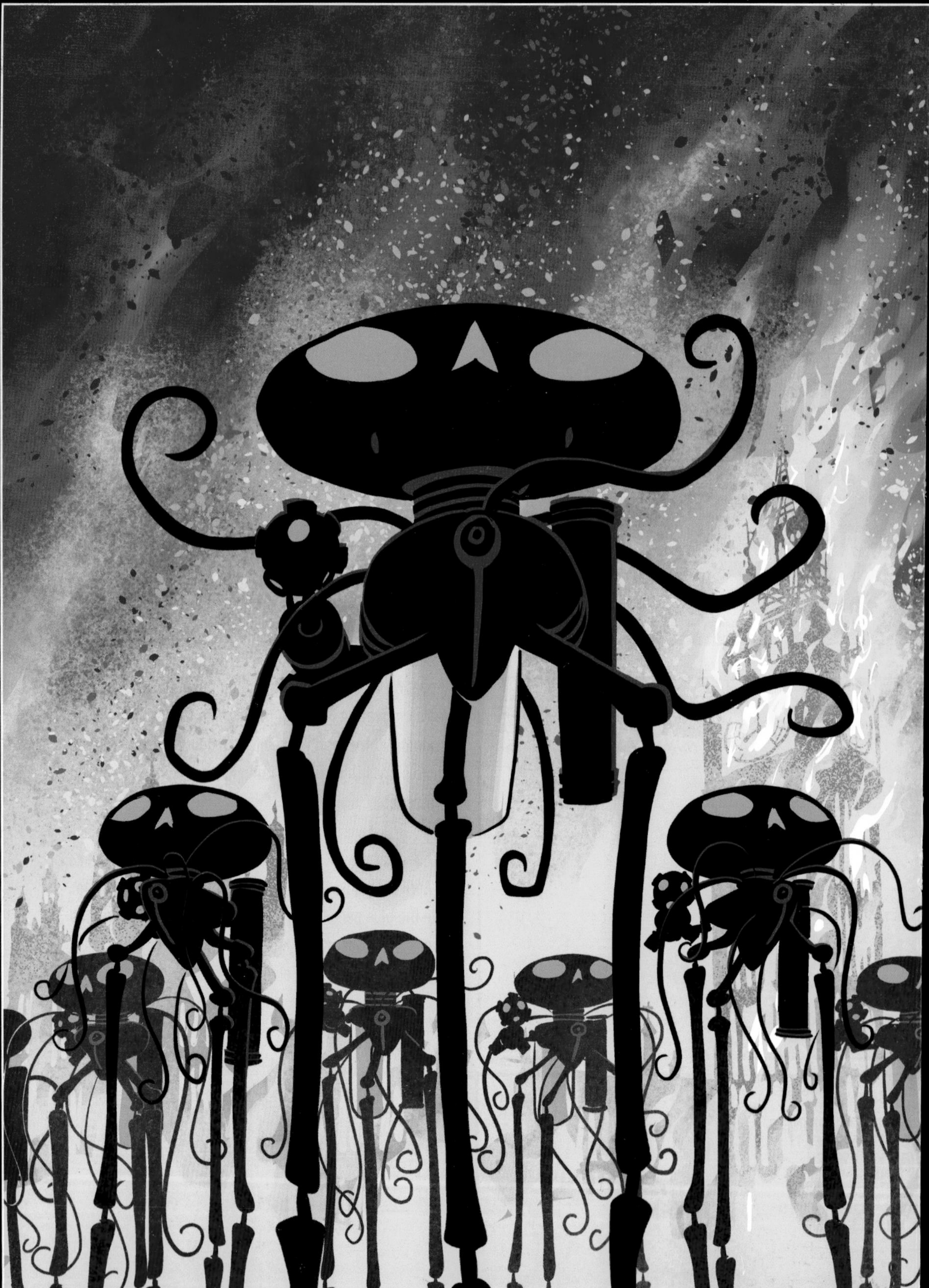